ON THE TRAIL OF VANISHING BIRDS

# ON THE TRAIL OF VANISHING BIRDS

*Robert Porter Allen* RESEARCH DIRECTOR,
NATIONAL AUDUBON SOCIETY



McGRAW-HILL BOOK COMPANY, INC.
NEW YORK TORONTO LONDON

ON THE TRAIL OF VANISHING BIRDS



*Library of Congress Catalog Card Number: 57-7225*

*Published by the McGraw-Hill Book Company, Inc.*
*Printed in the United States of America*



The author is grateful to the editors of *Blackwood's Magazine* and *Audubon Magazine* for permission to reproduce in this book material that has previously appeared in their publications.

# Preface

For more than fifty years the National Audubon Society has worked for the preservation of our native bird life and, over the last twenty years, has initiated and carried out studies of the lives and special needs of a number of North American birds that continue to be threatened with extinction, in spite of the great advances that have been made in the conservation field in recent years. One phase of these studies has been the publication of monographs on each of the species concerned—complete life histories that summarize everything that is known about these birds, with practical recommendations for arresting their decline and thus preventing their disappearance from the American scene. Although such publications represent an important and essential part of the over-all contribution that is made by these projects, they are not an end in themselves. Our efforts to follow through along the lines indicated as a result of each study are a continuing responsibility, a job that must end in eventual success or complete failure, or not at all.

Nevertheless, those of us who have been actively associated with this program experience an understandable sense of relief and a certain feeling of accomplishment when the painstaking search for facts and for clues that may lead to a happy solution are finally assembled, in more or less readable form, between the covers of one of our monographs. At least that has been this author's reaction to the publication of our reports on the whooping crane and, more recently, on the American flamingo. Together they represented nearly six years of hard work in the field and of even more strenuous effort digging through dusty library shelves and bent over a typewriter.

In my own case, however, a feeling of having written *finis* to something worthwhile was short-lived. Not only was there still much to be done for both birds, as new problems cropped up and clamored for attention, but I soon found that such widespread interest had been aroused in both the whooping crane and the flamingo and their separate struggles for survival that I would have to go on and tell the entire story. People wanted to know about those experiences that were not mentioned in the relatively formal pages of the monographs. How had we conducted our long search for the Northern breeding grounds of the whooper? Why had it taken so many years and just what had been our feelings about it in the process? How had we lived on the flamingo islands of the West Indies and what was it like there? So many questions were asked that something had to be done about it. This book is the result, and while it doesn't relate all of our adventures or describe every one of our many difficulties, it is a faithful account of much of what happened to us.

There is even a brief explanation that will have to stand as an answer to the frequent question, "How did you happen to get into this kind of work in the first place?" As you will see, even so improbable an event doesn't just happen, but is a result of simple cause and effect, as are most events. Provided, of course, that the essential cause is present and that the natural effect is permitted to follow, which it was in my case.

One half of the book is about the whooping crane, which is certainly fitting, as this great bird continues to dominate the entire picture so far as vanishing species are concerned. None of our endangered birds is so well known to the public at large, and yet here are yarns about them that are not generally known. The roseate spoonbill, much improved but still not out of the woods, has a chapter of its own, and the remainder of the narrative belongs to the flamingo, whose story is less well known and yet is eminently deserving of our attention. There is a final chapter that reviews our record with regard to extinct North American birds and that discusses the causes of extinction and the situation that is faced by our threatened birds of today.

I have tried to present this material in a realistic manner, from the very special point of view of the active field ornithologist, for it has been my privilege to work at close hand with most of these birds in their natural wilderness habitats. These have been my own experiences and heartaches and adventures, and for the most part this is my personal account. But it is also, and perhaps more significantly, a part of the history of the National Audubon Society, the organization that has fought so valiantly for the birds of America and that has made these studies of our threatened species possible. It is the author's hope that those who read this book may have as a result a better understanding and appreciation of the scope and importance of the Society's high purpose and many accomplishments.

ROBERT PORTER ALLEN

## Contents

## List of illustrations

*. . . All my nature craved for knowledge of these things, but there were neither books nor birdmen to help me. I wonder if other boys suffer so. . . .*

ERNEST THOMPSON SETON *

# I : The education of a Seton Indian

I no longer have a copy of Ernest Thompson Seton's *Two Little Savages* on my bookshelf, having lent it out years ago, but it is a book that held between its covers the very essence of life for me when I was a boy of ten. Forty years ago boys of that age were much the same as they are today, but the world itself was certainly a different place. Perhaps the total lack of diversions made us a little more self-sufficient. We were never at a loss for things to do. And because my brother John and I spent most of our spare time in the woods and swamps and along the river, *Two Little Savages,* when it came finally into our hands, was the perfect textbook. We became Seton Indians, sitting cross-legged around tiny campfires, Indian-fashion, discussing important current events in the *Tutnee* language and planning expeditions and cruises to far places (three or four miles away!) for the purpose of adding to our knowledge of local natural history. Our little world was filled with reality and with a high regard for birds, first spring flowers, woodcraft, canoe

* *Boyhood Days in Canada.*

travel, and an endless array of kindred matters. These things had substance and durability. They were real then and they are just as real today. If Seton had never written another book or drawn another picture, our debt to him and our regard for his particular brand of magic—a regard that has grown with the years—would remain unchanged.

My birthplace in northern Pennsylvania lies in the West Branch Valley of the Susquehanna, at the foot of a range of mountains. Black bears, deer, wild turkeys, bobcats, and other game roamed the oak scrub in abundance. I can remember my Aunt Georgiana coming into the house one winter morning, breathless. The wind had drifted the snow clear of the long plank walk and when she had turned to see who was following her, and making so much noise about it, there was a big ten-point buck standing right behind her! In the surrounding countryside roads were few and unimproved. Winter and summer my brother and I could tramp all day along the hogbacked ridges, guns in hand, without meeting another human being. And this meant a lot to us, for we were actually living a dream of the wild. We were still pretty young when Uncle John loaned us his Winchester and we set off in an early fall of snow to kill a bear. We had seen the bear's tracks on the slopes of Bald Eagle Mountain, and by luck we came across them again. They were undoubtedly fresh as we began our stalk. At one point, on the crest of a ridge that dropped off toward a great pile of rocks where the bear may have had a den, we could hear him bumbling down the steep slope just ahead of us, but the snow was wet and heavy and he was quite invisible. I wanted a shot at that bear more than anything in the world. I recall getting down on my knees, while making my brother do the same, and praying earnestly for a chance at him. My brother, who was always very sensible, objected at first on the grounds that it wasn't right to ask God's help in killing something. But I pointed out that we would only ask that the snow let up enough to give us a clear view. "Damn it, John," I whispered, "get down on your knees before the bear gets away!" John did so, reluctantly, but in spite of our entreaties the snow continued and the bear escaped. Such disappointments are mighty serious when you are a boy and have your heart set on living out in the woods forever.

As far as I know there were no naturalists in my family background. My father was a lawyer, and one grandfather and one great-grandfather before him. Mother had been a schoolteacher, and her father had been a law student turned minister in the Methodist Church South, a change of route brought about by his marrying a remarkable woman who started out to be a missionary in China, but settled for the Methodist Church South and eleven children of her own instead. There wasn't a scientist in the lot, but there was a great deal in the way of speaking and writing and expostulating and devotion to Causes. All of which not only made important and inevitable contributions to my own character, but, since the sum of all these talents had in some mysterious way produced in me a Seton Indian, it would seem reasonably logical, or at least not surprising, that in course of time my path should lead to the Audubon Society, and to an opportunity to work for some of that society's great causes.

In early summer, when the valley and the town were hidden beneath a thick fog, we would climb to the peak of Bald Eagle Mountain and see below us a white blanket of wool filled with muffled sounds and mystery. Off there close to the sky, without visible connections with the rest of the universe, it was like being in another and less complicated world, or perhaps in our own world as it might have been at an earlier time. Yet this was not a feeling of escape, for there was almost as much in the world there below us that we loved as in any other place. We simply enjoyed the peace and the beauty and the solitude of the mountain slope without wondering why. If the pleasures we found on those mountain ridges—the soaring flight of a red-tailed hawk, the song of a veery, the fresh beauty of the first wild honeysuckle—if this was escapism, then what could one describe as reality? Without really knowing it, my brother John and I had stumbled upon something of great value, an easy kinship with the world of nature. And all this was real, every bit of it—the trees in their strong grandeur, the bird song in its sweetness and variety of meanings, the depth of sky, the river curling around the foot of the mountain—while there in the town below, under its pall of fog, we could hear the whistles tooting and the wheels grinding, but not for us. Somehow, for us, the mountain was a better place.

But there are other factors besides environment. Every other boy of the same age in our town in those years was exposed to the same surroundings as we were, yet only a few of them made the same discoveries. They did not seem to find what we did in Schooley's Woods, where the scarlet tanager nested, or in Gibson's Swamp, where we saw our first pileated woodpecker and where the cardinals stayed all winter long at our feeding station. If they looked at the river they did not see the flock of bluebills, or take a chance on being late to school in order to watch the pintails that splashed about in the wet meadow west of town. Other boys discovered that for them reality was made of something else —they found it in the engine of a Model T perhaps, or in the clattering presses at the newspaper building, in test tubes in the high-school chem lab, or in their first crystal set.

In the face of all the variety and wealth of interests that were opened to us, my brother and I gradually drifted more and more toward birds as the primary object of our busy lives. And it became a serious interest, as attested in the detailed writings of many a notebook. One late February afternoon, with two companions, John and I were in Gibson's Swamp. My brother wrote in his notes that we were looking for the cardinals that had wintered there that year. Alan and myself walked along the north side of the swamp while John and Maynard "pushed through the center." Suddenly, he went on, in rather self-conscious prose for a thirteen-year-old:

> ...while sitting astride a rather high tree I noticed that Bob and Alan were showing signs of glee and constantly gazing at some bird through their glasses. Climbing from my lofty perch I hastened toward them to learn the cause of all the excitement. Bob told me, "Fox sparrows, two of 'em!" That was enough, and with fast beating heart I crept towards the spot where I thought they were hidden. Soon I heard unfamiliar notes—long-drawn-

out *tsee-eep, tsee-eep*—and later saw one of the objects of my search. Then I made a sound which alarmed him and, calling louder than before, he flew away followed by five of his fellow-men. Or women.

Obviously, my brother John had the makings of an ornithologist.

It was in high school that these interests, until then rather vague and pleasant and undemanding, began to crystallize and to assume some purpose. It was a gradual process, aided by a wise biology teacher who enlisted a large number of us in an Audubon Junior Club. It was through this club that I met for the first time ornithologists like Arthur A. Allen and Louis Agassiz Fuertes—who lectured in town under our sponsorship—and corresponded with Frank M. Chapman and T. Gilbert Pearson. All this broadened our horizons and taught us that there were more rewarding ways of studying birds than by looking at them along a gun barrel. I deserted the ranks of mighty hunters and trappers forever and became a dedicated ornithologist and conservationist.

At fifteen I was an extremely active youngster, and although my allegiance to forest trails, to sunlit reaches of the Susquehanna River, and to the fauna of the surrounding area was unimpeachable, I also managed to find time for other things. Since the age of nine I had been maintaining an increasingly bad treble in the boy's choir at Christ Church in Williamsport, where a completely improbable English choirmaster named Frank Gatward, aided by a Conan Doyle mustache, an old-fashioned dickey, sleeveless cuffs, an alpaca coat, and jokes lifted from *Ally Sloper's Holiday*, was one of the great delights in the lives of all of us who came under his stern choirmaster's eye. I had nearly ten years of it, which included three week-day practices and no less than two services on Sundays. But sometimes, for a dedicated outdoorsman and budding ornithologist, the strain was evident. At Sunday services we were forced to wear "Buster Brown collars." It was one of the sacrifices that had to be made. Most of us removed these collars with cassock and surplice after service. But the worst ordeal of all was wearing them on the way to church on Sunday morning when all the world could see. This requirement not only kept the collar clean, of course, but was definite assurance that we would proceed straight to church by the quickest, most direct route and not stop along the way to watch a flock of ducks on the river or to climb a tree and stick an exploring hand in a flicker's nest. Mother was our most sympathetic ally when it came to our exploring, but on certain points, like all mothers, she was adamant.

I had a deep desire for adventure and a determination to seek it out. I remember the day in 1916 when our local National Guard battery boarded a troop train and left for the Mexican border. One of the officers brandished a sporting rifle that was fitted with a telescopic sight, and I can hear him now, shouting from the rear platform that this was the gun that would kill Pancho Villa. It was an exciting and never-to-be-forgotten moment. I was only eleven, and I never wished more fervently for anything than that I might be a few years older. So when the battery returned from France after World War I and was eventually reorganized in 1920, I successfully advanced my actual age and enlisted. There were drills on Friday nights and two weeks of artillery range experience each summer. But even these adventures were mere fillers. In an old notebook under date of April 24, 1921, my sixteenth birthday, I find this sober and, as it turned out, significant entry: "At drill Friday evening I was paid for the six months ending Jan. 1, a check for $26.67 . . . Now I can get a pair of good field glasses. I find that they are indispensable for the study of birds."

With high school behind me, the question of a career had to be considered. Though still as interested in ornithology as in breathing, I found little basis for hope and almost no encouragement. In those years there were few specialized courses in the universities, and in the field in which I was interested there were scarcely any openings. I entered Lafayette College at Easton, where my father, grandfather, and numerous uncles and cousins had graduated. I found that in my outmoded Norfolk jacket I was a trifle rural among my new friends, and although I knew that I could outrun the whole lot of them on a mountain trail, outpaddle them in a canoe, and make jackasses out of them in a river-bottom swamp, this was another world, in which they were so much at home; and I would have to learn about it if I was to survive there.

So far as any sort of career was concerned the two years I spent at Easton were completely wasted, although I did learn a few things about the rest of the world that lay beyond the shadow of Bald Eagle Mountain. But I remained an undisciplined nonconformist, incapable of learning many of the graces and determined to find a way of life wherein the kind of shoes you wore and the sort of knot you tied in your tie were of no importance whatever.

During my second year I corresponded with the artist Fuertes, and at his invitation visited him between terms at his home in Ithaca. At his suggestion I applied for a transfer to Cornell University, and landed there in the autumn of 1925. Meanwhile various difficulties had arisen. My father had died unexpectedly, and there wasn't as much money on hand as we had thought there would be. Mother, who had taken a job at a girls' school near New York, would have seen me through at any cost, but other members of the family could see no future in ornithology worth an actual investment. So after only three months I dropped out.

In the winter of 1925 I turned my back on everything and set out to see the world. This phase had its beginning in the books of Stevenson, Conrad, and McFee, moved on to the throbbing engine room of a freighter bound for Singapore, and ended more than three years later when I came home with exactly forty-eight cents in my pockets. While I was at it I sailed twice around the world, and got shipwrecked on an island in the Sulu Sea before I was old enough to come back to my home precinct and cast a legal vote. In the process I learned even more of the world that lay beyond Bald Eagle Mountain.

My brother John, a far more adaptable nonconformist than I, stuck it out at college and eventually graduated. When I came to New York just after the '29 market crash, John still had a job in an advertising agency and from there he moved on to *Fortune* magazine as one of the original staff. I had come to the city to visit with John and fully intended to study for my third mate's ticket and go back to sea. But in December I met a young lady named Evelyn Sedgwick, who had finished at Julliard and was preparing for a debut piano recital at Steinway Hall. We met at a party, and afterward we sat on a park bench in Washington Square and talked for half the night. It was snowing, but we didn't seem to notice it. We talked and talked, on and on, endlessly. By some strange miracle each of us seemed to have things to say that the other wanted very much to hear, and although we had met purely by chance the lives of both of us were changed from that moment on.

In the summer of 1930, I had a talk with Dr. Chapman, the illustrious head of the Bird Department of the American Museum of Natural History, with whom I had corresponded during my high-school days. He said that I could work with him as a volunteer, without pay, on the chance that a regular job might be available in about six months or so. At the moment I had just enough of a cash reserve to get me downtown on the subway—five cents—and I told him so. He then suggested that I go to 1974 Broadway and see Dr. Pearson, who was then president of the Audubon Society. There might be something for me there. I was determined that if I had to give up the sea I must find employment that was close to my heart. Dr. Pearson saw me and we talked for a full hour. He asked me endless questions, and as he was a former college biology teacher some of them, touching on the extent of my formal education, were more than a little embarrassing. But he had also been a personal friend of Seton's, and although Seton's name was never mentioned, somehow or other the reflected glow of a hundred campfires must have shown through. When I left Pearson's office I was a staff member on a trial basis and temporarily assigned to the job of assembling the library, then stored in several dozen huge packing cases in the basement. I reached the street walking on air and hurried to a friend's apartment to write the good news to Evelyn, who was at her parents' home in St. Louis. Now we could make plans.

It was five years later, shortly after John Baker had taken over the executive duties of the Society, that the research program was first set in motion. This vigorous, imaginative, and urgent undertaking was the natural outgrowth of a grave need for more precise and more detailed information on the habits and requirements of certain North American birds that were either in immediate danger of extinction or on the road that would lead to that state. Through the years the National Audubon Society had become primarily an educational institution and instrument, but its first breath of life had been taken many years before on a note of urgency and of militant action. As a minority group with a dramatic cause to plead, it had reached the hearts of men (and of legislators!), and thereby not only saved the egrets in this country but made bird protection a matter of popular and public-spirited concern. Now, with the rapid growth of human populations and the unprecedented advance of the relentless tentacles of the Machine Age, certain highly specialized bird species faced new dangers. The combined protection of laws, wardens to enforce them, and inviolate sanctuaries, a formula that had worked so well heretofore, was no longer enough in the case of birds like the ivory-billed woodpecker, the California condor, the roseate spoonbill, and the whooping crane. An entirely new concept and method of approach was needed, and this the Audubon research program set out to discover and put into operation.

During these intervening five years from 1930 to 1935 a great many things had been happening, to me as well as to the Audubon Society. For one thing, I had become an active member of the Linnaean Society of New York, a scientific group interested chiefly in observations and studies of birds in the New York City region. The membership was made up of amateurs and professionals alike. Here I met men like Joe Hickey, Allan Cruickshank, Bill Vogt, Charlie Urner, Lester Walsh, Roger Peterson, and many others. With some of them I was to be associated, as close friend and coworker, throughout the rest of my professional life. And here too I began an important phase of the educational process I was already undergoing in the course of my duties with the Audubon Society. Ernest Golsan Holt had been added to our staff in 1932 in the newly created post of Sanctuary Director, and I was to learn much from his long experience and careful scientific methods. When Evelyn and I were finally married the following year, Ernest and Margaret Holt stood up with us, beside my mother and my brother John, for the simple service in the Presbyterian church on lower Fifth Avenue.

These were the Depression years, and they were also years of change and of experiment. Even in established scientific institutions like the Linnaean Society the air was stirring with new ideas and unexpected energies. A Field Work Committee had been formed, largely as a result of the active mind, charm, and persuasiveness of one Joseph J. Hickey, who was later to take over the late Aldo Leopold's job as teacher of wildlife management concepts at the University of Wisconsin, and write such books as his challenging *Guide to Bird Watching.* I worked closely with Joseph Hickey on this committee, and for me, at least, our efforts were both instructive and rewarding. There are many sides to the science of ornithology, as I had been learning. If a man says that his field is music and fails to go into details about it, you may not know whether he conducts a symphony orchestra or merely sells sheet music. I found that there are ornithologists concerned solely with taxonomy, or the classification of birds. Others specialize in ecology or distribution or migration, while still others spend most of their time making collections of bird skins from remote corners of the globe so that the taxonomist may study them and add to our knowledge of classification and avian evolution. At the time of which I write there was a growing interest in this country in the study of bird territories and bird behavior, fields in which considerable progress had already been made in Europe. Ernst Mayr, then at the American Museum, was a helpful mentor in these subjects within Linnaean ranks, and the visit of Niko Tinbergen a few years later gave much encouragement to behavior students on this side of the Atlantic.

As a base for all of these specialized facets of the science there is always the great army of zealous amateurs, most of whom must watch birds in their spare time, which means chiefly on weekends, and thus have to be satisfied with merely listing birds as they see them, from season to season and from one habitat or locality to another. It was this group of amateur "list-chasers" that our committee sought to interest in field projects designed to result in contributions to our knowledge and, at the same time, as we hoped, add immeasurably to the personal enjoyment and intellectual satisfaction of the participants.

In the hope that I might be able to assist with one of our research projects, I went to John Baker and asked that I be permitted to come into the office an hour late each day during the period from late March to early June. We were then living in Amityville on the south shore of Long Island, where we had moved after the untimely death of my brother John. It was my plan to get up at 4 A.M. and pedal my bicycle some three miles west to Massapequa, where a colony of black-crowned night herons was established each season in a cedar swamp. I wanted to make a nesting behavior study of these birds, and if I could arrange to have a reasonable amount of time in the colony each morning, and still reach the office only one hour late, I felt that the results might justify all the trouble involved and perhaps increase my ultimate value to the Society. John Baker immediately agreed to this plan and I set to work on it at once.

Without question the field experiences of the next three seasons were of immense help to me later on. I enlisted the talents of Fred Mangels as a working partner, and we later published our findings in the *Proceedings* of the Linnaean Society of New York (Nos. 50–51, October, 1940). In addition to increasing my knowledge of heron behavior in particular, and of the literature of the important and fascinating field of animal behavior in general, there were other lessons. I would leave the house in the darkest hour before dawn as stealthily as possible so as not to rouse my wife and small children. As I tiptoed out to the garage where my bicycle was housed I frequently had a near collision with the milkman. Since we didn't know each other by sight, and as I thought he might take me for a sneak thief and raise a hue and cry, I always managed to conceal myself in a shadow or behind the garage. My own garage! After he moved on I would emerge, feeling a little foolish, and proceed with my journey. These experiences were sometimes a little unnerving, but I soon learned to think of them as one of the occupational hazards in the career that I had chosen. But even more shattering involvements lay in store for me!

The day came when the young night herons had hatched and were large enough to be banded. Fred and I had worked out a complicated method of individualizing each young heron by placing a series of colored bands on their legs. The colors were so arranged, according to a system that Fred had devised, that each youngster could be identified on sight later on—a great advantage to anyone interested in subsequent details of its life history, as we were. So on this particular morning, somewhere on the nether side of four o'clock, I stole from my house and set off on my bike into the inky predawn blackness. And over the handlebars was slung a large sack containing notebooks, pencils, binoculars, pliers, and several hundred celluloid and aluminium bands, gathered together in strings according to color and number sequence.

I didn't know it at the time, but a gentleman referred to by the press as a "cat burglar" had been operating in that district for some weeks. The local police were determined to catch him. As I pedaled along, my sack over the handlebars and a faint spring breeze in my face, I was suddenly startled by a blinding light that was being directed straight at me. At the same instant a heavy voice shouted sternly, "Get off that bike wit' yer hands up!" Not understanding, I did as I was told. Behind the searchlight, which was attached to a prowl car parked along the road, were two burly policemen, just finishing a long and, up to this point, unproductive vigil. But as they came cautiously toward me and saw that bag they were sure they had at last caught the cat burglar.

"Wha's in that bag?" asked the first policeman. I began to see what they were aiming at, but I couldn't help grinning. "I don't mean to be funnny," I said, "but if I told you you'd never believe me!" Without a word the second policeman picked up the sack and dumped its entire contents in the dust of the road. "An' what th' hell," the poor man groaned, "is all this?" So I told them, without too much detail, but just enough to show beyond question that such things were possible. Utterly disgusted, they put away their guns and motioned me to gather up my possessions and move on. And as I started off the first one shouted, "An' see thatcha get a lamp fer that bike or I'll pull yuh in, so help me!"

It was in 1936—just twenty-one years ago—that John Baker laid the groundwork for the field studies that were to supply the basic facts uncovered by our research projects. The most critical species on the list was the ivory-billed woodpecker, of great size and even greater rarity. Though it was thought to be already extinct by the late 1920s, hope for its survival was revived in 1932 when a few birds were discovered in the Singer Tract in Madison Parish, Louisiana. Five years later other ivory-bills were reliably reported in the Stewards' Neck–Wadmacaun section of the Santee River bottoms in Georgetown County, South Carolina. Field work was begun in January, 1937, under an Audubon Research Fellowship that was established at Cornell University—my own short-lived Alma Mater—with Dr. Arthur A. Allen in charge. James T. Tanner, a graduate student, was selected for the job.

In 1939 two more projects were launched, one on the California condor and the other on the roseate spoonbill. The condor study was set up at the University of California, again under an Audubon Fellowship, and with Dr. Alden H. Miller and the late Dr. Joseph Grinnell in charge. A graduate student, Carl B. Koford, was selected as Fellow. Well along in that same year it was decided to assign the spoonbill study to me.

In Florida Bay the spoonbills arrive on their nesting grounds in October, and so it was that in that month, in the year 1939, Evelyn and I gave up our house in Amityville, lent piano, refrigerator, and a few other items to friends and, storing the remainder of our few worldy goods, packed our two small children into a shiny new and unpaid-for Ford, and hauling a not-so-new house trailer behind us, set off in the direction of Florida and a new life. It was also our hope that we might be able to work out a new life for the roseate spoonbill.

*. . . Can you understand that it is not only scientific results that are the recompense for all this trouble and annoyance, but more, much, much more?*
LORENZ *

## II : The spoonbill comes into its own

Even in the sparkling light of midafternoon an isolated mangrove key in Florida Bay has strange undertones of life, unseen stirrings, and an indescribable awareness. The human intruder may be alone, but there is the uncomfortable feeling of being watched. Such creatures as are visible—an osprey, a distant and alert great white heron—stare with persistent grimness. The osprey's thin, nervous cry is disconcerting. The heavy marl, filled with shell particles that scratch and irritate the skin of your legs and feet, sucks tenaciously as if trying to hold you fast. Great burrowing crabs retreat with gestures of crustacean anger and contempt, throwing tiny jets of liquid from their grotesque heads.

At every step the wall of mangrove shuts doors or drops opaque curtains. The air is still and the small but very maddening mosquitoes swarm in tireless droves, biting viciously. On the weather side of the key I could barely hear the winter breeze piling short, choppy waves against the solid bank of buttress roots that guard the shoreline. In the center of the area there was no movement of

* *King Solomon's Ring.*

air, and I could hear the silence of the mangrove, its deliberate, unhurried, unheeding silence.

I remember my first visit to the hidden pools near the southern tip of the key. Here the red mangrove is dominant. Where the Great Hurricane maimed and killed older trees that were intent on marching out across the broad flats of marl and turtle grass a whole new growth of red mangrove has come forth. A narrow tidal creek enters the key along this southern rim, but the entrance is lost behind the stiltlike fingers and glistening boughs of the red mangrove. Inside, where the less spectacular black mangrove has taken over the endless task of land building, one can trace the winding course of the little stream, and then it is once more lost in a series of tiny pools, silent and enigmatic. The red mangrove is on the march, as it has marched with unbroken stride since the Eocene.

As I stepped over and under tangled roots and brushed aside the network of branches, my legs sank to above the knees in treacherous mud. I pulled myself out by grasping at roots and boughs, half falling, half crawling, and moving forward slowly and painfully. The annoyed grunting notes of Louisiana herons, disturbed in their graceful and expert search for killifishes, the far-off, muffled protest of a fish hawk were the only sounds. Up ahead I saw a narrow opening in the wall of vegetation, and beyond, scarcely visible, a broad pool—mud and a thin layer of water. At the same moment I heard the low, rapid *huh-huh-huh* note of a roseate spoonbill and the startling *woof-woof* of its wings. As I emerged, wet and weary, at the rim of the opening, two spoonbills, necks outthrust, scaled in short circles close overhead, their delicate pinks and deep carmines brilliant against the blue space of sky.

Somewhere in that now immense tangle there was a nest. I felt sure of that because the spoonbills kept swinging by overhead, opening their incredible bills to protest in that steady, subdued note of alarm. With an uneasy coolness I began to search. The mud was softer and deeper away from the edges of the pool. I found it difficult to get across. Impossible! I fell down, in a ridiculous sidewise posture. I pulled my legs and feet from the tentacles of the mud and sat back, in mud and water to my armpits, exhausted. Sweat streamed down my face, blinded my eyes. Tiny mosquitoes stung me, and somehow I ignored them.

Across my path I saw a broad trail, a fantastic trail. There in the slime something as large as a Pleistocene lizard had crawled only a little while before. Its wide belly had left a sickening swath in the mud, wider than my two hands. And clawlike feet had planted themselves on either side, with measured, inexorable regularity. I knew, of course, that it was the trail of a crocodile, for a remnant of that race remains in that lonely corner of Florida. I peered into the silent wall of mangrove that fringed the pool, unable to see what lay just beyond and felt definitely unhappy because of it.

Other trails crossed and recrossed the muddy surface. At the end of some of the trails I found several slow, plodding, diamondback terrapins. When I picked them up they blinked without concern. Placed once more in the mud they barged on four or five feet and then huddled in their shells. They seemed oblivious of me, of the time of day, or of anything whatever.

The spoonbills hovered close overhead, and finally, with sudden good fortune, I found a nest. It was a pile of large sticks seven feet up in a red mangrove, and in it was a clutch of three dull-white eggs, their shells etched and dotted with various shades of brown and chestnut. I tagged the nesting tree and retreated, awkward and uncomfortable, but repaid for my pains.

This journey took place in the full sunlight of midmorning on a clear, fairly calm winter's day. But picture it at night when the mud disgorges creatures of myriad shapes and sizes! At the beginning of my second season in Florida Bay I built a camp on stilts, right over the marly flats at the south rim of a nearby key. The camp itself was hemmed in by mangrove except for a narrow entrance. Here I could study the feeding habits of the pink birds "on location," and here, too, I could share with them the sheltered habitat of mangrove by which they defeat the chill of winter winds.

By day it is a placid, almost uninteresting place. The milky waters are apparently lifeless. In the mangrove a prairie warbler searches for insects and a yellowthroat chatters amiably. But with darkness the mangrove seems to spring to life. Close to my tent a clapper rail unleashes his mad, yammering call and immediately three or four of his kind echo the sound. In that silent, lonely spot the clatter is wild, insane.

As the darkness deepens the waters crawl and churn. Tiny fishes stir the mud with little spirals that look like small clouds of thick, brown smoke. Crabs race sidewise, careening. Large fish, wraithlike in the beam of the flashlight, swim closer menacingly. Mollusks, as small as one's little fingernail, move by fractions of inches, some in straight lines, others whirling into the muddy film and engulfing smaller creatures with ponderous rapidity. The empty shells of dead mollusks race dizzily across the mud on the backs of hermit crabs.

On a warm, still night the movement of many hundreds of tiny fish is a sound as large as that of surf on a shoreline. Sometimes at night, listening, I would imagine that *Teleoceras,* the extinct rhino of Florida, had survived in this unvisited solitude and was now feeding along the edge of the flat inside the key. But it was always the hosts of tiny fish, none of them longer than an inch and a half!

In this atmosphere the cautious, truth-seeking naturalist must constantly sit back, clear his throat (*and* his head!), and start in afresh. He must destroy illusions, hog-tie his imagination, and scratch away at facts. If he can find any! In the marl and the mangrove they have a way of hiding, and their silence is that of the ages.

The fish that live in the mud are one of the common everyday items that were utterly obscure to me at first but that grew in importance and numbers in a gradual sort of way. I first found the fish in the bottom film of the pools of water, some three inches deep, far inside the outer rim of the key. Pneumatophores, the breathers of the black mangrove, dot the surface of these areas, and I was unable to drag an ordinary seine net through them. But I found little schools of miniature fish darting among the beds of quills, and by the careful use of a small dip net I eventually captured several specimens. Still uninformed as to the importance of my catch, I completed the season's work in Florida and moved nearly 2,000 miles to a new base camp on the coast of Texas. And there, in another region inhabited by spoonbills, I found the same tiny fish.

Meanwhile, I had learned that it is an exceedingly common, hardy, and widely distributed species, the potbellied minnow, *Cyprinodon variegatus.* I went back to Florida Bay definitely aware of *Cyprinodon.* Rechecking data on the actual stomach contents of spoonbills (there were only five such stomach contents on record!), I saw that one bird had consumed no less than 246 *Cyprinodon* and other killifishes, in addition to 152 small shrimp. This fish must be incredibly abundant. During my preliminary studies of the previous winter I had missed its significance completely.

Once again I was deep in the mud and mangrove. The hot sun scorched my neck as I leaned over the gunwale of the skiff, peering into the shallow waters for some sign of *Cyprinodon.* I saw nothing. The muddy bottom was apparently lifeless, the water seemingly dead. In a far corner, half hidden by the secretive mangroves, was an area marked by the tracks of a good-sized wading bird whose toes were partially webbed. And floating idly on the surface film was a small pink feather, delicate and symbolic. An even closer search disclosed semicircular lines in the mud, lines an inch apart and in pairs, lines that curved through 180 degrees in a strange crisscross of patterns. Spoonbills had been here, plying their partly opened mandibles back and forth in the sweeping motion that typifies their manner of feeding.

But still no sign of life. No swarms of fish, no expected multitudes of *Cyprinodon.* Nevertheless I took my short seine and, stepping cautiously into the water, I made a quick, darting sweep. Pulling the net aboard, I saw that for me the mystery of *Cyprinodon* was forever dispelled. There, in the belly of the net, lay a wriggling, quivering mass of *the* fish. Out of the mud, where they lay protected from enemies and from the direct heat of the subtropical sun, I hauled them by the score.

Perhaps I have given the impression that the mangrove is fearsome. It is, in a way, but it is also one of the most interesting, most challenging of North American habitats. Gaze at a mangrove key from the deck of a boat. It is drab or wild-appearing or uninteresting or even unnoticed, depending on your individual point of view. But go ashore, alone. Above all, camp there overnight. It is no longer drab or uninteresting, and certainly not unnoticed. And as for its being wild, you will revise your private connotation of that word before the night is over. A million years have done little to change the aspect of a hidden pool inside the mangrove. If you don't believe it, crawl with crocodile and terrapin through the slime and watch the lowly gastropod leave his smooth track beside yours. A million years have not changed them. Best of all, stay out there at night. You will listen to the silence of centuries and you will hear, as I have, the noiseless murmur of the Pleistocene.

At 6 P.M. the *Croc* was hard aground on the mud flat where the falling tide had left her. She was probably there for the night, and I along with her, although I figured there might be enough water to get her off around midnight if I could manage to wake up. Then I could run her slowly out into the middle of the lake and anchor until daylight. There was a freshening wind out of the west, and after dark it started to rain.

It was April, 1941, the second spring of my spoonbill studies, and I was stuck in the mouth of Little Sable Creek at the northern end of Lake Ingraham, but anxious to leave so as to move on up the coast toward Alligator Cove, where I knew I would find spoonbills. As it turned out, I got up five times during the night but was unable to get clear. Next morning there were three white pelicans loafing on a mudbank in the lake, watching me with disinterest. As I made my coffee I counted sixteen willets feeding in the shallows nearby and bathing in the nearly fresh flow of water. Overhead flashed scattered flocks of shore birds and small groups of lesser scaups. I had seen no spoonbills. To pass the time I took the small skiff and poled up the creek, with snowy egrets rising ahead of me. Turning into the ditch leading to Cattail Lakes, I soon reached the sawgrass. Along the bank a clump of yucca was in full bloom, their white flowers lovely in that desert-like setting of dead mangroves and the broken stubs of hurricane-killed cabbage palms. Schools of small silver mullet and slender needlefish darted before me, moving much faster than I could against the current in my squat, flat-bottomed little craft.

A half hour later I ran up against a crude bridge of palm logs, so I had to unload and pull the empty skiff over it. The Cattail Lakes were now visible just ahead. Spoonbills had been reported from here a number of times and were said to have nested somewhere in the area. I pushed on for nearly two more hours, stopping now and then to drag my net in the water and catch a few specimens, most of which were killifishes. The channel narrowed to about four feet in width and was now very shallow and obstructed by brush and fallen trees. There were great numbers of alligator gar, a fish of prehistoric appearance with heavy scales that cover its body like armor, but I was more interested in the tiny killifishes, which are an important spoonbill and heron food. They were quite numerous and included several varieties—top minnows, banded killifish, sail-fins, and the ever-present *Cyprinodon.* But still I had found no spoonbills, and once again I was impressed by the fact, so often to be repeated, that here was what appeared to be an extensive habitat, suitable in every way except that it was empty of spoonbills. There were other birds, all of them the usual associates of the spoonbills in this region. I counted four shovelers, some fifty or more Florida ducks, many yellowlegs, Louisiana herons and snowy egrets. A brown pelican and several white ibises flew by.

In those days, some fifteen years ago when we were just beginning to learn something about the spoonbill and its problems, the only breeding colony in Florida was located on Bottlepoint Key near Tavernier.* It was a winter colony, and now that April had arrived the birds had completed their nesting cycle and scattered to parts unknown. The most that we could hope for at that time was fifteen breeding pairs, with an average of surviving young that ran about 2.7 or less per nest. We weren't getting ahead very rapidly at this rate, especially considering the fact that the

* Of the joys and vicissitudes of my first season on Bottlepoint Key I have told in *The Flame Birds* (Dodd, Mead & Company, Inc., New York, 1947).

roseate spoonbill requires three years to reach mature breeding age and that the normal mortality during the first year is probably in excess of 50 per cent, and perhaps as much as 70 per cent. But we had a few ideas and a good deal of hope, and we meant to keep at it. Today, twenty-one years after we first began our protection program in Florida Bay, roseate spoonbills nest on seven or eight different keys and their numbers have climbed to 150 or more nesting pairs which rear more than 300 young every winter. The improvement has been slow and they are by no means out of the woods, but if you had had a part in nursing them along through those early years, as I did, you would be pretty happy about it.

The roseate spoonbill is no ordinary bird. It is large, with a wingspread of over four feet, but it is the color of the plumage that is the outstanding characteristic. It is unbelievable! And the shape of the bill—elongated, flattened toward the tip, and spoon-shaped. There is nothing else quite like it. At the start of the breeding season a fully grown adult is a vision of pinks, carmines, orange-buffs, saffron yellows, lake reds, and subdued greens. The sexes are plumaged alike. The head is bare of feathers and the skin is a soft apple green, which changes to a glowing golden buff at the height of the nuptial period, probably at the time of pairing. Against this setting the cherry-red eyes are like jewels.

The longish but sturdy neck is white and the over-all body plumage and wings are a rich pink, with the elongated feathers of the upper and lower tail coverts an intense carmine. When the wings are folded there is a splash of deep carmine in a horizontal line from shoulder to back—the lesser wing coverts. In the middle of the breast there is a patch of stiff, curly feathers that are also carmine in color, and as if this wasn't enough, this is surrounded by suffusions of pink and orange-buff, with splotches of soft saffron yellow toward the shoulders. The short tail, beneath its brilliant coverts, is a startling orange-buff. The legs, which are long as in all wading birds, are thicker than those of a heron and are a dark lake red.

The day that Nature chose the roseate spoonbill's colors must have been a very special one. There are five other species of spoonbills in the world, but none have the brilliant colors of the New World form. These other spoonbills inhabit parts of Europe, Asia, Africa, and Australia, and in general they are white birds with some black or yellow in their plumage. As if to make up for their lack of brilliance they sport long, pointed feathers on their heads, a nauchal crest that is quite striking.

The evolution and purpose of these varied plumages and soft-part colors is in itself a fascinating subject. When we were studying the black-crowned night herons back on Long Island we observed that head plumes and the colors of the legs, the bill, and the loral space in front of the eyes had a direct bearing on the selection of a mate and pair formation. These ceremonies are initiated by the male night heron, who reaches unexpected heights during these two or three weeks of high-pressure courtship. Normally, during the remainder of the year, a rather unspectacular little heron with inconspicuous black, gray, and white plumage patterns, dull-yellow legs, and creaking vocal attainments, the male reacts in a most wonderful manner to the arrival of April and its warmer temperatures. As a result of a partial prenuptial molt, his plumage is sleek and glistening. The heavy bill is a glossy blue-black and so is the bare skin of the lores. The slender white plumes on the head are long and resplendent. But the most striking transformation is in the color of the legs. Their usual yellow is now a pinkish red, and we soon learned that there is a definite purpose in these changes. It was our conclusion that the acquisition of red legs in the night heron is an inborn character limited to a period of two to four weeks out of the year. Its chief function is as a releasing stimulus that serves as an indicator of readiness for pairing.

When you consider that birds have no intelligence as in man, and when you ponder the obvious fact that flocks of birds such as these night herons still manage to get together in the same place at the same time and eventually produce young, you can appreciate the importance of studies such as these. In my researches into the habits of a rare species like the roseate spoonbill the part that behavior studies played in our understanding of these little known birds was considerable.

In the spring of 1940 I had shifted my base of operations to Texas and found there that the spoonbill colony on the Second Chain-of-Islands in San Antonio Bay offered much better opportunities for observation than the few pairs nesting in the tangled mangrove thickets of Florida Bay. I discovered for the first time that in the spoonbill it is the female who isolates herself in a tree or bush that will later be the nest site. Her role is a relatively passive one, which is in marked contrast to that of the male of this species. She merely sits there, now and then reaching out to grasp a twig or small branch in her bill and agitate it. The male spoonbill, on the other hand, demonstrates his "maleness" by moving about with a great show of activity and purpose. When he sees an unattached female occupying her pairing site he flies toward her, bobbing his green and golden head and beating his resplendent wings. She may repulse him at first, but if he is persistent and if no other male dislodges him during these advances, he may shortly find a perch beside her and together they may begin the touching betrothal period of their kind. Of course, to accomplish these things, both the male and female spoonbill must have reached breeding condition at a high level, as demonstrated by the color and appearance of plumage and soft parts, and by the production of the limited and generally improbable behavior that is required. As in night herons—or, indeed, as in all animals, man included—boy meets girl and by means of certain inherently established signs and signals peculiar to each separate species, an understanding is accomplished. Watching the courtship behavior of birds, in which there is no intelligence remotely comparable to that of the higher mammals such as man, we must confess our wonder and admiration. Beside them we ourselves are often inept and frequently confused, but I suppose that this is one of the many penalties that we must pay for our superior intellect.

One significant fact concerned with the survival of the spoonbill could have been uncovered only as a result of behavior studies. From what I saw in Texas it was clear that their inherent ability to gather in suitable habitats and reproduce their kind was in no way impaired genetically. Though the elaborate courtship and its logical follow-through are complicated enough, there is no impairment, no genetic deficiency that can be observed in the birds themselves. Not that we really suspected that there was, but once any creature is classified in the "rare" category, all sorts of suggestions are made as to the reason for this condition. This was one of them. Another had to do with food. Was sufficient food available for a species that must have highly specialized feeding habits, considering the unique shape of its bill, etc.? As is often the case, we found that their habitual environment contains more food of the character preferred by spoonbills than our small population could possibly require. No problem in this field at all. The reasons behind the spoonbills' rarity are abundantly clear and quite logical once you are in a position to comprehend them. But it was necessary to do a lot of spadework first, and that takes both time and hard work.

In the course of my study of the roseate spoonbill there were many problems that could not be solved by the usual or the ordinary or the conventional research methods. I was forced to devise methods of my own. One puzzle of major importance was the status of the several hundred spoonbills that spend the summer on the southwest Florida coast without breeding. For some years we had observed these scattered flocks and hoped that they might nest somewhere in that area, as they once had years ago. Our wardens went to considerable lengths to report on their movements and to provide them with special protection. From what I had seen of them it seemed to me that the first point to be cleared up was the question of the age groups represented in these flocks. How many of them were actually of breeding age?

It had already been established that the roseate spoonbill goes through several molts and plumage changes before attaining the full splendor of the adult garb. And it was estimated that this entire process requires perhaps as much as thirty-six months. In addition, according to our observations, these birds do not breed except in the complete adult plumage, or not until they are at least three years of age. How was I to go about determining accurately the ages of some four or five hundred spoonbills that live during the hot summer months along a wild, mangrove-lined coast nearly 150 miles in extent? A number of methods suggested themselves but were discarded, one by one, as impractical. With a species as rare as *Ajaia ajaja* it would be impossible to even so much as lay a hand on a single one of them. How was it to be done?

There was also the less immediate but equally important question of the origin of these flocks. Where did they come from? With our Texas spoonbills quite obviously migrating in an opposite direction toward Mexico and our little Florida Bay colony producing only a handful of young each year, it seemed clear that these particular individuals must be hatched and reared in colonies outside our boundaries. But where?

Actually it wasn't as difficult as you might imagine, and I never have had so much fun in my life as I did in working it out. I eventually decided that there was only one way to acquaint myself with the age groups in the summer flocks, and that was to seek them out, observe them at close hand, and analyze their plumages in as much detail as I could. Fortunately for my purpose, the flock as a whole was broken up into many small units, beginning with the southernmost unit in the vicinity of the East Cape Canal in back of Cape Sable. There were other small flocks near Wood Key, Alligator Cove, Shark Bight, Duck Rock and Duck Rock Cove, Joe's Grasses, Rabbit Key Grasses, Pink Curlew Flats, Bluehill Bay, and still farther north in Pine Sound. In other words, if I could spend enough time with each separate unit to observe the plumages represented, then by the end of the summer I might learn what we needed to know.

This inquiry was the chief purpose of the cruise of the *Croc*, the shallow-draft, eighteen-foot boat that I fitted out just for this job. I could live aboard her for ten days at a stretch without setting foot on shore, if need be, and in her I could reach every one of the remote coves and the half-hidden bays where the spoonbills came in to feed. I let the tide drop me on mud flats close to where I conjectured the pink birds would appear, and by trial and error I finally managed to work over the entire route and fill my notebooks with detailed descriptions and sketches of a total of 305 spoonbills, or nearly 60 per cent of the entire summering flock. On a basis of their plumages, none were juveniles, 109 were birds just over one year of age, 174 were in the first postnuptial plumage, or just under 20 months of age; 20 were in the second postnuptial plumage, or just under 30 months of age, and only two showed the full adult feathers.

A careful check on their arrival and departure dates on that coast, the observation of migrating birds that headed out from Cape Sable to Key Vaca and apparently off beyond Sombrero Light toward the Cay Sal Bank and Cuba, as well as new firsthand information on Cuban spoonbill colonies, convinced us that these summer flocks represented a postbreeding season dispersal from Cuba. We still believe this to be the case, but it would be both interesting and of considerable value to place colored bands on the legs of nestling spoonbills in several Cuban colonies and see how many of them turned up on the Florida coast. Perhaps this can be done someday.

During the war years of 1942–1945 many of us, the writer included, were almost completely out of touch with such pleasant subjects as the love life of the roseate spoonbill. We learned later that a few of the flocks had been among the innocent bystanders which suffered quite needless casualties. Most of the losses were on the Texas coast, where local training fields sent out aircraft manned by eager and trigger-happy youngsters who fired on any object that seemed to them a safe target. Others dropped practice bombs which exploded a 10-gauge shotgun shell when they hit. Unfortunately, spoonbill flocks in open, uninhabited areas made tempting targets, and during those years their numbers were definitely reduced on the Texas Gulf Coast. In Florida we were luckier, and when I returned to the Keys in 1946, after an absence of four years, I learned that our Florida Bay spoonbill flock had actually shown an increase. This was the year before Everglades National Park was dedicated, but the U.S. Fish and Wildlife Service had held the fort by taking over Florida Bay and operating it for the time being as a Federal Refuge. An effective patrol had been set up by Jack C. Watson, and this meant not only thorough coverage of the entire region by boat, but a public relations job that had made a conservationist—or if not a conservationist then at least a Christian—out of every fisherman, boatman, tourist, and resident in the area. In the winter of 1950–1951 the spoonbill population had increased to seven separate nesting colonies, and a total of 64 occupied nests. This number reached 81 nests the following winter. By this time the entire area of Florida Bay was within the boundaries of the National Park, and protection was in the hands of regular park rangers.

Also at this time the National Audubon Society instituted wildlife tours in this and other parts of Florida, so as to take the public by car and boat, with competent guides, to see such spectacles as a colony of roseate spoonbills in Florida Bay. When I think of the lonely days and nights of that first difficult winter on Bottlepoint Key at the start of our spoonbill studies in 1939, it is hard to realize that more than 12,000 people have now taken part in these tours, the greater part of them visiting Florida Bay, chiefly to see the spoonbills. Only a few people had seen this beautiful bird a few short years ago, but it can be said now that its friends and well-wishers number in the thousands. Once you have seen the spoonbills flashing their pink and carmine wings against the blue of a Florida sky you'll get some idea of the satisfaction of those who have fought to protect this bird.

In this way the main purpose of our roseate spoonbill study has been served. The new knowledge that has been gained as a result of our research is important. Because of it we have known what steps must be taken and where and in what direction to take them. In our continuing efforts to increase this lovely bird on our shores we will not be working in the dark. But the main job has been to interest the public in the spoonbill, including the local public that, in considerable measure, has a part in controlling the destiny of these birds. I now make my home in Tavernier on the lower end of Key Largo. It looks out on the open Atlantic on the one hand and on the shallows of Florida Bay on the other. From the roof of my study I can see Bottlepoint Key, and from this vantage point I have also seen spoonbills flying across the harbor toward their feeding place on Dove Creek Slough, just north of town. When I first saw the pink birds here, more than twenty years ago, they were frequently shot as they crossed the old Key West highway alongside this same slough. Once we had to put up a warning sign and employ a man to try to prevent these birds from being killed there.

Today this same community is proud of the fact that this is the only town in the United States where roseate spoonbills are a daily sight each winter. You can see them feeding in ditches along the highway and you can stand in front of the drugstore and point them out to visitors. "Look, right overhead—there goes a spoonbill!" Two years ago the Upper Keys Chamber of Commerce distributed a brochure that listed all the motels, restaurants, fishing guides, and places of interest to tourists. And on the cover was a picture of one of the star attractions. It wasn't a Marilyn Monroe figure in a Bikini, nor was it the usual Florida palm tree. You've probably guessed it! The picture was that of a roseate spoonbill—none other than *Ajaia ajaja*—and when I saw it I knew that the spoonbill had finally come into its own. It couldn't have happened to a more deserving citizen!

*. . . The crane the giant, with his trompes soune.*

CHAUCER *

# III : A giant of beauty and grandeur

In the journal of Meriwether Lewis, under date of April 11, 1805, there is this entry: "...we killed two geese, and saw some cranes, the largest bird of that kind common to the Missouri and Mississippi, perfectly white except the large feathers on the first joint of the wing, which are black." The location was just above the mouth of the Little Missouri River, in what is now Dunn County, North Dakota. These birds were undoubtedly whooping cranes, possibly a migrant pair moving north from wintering grounds on the Texas Gulf Coast. At that time, a century and a half ago, the continental population of *Grus americana* was relatively undisturbed. During the breeding season they ranged from northern Illinois northwestward across the Prairie Provinces of Canada and far into Northwest Territories. In winter they scattered out across the broad spread of the entire continent, from the vicinity of Cape May, New Jersey, and the river deltas of the South Carolina and Georgia coasts to Louisiana, Texas, and

* *Canterbury Tales.*

the interior plateau of old Mexico to a point scarcely 100 miles from the Pacific Ocean.

Today the picture is somewhat different. It is possible that you still might see a pair of migrant whooping cranes at the mouth of the Little Missouri, for the few members of this splendid race that survive continue to fly across the country in their migrations and pass very close to that location. But I wouldn't make any bets on it. For these birds are now reduced to little more than a couple of dozen individuals, and their breeding and wintering ranges are, by comparison with their original limits, mere pinponts on the map of North America.

What has been the cause of this tragedy, and why should we be concerned about it? For we *are* concerned; there is no denying it. In the last ten years or so the welfare of the whooping crane has become front-page news. Their photographs have appeared in magazines of nationwide circulation, and every official report of their nesting success and current numbers is sent out by the wire services and printed in countless newspapers. Editorials have been written about them, hopeful, earnest commentaries on their precarious situation and their chances of survival. In 1952 a great oil company proudly announced, in a full-page advertisement in *The Saturday Evening Post,* that they had agreed to limit drilling operations on a part of the wintering grounds of these birds as a contribution toward their preservation. In addition, this same corporation relocated a loading dock, pipeline, and access road to avoid further disturbance of the wintering area. They did these things at considerable cost, acting simply as "good neighbors and good citizens."

What is behind this new awareness? In a recent article in *The New York Times,* John Oakes wrote:

> The immense latent strength of conservation as a political force in the United States is becoming constantly more apparent. People generally—and that means voters—are gradually awakening to the fact that the natural resources of their country, and much of its natural beauty, have been disappearing before their eyes; and, though there are constant setbacks, there

is also much evidence of a growing determination to do something about the problem.

An editorial in the *Christian Science Monitor*, in commenting on the whooping-crane situation, expressed the opinion that our civilization, although outwardly unaffected, does not wholly survive the needless extinction of a species. "Can society," this editor writes, "whether through sheer wantonness or callous neglect, permit the extinction of something beautiful or grand in nature without risking extinction of something beautiful and grand in its own character?"

And the whooping crane, tallest and most imposing, as well as the rarest, of North American birds, is in truth both beautiful and grand. An adult male stands nearly five feet tall and has a wingspread of seven and one-half feet. His carriage is proud and alert, and this, with the cold yellow brightness of his eye, is eloquent testimony of his fierce, untamed, and fearless nature. The plumage is a satiny white, except for the jet black of the wingtips. The female is similar in appearance, but slightly smaller and more gentle in character. The head, which is usually held high so as to look an alien world squarely in the face, is bare on the forehead and crown except for sparse, black, hairlike feathers. The exposed skin is a carmine red, as is that of the cheeks and the space between the eyes and bill, but there is a heavy, black "mustache" of bristle-like feathers across each cheek, rich and glossy in a healthy adult. The heavy, spear-shaped bill is pink or flesh-colored at the base, dark olive green on the middle portion, and a yellowish-olive color on the tip. The legs are black and so are the upper sides of the toes, which are flesh-color beneath.

As in other species of cranes, the tertials, or innermost series of flight feathers, are longer than the primaries and are exquisite and plumelike. They trail over the after tips of the folded wings and can be raised over the back at will in certain types of display.

The young whooper begins life as a downy chick with cinnamon and russet-brown colors on the back and grayish buff beneath. As a juvenile in its first feathers it is a brown to almost pinkish buff in over-all color, with white beginning to appear on the lower breast, belly, and back, and especially in the wings. There is considerable individual variation. In March, at close to ten months of age, most of the browns and buffs have disappeared entirely except for some feathers on the head, upper neck, and in parts of the wings. The head is feathered until about this same age.

With the broad extent of its original distribution the whooping crane has had quite an array of local names. Because of its great size it was once called the "flying sheep" in Manitoba. In Texas its voice earned it the resounding names of "bugle crane" and "trumpet crane," and the young were spoken of as "pink cranes." In Mexico and along the borders of Texas, various Spanish names were applied: *mal ojo* for the "fierce eye," *grulla blanca* or "white crane," and the poetic *viejo del agua* or "old man of the water." Far to the north, in Canada, the Cree Indians called it *wapow oocheechawk* and the Eskimos along the west shore of Hudson Bay, *tutteeghuk,* both of which probably mean the same thing.

Laymen frequently confuse the cranes with the herons and egrets. Except that both have long bills, long necks, and long legs, they belong to entirely different families. In the accepted order by which birds are classified, with the lowest orders at the bottom, the herons follow such families as the pelicans, gannets, cormorants, and man-o'-war birds, while the cranes are considerably higher on the scale, on beyond the ibises, flamingos, swans, geese, ducks, all of the hawks, as well as the grouse, quails, and turkeys. Cranes properly belong in the Order Gruiformes, which includes all cranes, rails, coots, gallinules, sun grebes and sun bitterns. In the evolutionary scale they follow immediately after the grouse, turkeys, and their kin, and are followed in turn by the ploverlike birds—plovers, snipes, sandpipers, and so on through the terns, gulls and auks, and their relatives. This may not tell you much more about the cranes, but it seems appropriate to give them their full due. The cranes are a magnificent group of birds. There are twenty-three species and subspecies extant in the world, some of which are fully as handsome and even larger in size than the whooper. Only *Grus americana,* however, is currently threatened with extinction. Asia is the great home of the cranes, with eight distinct species and two subspecies, but they likewise occur on all other continents except in South America. In North America, besides the whooping crane, we also have the more abundant sandhill cranes, which are divided into one species and three geographic races.

The heyday of the larger cranes appears to have been the Pleistocene, conditions having been more favorable for their existence then, perhaps, than at any time since. From what we know of these conditions it seems likely, however, that the whooping crane entered upon what we term "recent" time—say a mere one million years ago—in lesser numbers than was good for them. The reasons for this are forever hidden in the darkness of the prehistoric past, but certain clues remain. We picture the salt seas as the birthplace of all organic life; and in the endless struggle toward perfection and improvement that is the motivating force throughout the animal kingdom, we can see abundant evidence that most living animals have escaped from their lowly origin in the sea and found the means for development and fulfillment on the land. Even today there are countless creatures still struggling to make good this escape—first from a marine environment to a brackish- or fresh-water existence, then the final and more difficult advance, from water to the land.

Nature is dynamic, and the evolution of an organism, in very general terms, may be described as a constant adaptation to change. When, for example, a certain environmental condition alters so that an organism is unable to secure its habitual food in the usual way, it must broaden the scope of its food preferences or find a new way of securing the food it is used to eating. Otherwise it will perish. It is evident that the ancestors of the cranes were marsh dwellers, denizens of fresh-water or brackish marshes whose inhabitants were one step removed from the sea of their ancestry. As conditions changed, most of the cranes moved more and more into the uplands and in time were land birds for more of their life than they were water birds. The sandhill cranes, which are far more abundant than the whoopers, are an example. The whooper, for reasons of its own, has been less adaptable, more resistant to change, and not only continues to spend nearly all of its life in the marshes of its progenitors, but spends one half of the year on the very rim of the original salt sea. On their winter quarters in Texas, the whooping cranes are seldom seen above the three-foot contour line, just beyond sea level, whereas the sandhill cranes are rarely observed below that line. The ratio of lesser sandhill cranes to whooping cranes in the Pleistocene deposits of Rancho La Brea were 29 to 1, and, even more significant, the comparison between these two species today is some 150,000 sandhill cranes to 20 or so whooping cranes.

So, while we can readily understand the survival problem that has faced *Grus americana* for so long a period, perhaps since the end of the Pleistocene, this understanding does not detract in the least from our admiration for his invincible will to survive, against all the accepted rules of biological inevitability; nor does it deter us in our current efforts to perpetuate his noble existence, by whatever means we have at hand.

This last has not been easy, the world being what it is. In more or less recent years, when whooping cranes needed help more than ever before, the work of the Audubon Societies, and similar organizations, began to change public opinion with regard to such matters. This, if you will, was a step in human evolution. Then came the Migratory Bird Treaty Act and Federal protection for many species of birds, including the whooping crane. Perhaps the abolishment of the spring shooting of waterfowl did as much to prevent their extinction during the last forty years as any other move that has been made in that time. But the most telling blow in their favor was struck by the U.S. Fish and Wildlife Service in 1937, when the Aransas Refuge was established on the Texas coast. Although the refuge was set up ostensibly as a winter haven for ducks and geese, the Service had not been unaware of the fact that more than half the remaining whooping-crane population spent the winter within a portion of its area. This move has been responsible in a very large measure for the continued survival of the species.

Aransas is now an accepted and widely regarded addition to the important wildlife refuge system of our Federal government, but its early days were not without their difficulties. As is so often the case, local factions did not fully understand the purpose of the refuge and resented the invasion of governmental authority, especially Federal authority. James O. Stevenson, the first refuge manager at Aransas and an old and valued friend of mine, was an able student of the whooping crane from the day of his initial contact with it. He wrote several articles about these birds that stirred wide interest in the need for greater knowledge of their entire life cycle and a more comprehensive program for their protection. In one of these he described the local reaction to the establishment of Aransas Refuge.

> Back in 1937, the boys used to gather around the old coal-burner in Cap Daniel's store in Austwell, Texas, commenting from time to time on the fate of the farmer. A visitor could have heard them mulling over the latest news: "I hear the government is buying up the Blackjacks for a pile of money just to protect a couple of them squawking cranes! They tell me they ain't bad eating but there's no open season on them." To this came the inevitable reply: "If you can't shoot them, what the blankety-blank good are they?"

But, as Stevenson commented, "Facts are invariably garbled in any hot-stove league."

When Jim Stevenson left Aransas in 1941, local savants were rapidly changing their opinions. A few years later, when I lived near Austwell for two winters, the irrepressible Cap Daniel's combination store, beer parlor, gas station, and garage was also Whooping Crane Information Center. The price of crops and the recent war were high on the list of major subjects under discussion, but whooping cranes had become topic number one. Cap is a great collector of antiques, especially old firearms and other engines of war. The walls of his little place are heavy with relics from many periods, and he never tires of adding new exhibits. One day he said to me, "Mr. Allen, I wonder if you couldn't get ahold of some whoopin'-crane pitchers I could put up on my wall. People ask me about 'em every day an' I oughta have a pitcher or two." I brought him some pictures a few days later, including one large drawing of a pair of the great birds. It was then that Cap showed his true mettle. Without a moment's hesitation he walked to the most prominent wall in his establishment and yanked down the large reproduction of Judge Roy Bean holding court west of the Pecos, a beer advertisement that is justly famous throughout the Lone Star State. In its place he hung the portrait of the two whooping cranes and, as far as I know, there it reposes, in that place of honor, to this day.

You must understand that it took several months—one entire winter season and an absence of some months more in the North—to get to this point, even with such a genial character as Cap Daniel. And with all of the other characters, some of them less genial, who made up the human elements of the whooping crane's winter environment. You can be sure that it wasn't easy—it never is—but getting people lined up and in a sympathetic and cooperative frame of mind is vitally important on any job. There is no need to go into it to any extent, but when my family and I arrived in Texas in November, 1946, we found ourselves in a hostile camp. We were "outsiders," and therefore we were expected to be foolishly impractical and naïvely critical. Furthermore, we couldn't possibly know anything at all about whooping cranes. This last I was so willing to admit, right at the start, that it was relatively easy to enlist nearly everyone's help in learning all there was to know about them. We began with a clean slate, which is a very good way to begin. I find that my first field notes read as follows: "Two adult wh. cranes on wet mud flat in Redfish Slough. Fed a little and rested, preening. ½ to ¾ mi. distant from our position on dyke." What could I learn about them and their existence? My job was to dig into their lives as deeply as possible and come up with some answers that would assure their survival.

I remember that those first two birds seemed very far away—"½ to ¾ mi. distant"—but not only in a physical sense. Their arrogant bearing, the trim of their sails, as it were, would intimidate the most brash investigator. I reached our cabin that first night feeling very humble and not too happy. And that, also, is a very good way to begin.

It was in October, 1946, that I was asked to take over the whooping-crane investigation. I shut up my house on the Florida Keys, packed my family, bag and baggage, into a car and luggage trailer, and headed for New York for a briefing. Sewall Pettingill, who had been studying the cranes for the past year, was there; also Clarence Cottam, Gus Swanson, and Phil DuMont of the Fish and Wildlife Service, and John Baker, president of the National Audubon Society. When I had been sufficiently stuffed with information and good wishes, we resumed our travels, heading for Texas, where most of the whoopers spent the winter and where my studies of this phase of their life would have to begin.

The Whooping Crane Project was set up in 1945 as a cooperative undertaking between the U.S. Fish and Wildlife Service and the National Audubon Society. Some years before, when on the Texas coast working with roseate spoonbills, I had seen my first whooping cranes and wondered idly what poor, unsuspecting soul would someday be assigned the rugged task of making a full-scale study of them. I hadn't the slightest notion that it would be me! The initial investigations were begun in Canada by Fred Bard of the Provincial Museum in Regina; and Dr. Olin Sewall Pettingill, Jr., of Carleton College, was appointed Research Fellow and made the first field studies in 1945–1946, including the first airplane search for the northern breeding grounds. When Pettingill returned to his teaching chores at Carleton the job fell to me.

For almost half a century these birds have been advertised as on the verge of total extinction. As early as 1912 Forbush pronounced them "doomed to extinction," and the following year Dr. Hornaday predicted that "this splendid bird will almost certainly be the next North American species to be totally exterminated." Ten years later, in 1923, an article in *The Saturday Evening Post* actually announced that "the Whooping Crane, perhaps the most majestic bird of all our feathered hosts, has traveled the long trail into oblivion." To use the familiar phrase, this report of its demise was somewhat exaggerated. The truth is that while seriously reduced in numbers by that year, the whooper was far from being at the end of its long trail. And in the thirty-three years that have passed since that premature announcement it has held its own with an amazing vigor and stubbornness.

The causes behind its depleted range and reduction in numbers should be crystal-clear. The Illinois marshes at the southwest tip of Lake Michigan where it once nested are now occupied by the sprawling city of Chicago. The sloughs of northwestern Iowa have long since been drained for the raising of corn and hogs. Reed-bordered lakes in central and northern Minnesota are populous summer resorts, and other former nesting sites in northeast North Dakota and in the lowlands and parklands of the Prairie Provinces are rich crop lands. Even peripheral nesting sites along the Slave River and elsewhere in the Northwest Territories no longer provided the vast isolation these strange wild creatures require, and they too have long been deserted.

On top of this, the wintering range on the Gulf Coast, and the once broad migration highway between there and breeding areas to the North, gradually and inevitably were overrun with enterprising and restless representatives of the human race. More and more whooping cranes were killed, for sport and for food, a peak being reached during the 1890s. The greatest number reported as killed met their end in Nebraska, with Texas, Louisiana, Saskatchewan, North Dakota, Iowa, Illinois, South Dakota, Kansas, Manitoba, and Minnesota close behind, in that order. They were shot on the breeding grounds as they sat on their eggs, and they were shot on migration as they came to earth to feed and rest. On the wintering grounds they were shot when they raided sweet-potato fields in Louisiana, and for sport along the Texas coast.

From 1912 onward a yearly record was kept of the number of migrant whooping cranes passing over the Platte River in Nebraska. The reports were often inaccurate, and the result was usually an exaggerated picture of the actual total. Nevertheless the publication of this information, contributed almost entirely by amateurs, did much to keep alive an interest in the fate of this species. In 1941, however, observers in Nebraska reported the sighting of only three migrating whoopers, in 1942 only four and in 1943, just one lone bird. Ornithological and conservation circles were immediately aroused and there were pleas for immediate action. As I wrote in my monograph on the whooping crane (National Audubon Society: *Research Report No.* 3, 1952): "The conflagration that had been smoldering along for more than eighty mortal years had at last blazed into a four-alarm fire! *It was about time.*" The Cooperative Whooping Crane Project was the natural outgrowth of this situation. In addition to the leading role undertaken by the two cooperating agencies, many other organizations answered the plea for action in every way that they could, among them the Canadian Wildlife Service, the Saskatchewan Department of Natural Resources, the Royal Canadian Mounted Police, the Saskatchewan Fish and Game League, Ducks Unlimited, the game commissions of those states through which the birds migrate, and a long list of others. And this was only the beginning. In the ten years and more that have passed since this campaign got under way the public has learned about whooping cranes. To quote once more from the editorial in *Christian Science Monitor:*

> Some millions of Americans will hope, we are sure, that the whooping cranes are spared for their own sake. And we have an idea that most of them will at least sense, also, that each of these beautiful birds, as it flies southward, carries a Yellowstone or a Quetico-Superior Wilderness between its great wings.

But this widespread response and this brand of understanding has not been accomplished all at once. It has taken time. In 1945, when the whole thing began, the immensity of the problem and our ignorance of the facts were appalling to contemplate.

In December, 1945, previous to my arrival at Aransas, after two flights over the area and consultation with Fish and Wildlife personnel, Pettingill estimated the Texas population at twenty-five birds, adults and young. Sixteen of these were on the Aransas National Wildlife Refuge and nine on Matagorda Island, which is privately owned and lies immediately to the south facing the open Gulf of Mexico. In Louisiana, the Service's flyway biologist, Bob Smith, reported the continued presence of two whoopers between White Lake and Gueydan, all that remained of the flock of thirteen observed by Johnny Lynch in 1939. As there were reportedly two additional birds that had been injured and were being held in captivity, the best we could count on, as of the previous winter, was a total population of twenty-nine whooping cranes still surviving. However, a number of interested people, myself included, wondered if others might not exist on other wintering grounds, elsewhere on the Texas coast or in Mexico. This was one of the important little items that must be dealt with as soon as possible, preferably that same winter.

The winter home of most of these cranes is on the mud flats at the tip of the Blackjack Peninsula, so named for the blackjack oaks that grow there, a jutting, heart-shaped tongue of land lying between San Antonio and St. Charles Bays, some 25 miles to the northeast of Corpus Christi Bay. A few may pass the winter on Matagorda Island or on nearby St. Joseph Island. Since 1937 the Blackjack Peninsula has been established as the Aransas National Wildlife Refuge, operated by our partners in the study project, the U.S. Fish and Wildlife Service. Even before setting up a field camp, I had begun a series of counts on which to base an up-to-date estimate of the current whooping-crane population. At that time we had two very simple methods: We could cover the area on the ground and hope that we didn't miss any of them, or we could fly over in Bob Tanner's light plane—and hope that we didn't miss any. Some of those ground counts were pretty rugged, as our initial equipment was nil and we had to improvise by hitching a big farm wagon behind a slow and noisy tractor. Eventually we used the airplane for all more or less "final" or official counts.

Although it was early November when we made our first count, the damp air was already chilly. If they had any sense, I thought, the transplanted Brahman cattle would begin dreaming unhappily of the humid valley of the Brahmaputra, but, looking at them, I decided they had been in Texas so long they didn't remember. As the day progressed the leaden sky grew even more oppressive and it was colder. We had worked over the east section, including a rough side trip to Jones Lake and Mustang Lake, and were now moving more or less steadily down the long stretch of East Shore Road. Up ahead on the tractor, Bud had his wide Albuquerque Special cocked over the bridge of his nose, probably in an effort to keep some of the wind out of his eyes. His feet, on the clutch and brake pedals, were thrust into high-heeled cowboy boots. The boots were tight and he was trying, without obvious success, to wriggle his numb toes and still keep the tractor moving over the rough trail.

Now and then one of us in the wagon box would spot a white blob in the distance and then we set up a fearful howl until Bud heard and, with much clanking and bumping, brought the entire equipage to a halt. Standing up on a plank thrown across the wagon box, we looked long and carefully at the white blob, trying to decide if it might be a whooping crane. Aside from pure figments of imagination or optical illusions, we had to eliminate white pelicans and egrets. The pelicans are huge brutes with heavy bodies and a nine-foot wingspread. On the water or squatting lazily on shore, they are bulky and built close to the surface. Also, they are a sparkling, alabaster white, of a different degree of whiteness from the whooping crane. The much smaller egrets are slim and usually alert, leaning forward slightly and rather quick in their movements. When you do spot a whooping crane you wonder how you could mistake him for anything else or anything else for him. He looks like a great, flightless, prehistoric bird, prancing about over the mud flats. His stride, the length and thickness of his neck, and the long, sloping back with its dangling plumes over the tail are completely characteristic. Most of those we saw were at least a half mile or more distant, but on one occasion, as we came from behind the cover of a thick *motte* of live oaks, there stood a pair of them not fifty yards away. At the moment we saw them they were already moving, sounding off with their bugle-clear trumpet blast of warning and running with amazingly lengthy strides before getting airborne. The red skin on top of their bare heads stood out clearly, and so did the grim, almost fierce cast of their features. They seemed like great satin-white bombers, with their immense wings flicking upward in short arcs and their heavy bodies fighting for altitude. Still calling, they glided over the tops of the scrub, slowly gaining elevation. Nothing flightless about them!

When they had moved more than a mile to the south of us, to the rim of Mullet Bay, we came up for air, for we had been watching them with bated breath. I found that I had forgotten how cold I was and my hand was shaking when I started to write in my notebook.

The campsite we selected was an oak *motte* affording shelter, of a sort, from the full blast of rampaging north winds and at the same time commanding a good view of the salt flats. Also, as Bud pointed out, there were no "hooty owls" living in it to keep a fellow awake at night, for there are great horned owls living in many of the scattered *mottes* of the area, and now and then, under cover of darkness, one would visit Camp Cowchip. When my wall tent, grub box, and water barrel were in place and the barbed wire stretched, we fixed up a neat fireplace, built a good oak fire, and made coffee. Then, as it was getting late, the boys departed, leaving me with my two companions. These were my thirteen-year-old son, Bobby, already an experienced and inveterate camper, and a light Ford truck of ancient vintage that had been lent to our project temporarily. When supper had been stowed away, we sat close to the open fire for a while, as it was growing quite cold, and then retreated to our sleeping bags feeling that the job was now really under way. For out there in the darkness, not a mile from where we lay, two whooping-crane families were standing in one of the shallow ponds where they spend the night. At dawn we would be hiding in the oak brush watching them. From here on out, barring necessary interruptions, there wouldn't be much these birds did that we wouldn't know about. Or so we planned it. In practice, of course, there were many interruptions and a long list of unexpected problems that had to be tackled as we met them, and overcome if possible.

When we awoke next morning it was to come smack up against a sample of these unforeseen difficulties. It was raining, a chill, penetrating rain that was giving the grass clumps and oak thickets a thorough dousing, so that we were shivering and soaked to the skin before we had gone a quarter of a mile. Our oilskins had been left at home! We stuck it out, but without very notable results. From the shelter of a thicket that stood at the edge of the open salt flats we could barely see a family group of three whoopers nearly a mile to the southwest. They seemed to be just standing there. Another group, which had been feeding the evening before in a pond just to the east, was not visible at all. It was misty, and visibility was lousy. Besides this, our spotting scope, set up quite conveniently on its tripod, was also getting soaked, and very shortly we had nothing dry about us for wiping off the lenses.

It was some months, and many similar drenchings and disappointments, later that we learned the story of the whooping cranes' winter territories and understood what to expect with regard to their daily habits. Jim Stevenson, the first refuge manager at Aransas, Earl Craven, and others who had worked there with the birds noted the tendency of pairs and family groups to remain for an entire winter season within the invisible boundaries of a selected area. Only drought or other habitat failure would ordinarily cause them to desert, although when the high grass and live-oak brush on a section of cattle range was burned to produce fresh growth, the whoopers, as well as small flocks of sandhill cranes, frequently came to these blackened areas for the acorns that were exposed and for other special delicacies. In the course of two winters, by careful observations and repeated mapping, we decided that under normal conditions each family or pair, with or without young, occupied a distinct territory that approximated some 400 acres of true salt flats, including ponds and estuaries. Territorial claims were made soon after birds arrived from the northern breeding grounds, but were not defended with vigor until after the entire flock was in, for the pairs with new young in tow were the last to arrive and invariably grabbed and successfully defended the most valuable territories.

The best territories are almost 100 per cent salt flat, like the one at Middle Pond which is the area chosen by any cranes who fail to join in the spring migration—as sometimes happens—and who spend the entire summer on the refuge, with freedom to pick and choose any territory they wish. Less desirable areas have a certain percentage of oak brush on the higher ground; but this is really a matter of contour lines, for oak brush doesn't flourish below the three-foot mark. All of the fourteen territories that we studied and mapped had frontages on one of the bays, and these vary in width from about one mile to slightly less than half that distance. It seemed obvious that these tidal shores were the main source of food for the cranes. However, the narrow fringe of salt flats that lie between the bay shore and the three-foot contour is the habitat in which the birds spend most of their time. These flats are made up of a series of ponds, some of which are elongated in character (they are actually relics of depressions between ancient beach ridges washed out by the changing Pleistocene shorelines), while others are more or less round in shape and isolated. The elongated type are connected with one another by narrow estuaries and with the tidal bays, so that, with a certain wind direction, the tide flows from one end of the pond system to the other, bringing with it the fish and the crabs and other arthropods that are the principle food of the whooping crane. On the other hand, with a prolonged wind in the opposite direction the entire pond system can go dry, forcing the birds to desert it for the shoreline of the bays, where marine life is less concentrated and less easy to secure.

The isolated, smaller ponds are ephemeral in nature, mere depressions or mudholes in the marsh. These depend on the high tides of the autumn season for their quota of food animals. As the winter advances the cranes empty them of this stock, and as the water in the ponds slowly evaporates they become strongly odoriferous and yellow with algae. There are also large ponds that are a part of the drainage or run-off system of the peninsula, with fresh water pouring in at one end and salt tide at the other. They too have their value to the cranes.

It was a long and difficult job analyzing the relative merits and deficiencies of these ponds and understanding what makes them tick. Most fortunately for me, preliminary work had already been started by two valued friends, Dr. Gordon Gunter, then head of the Institute of Marine Science of the University of Texas, and Dr. Joel W. Hedgpeth, who was connected with the same institution, as well as with the Department of Zoology of the University of California. Among his many talents, Gordon is an expert on the fishes of the Gulf of Mexico and on salinity problems, while Joel is a specialist on marine invertebrates. Both contributed tirelessly of their knowledge, in the field and in the laboratory.

Many cold days had to be faced, wading the ponds, probing in the mud, and tearing our hair out by the roots in frustration, before a true and logical picture emerged. Although the initial work of Gunter and Hedgpeth gave us a list of the marine inhabitants of the salt-flat ponds, as well as many suggestions as to the way these tied into the whole environment, there were countless details still to be investigated. For each month brought a change in conditions and each season was different in some way from that which had preceded it and that which followed.

When he could get off from school (which was in Tivoli—locally pronounced *Ty-vola* or *Ty-voler*—more than twenty miles from camp) my young son stayed with me and helped with the work. One such day in early January, I made this record in my notes:

> 9:30 a.m.—Finally managed to get our collecting equipment reduced to pocket size, pulled on oversized hipboots on top of our shoes, restrung the 50 ft. seine on new poles and, the whoopers having moved, set out for the spot in Camp Pond where the South Family fed last evening. Rain coming down steadily, but only a little wind and the temperature up to 46°F. Another family group is feeding in Camp Pond. They called, apparently a duet, as we walked across our end of the pond, a half mile away. The call was an alarm, a high bugle note, then a rolling downward note, less prolonged than the first, and a third note that was a repetition of the first. Pintails in the air, passing over our heads. In the pond, just ahead of us, a single white pelican and a scurrying flock of red-backed sandpipers. In the deep mud we had trouble at once keeping our boots on, in spite of the precaution of binding the feet with rope that was brought up and pulled tightly around our ankles (eventually we abandoned boots for sneakers). The recent norther and a steady northerly breeze since yesterday has driven the water out of the pond until the north shore is a bare mud flat extending more than halfway across. In it we found whooper tracks (seven inches across the tips of the outer toes) and the empty shells of blue crabs. From our observations of last evening it appears that they were feeding on crabs, as well as probing in the mud for something else (which proved later to be marine worms).

We finally attempted to drag with our seine, but moving about with any purpose in that mud proved disastrous. First Bobby's boots came off, then mine. We fell down, got ourselves covered with mud from head to foot and finally gave it up as a bad job. Managed to collect a few small crabs, killifishes and small fry. However, in struggling to keep on my feet I broke the thermometer, which was the last straw. Also the last thermometer!

Question: does Camp Pond have an outlet to Mullet Bay and will a south or southeast wind push water back into this area along with a renewal of the crustaceans, fish, etc. [in the margin the word "Yes!" is written in a large hand, evidently added at a later date when this particular problem had been solved to our satisfaction].

This sort of thing was not only routine, it was the only way in which the job could be accomplished. In my notebook, page was added to page and one notebook followed another. Investigating the winter life of the whooping crane meant a great deal more than simply watching the activities and the behavior of the birds themselves. Those activities were only the signposts that pointed to the interrelated patterns of the entire environment. Maps were studied, the influence of winds and tides checked, marine animals were collected and their identity, relative numbers, size, apparent age and sex considered under one set of conditions and then under another. With planned patience we sometimes waited weeks for anticipated conditions to appear. Besides calculating the probable food of the cranes by direct observation, and by examination of areas in which they had recently been feeding, we followed Stevenson's example and collected as many specimens of their droppings as could be found and unquestionably identified. All of these were carefully preserved and shipped to Fran Uhler at the Fish and Wildlife food habits laboratory outside of Washington. Uhler's expert analysis of the contents—down to such minute items as the highly chitinized mandibles of tiny annelid worms!—were our final and most definite clue to actual food preferences.

Of course there were other fields to plow, and in addition to ecological problems it was equally essential that time be alloted to other phases of the life cycle and to an appraisal of the whooping-crane situation as a whole. During that first winter I flew on several aerial surveys with Bob Tanner, including a painstaking search along the entire coastal strip from the Louisiana border to Mexico, a total of nearly 1,000 miles of actual observation and search from the air. No additional whoopers were found. In Mexico, Dr. George Saunders, of Fish and Wildlife, undertook to cover possible wintering areas during his aerial surveys of the wintering waterfowl population. In many years of similar flights in that country, George had never observed any whooping cranes, and he was unable to find any on this occasion. With his help, and the testimony of old records, I eventually pieced together the place that Mexico occupied in the whooping-crane story. It proved to be entirely a matter of history. Except for a fine wintering group in nearby Tamaulipas on the Rio Grande Delta Plain, now long since gone, the whooping crane's presence in Mexico had not been of outstanding importance.

These were some of the experiences of that first Texas winter when we began our intimate acquaintance with the whooping crane. As spring aproached and the big birds began their spectacular dances and demonstrated in other ways their growing restlessness, we too began to cast our eyes to the North. For it was our plan to trace their flight as far along the trail as we could follow. Many of the answers lay in that direction, and the breeding grounds were still a very big and incomprehensible unknown.

*. . . The whooping cranes still dance, but unless we are able to discover some means of assisting them to gain a much improved nesting and rearing success they will not dance much longer. It will be the end of the line.*

R. P. ALLEN *

## IV : The whoopers still dance

The whooping cranes undertake prodigious preparations for their spring departure—so remarkable, in fact, that they must begin soon after the birds have settled down for the winter season, which usually has been accomplished by late November. I wanted to see as much of these rituals as I could, but as the season progressed I had still been unable to get really close to them. These attempts culminated that first winter in the construction of a very special sort of blind. We had seen how the cranes walked by a group of cattle without batting an eye, and it occurred to me that if I could just conceal myself inside of something resembling a cow—well, you get the idea. I hate to say this, but it was a bum steer! And I wasted a lot of time finding this out. Back at Refuge Headquarters, with Russell's ever-willing help, I put the thing together. Because of their immense size we decided on a big red Santa Gertrudis bull as our model, and first of all we constructed a light framework of wire in the rough form and vague

* *Audubon Magazine* (1947).

semblance of such a creature. Over this frame I stretched and sewed tightly a "skin" of heavy red canvas, which happened to be a rust-red color that approximated the shade of the Santa Gertrudis breed. Ears were made of folded pieces of canvas, properly shaped and sewn in place. There was also a very convincing tail, made of rope frayed out at the end and the remainder wrapped tightly in canvas. The eyes, with what was intended to be a glowering or baleful expression, were painted on, as was the nose, the line of the mouth, assorted wrinkles in the neck, etc. Actually, as it turned out, the expression of the eyes was quite demure and un-bull-like. In fact, everyone came to refer to my artificial beast as a "cow," and perhaps the eyes were the reason for this. To provide peepholes I cut openings in the "nostrils" and daubed their rims with red paint for realism. I could stand upright in the forepart, and by stooping slightly I could peer out through these apertures. In addition, there were wood handles fastened inside for picking the whole thing up and carrying it when under way. Along the bottom there were two wood shoes, or skids, on which the entire structure rested.

By the time it was completed I was quite enthusiastic about it. I climbed inside and pranced around the driveway at headquarters. Bud's old dog, which was half blind but had a lot of sense ordinarily, barked at me convincingly, and two of the workmen, driving up at that juncture, were pretty startled for a moment before they burst out laughing. By then I was completely sold on the whole idea and couldn't get it lashed on my truck and down "on location" fast enough.

When I had unloaded it at camp, with a family of whooping cranes moving slowly across the salt flats in the background, I began to cool off. With the caution of one who has begun to doubt his own judgment, I waited until almost dark and then carried the thing out on the marsh. Just before dawn, I decided, I'd get inside and give it a try.

Next morning, after a hasty cup of coffee, I waded across Camp Pond in the semidarkness, located my red bull, and crawled inside. For the next three-quarters of an hour I crouched uncomfortably in the mud and water waiting for daylight, enthusiasm only slightly dampened. When it was light enough to see any distance I stood and began peering through the two peepholes, moving the creature very slowly so as to scan the horizon. No cranes were in sight. Nearly two hours later, half asleep, I was startled to hear the clear *ker-lee-oo* of a crane. Jumping up so suddenly that the bull tottered in a drunken fashion, I stuck my head in its nose and stared through the peepholes. Two adult cranes were in sight, far to the east. I could scarcely see them at all without using my binoculars, which were difficult to handle because of the close quarters and the small size and spacing of the nostrils. After a little, with more whoops, the two birds disappeared beyond some tall grass near the bay. I was convinced that they had been calling to other cranes beyond my vision, and not at me, but I couldn't be sure.

The next day I tried the same procedure, but never caught even a glimpse of the cranes. As I was swinging my canvas beast so as to look across the salt flats toward Middle Pond, a large dark object suddenly appeared a few yards away. It was a live bull, and a red one at that! His head was lifted, as if he was trying to catch my scent, and his little eyes seemed to me to be glowing with sheer malevolence. I held my breath, while my heart pounded wildly. What to do? It occurred to me that perhaps a total lack of sound or movement might cause him to lose interest. For several awful minutes I stood perfectly still and stared into his uncharitable eyes, scarcely breathing and unwilling to look away for fear he would charge. If I saw him about to come at me, I thought, I might be able to move fast enough to sidestep him. Movies I had seen of bullfights flashed through my mind, and something I had read about the weak eyesight and lack of agility of a charging rhino, which seemed perfectly relevant at the moment. The words "Death in the Afternoon" kept going through my mind and I decided that it was a great misfortune that this should sound so much better, somehow, than "Death in the Morning." It was only 10 A.M. at the time. I was composing newspaper headlines—BIRD WATCHER GORED BY BULL, and so on—when my silent adversary suddenly turned and walked away. His expression, which had seemed so venomous a moment before, now appeared to be one of complete boredom. I waited until he was far in the distance before I crawled out from under the blind and walked quickly back to camp.

I must record (though shamefacedly!) that I placed a photographer from *Life* magazine in jeopardy by staking him out on the marsh in that same imitation bull a few weeks later. One day in January I had a long-distance call from Joe Kastner, one of the editors of *Life* and an old friend. They wanted to get some pictures of this rare bird I was studying. Could it be done? I told Joe that we couldn't get within a half mile of them. Cut that down to a quarter mile, said Joe, and our man Feininger can do it with a twenty-inch lens. Send him along, I told him, but I can't promise anything. So, not long after this, along came Andreas Feininger, whose beautiful landscape photographs of many parts of the country and spectacular telephoto shots of Manhattan you have probably seen. Andreas had never been in Texas before, and Austwell, while not much like Dallas or Houston, is typical in its own peculiar way. It was the first clear hot day in weeks, but I tried not to sound too encouraging. No doubt there was some unpleasant weather ahead. However, we made the long trip to camp and started operations at once. Andreas and his two big lenses fitted into the dummy bull all right, after we had performed an operation on its side so as to provide a larger aperture than the nostrils afforded. We also found him a stool to sit on. In fact, everything was splendid except that, as luck would have it, there wasn't a whooping crane in sight. This was what I had been afraid of.

The next day there was a southerly wind and thick fog, so thick that pictures were out of the question. In addition, the three cranes of the South Family were feeding so close to the blind that we couldn't make a move toward it anyway. On the third day, we took a chance on the fog clearing and crept out of camp in the darkness of early morning. With Bobby helping him, Andreas settled in the blind with his equipment, including some sandwiches and a jug of water. He was certainly determined. We watched for a while, from a safe distance, and after a little the fog lifted, leaving an overcast sky. The South Family then appeared, taking a stand directly south of camp and about a half mile beyond Andreas. At that point we went off with Olaf Wallmo, who was now assisting me in the field, and tended to other business. During the afternoon, after nearly turning over our truck getting past Jones Lake, we bogged down close to the head of Mustang Lake, nearly 10 miles from where Andreas, for all we knew, was by now being chased all over the marsh by that real bull.

Feeling suddenly concerned, we sat down to wait, while Olaf walked up the beach to Dagger Point for a tractor to pull us out of the mud. It was very late when we got back to camp. There was Andreas, safe and sound, but pretty well tuckered out after a weary and entirely unprofitable nine hours in the blind. He never even saw a whooping crane the whole time. At dark it looked as if we might have rain, and there was a gusty wind from the south during the night. The next morning it was do or die. Again we went out on the marsh before daylight, moving the blind to a more favorable spot. I wrote in my notes: "As we were working on it the fog lifted a little and the South Family group, already back on their feeding flats, saw us and started calling. We flopped, then managed to get Andreas inside the blind while Bobby and I crawled off on our bellies. However, with no apparent suspicion of *Bovus absurdus*, the whoopers came right on, and a short while later trooped past Andreas in single file. Then Andreas got excited and tried to follow them, dragging *Bovus* along through the grass. They sounded an alarm and have been on the alert since. Andreas, at the first note, froze dead in his tracks. *Bovus* is teetering slightly to port and the whoopers are still calling—several versions, all alarm notes—and are walking away in their stately fashion. The light conditions are nothing to scream about."

One good picture was all Andreas got, and it subsequently appeared in *Life* in the issue of March 3, 1947. I know that Andreas, who is one of the best of photographers, didn't think much of it, but it is one of the few pictures we have of a family of whooping cranes (the young bird's head and upper neck still show the rusty shading of immaturity) striding across the marsh sounding their magnificent call.

In 1947 we returned to Aransas from our first Northern

trip in late August, determined to find a way of bringing the big birds closer to us. For several weeks, in addition to resuming our studies of the habitat, we constructed carefully concealed blinds at a number of strategic locations. Then, when it was almost time for the first whoopers to return in October, I started baiting the vicinity of each blind with whole yellow corn. Although our birds feed for the most part on animal life, they are not by any means adverse to a certain amount of vegetable food, and we felt that corn might turn the trick. One unforeseen difficulty was the appetite for corn quickly developed by every raccoon, duck, and blue crab in each of the baited areas! We let them finish what had already been put out and then waited impatiently for the first whoopers to arrive. We would have to take a chance and hope to be able to place the bait after our birds were settled in.

There had been a hurricane off New Orleans on September 19, but clear warm skies in our region, in spite of a puffy breeze from the north. A few days later migrant hawks appeared—sharp-shins, kestrels, and marsh hawks (harriers). On September 24 a steady diurnal wind set in from the east and continued without letup for a period of two weeks, shifting toward the south on October 7. Other migrants began to show up, a peregrine and numbers of assorted shore birds on September 25 and a small flock of marbled godwits, then dowitchers, yellowlegs, pintails, widgeon, and blue-winged teal a few days later. Meanwhile, the prolonged east wind had filled the entire pond system to overflowing. Blue crabs, the most obvious crustaceans present, swarmed in every pond and puddle. Apparently our original picture of the relation of the autumn winds and high tides to the winter's food supply on the salt flats had been close to the mark.

Coot were observed on October 7, and green-winged teal two days later. Pintails were by now present in large numbers, and Jones Lake swarmed with them. On the eleventh we covered the area as far as the Point Pasture looking for the first whooping cranes. None had arrived. Next day the wind came around to the northeast. Finally, on October 21 the first migrant whooper showed up, a single bird that came to earth on the shore of Dunham Bay. By this time a few lesser sandhill cranes had likewise arrived, as well as white-fronted geese and Canada geese. I had now replenished my baited areas, and thirty-five sandhills settled on the corn in front of my blind nearest camp.

On the twenty-sixth more whoopers came in, a pair at the head of Mustang Slough and three more in the marsh south of camp. How glad we were to see them! There were now a dozen species of migrant ducks and geese on the refuge, including the first snow geese. We also estimated close to 5,000 coots, most of them on Mustang Lake and the adjacent Redfish Slough.

By November 1 the whooping-crane population had reached fourteen birds, but none of them was accompanied by new young-of-the-year. On the same date the wind came roaring out of the north with a velocity of 35 miles per hour, and more than that during gusts. The next day the first family group arrived, a pair with one brown-plumaged youngster, first seen on the east side of Mustang Lake. The little fellow must have been close to four months old, according to my calculations. His head and neck were a deep rusty brown and the paler brown or buff of his body plumage was much splotched with areas of white, chiefly on the wing coverts. We watched the family resting and feeding in the wet puddles near the lake, and they seemed very quiet and obviously tired out after their long and dangerous journey of 2,500 miles from the Northern breeding grounds. As we watched, there was a great flight of monarch butterflies coming in and stopping along the shore, covering every weed and bush with a fluttering blanket of orange and black.

The days that followed were filled with the excitement of the new arrivals. It turned out to be one of the best seasons in years, and a total of six young-of-the-year were finally counted. In all, the Texas population reached thirty-one whooping cranes. At first our bait was a grand success, the whoopers going after it with a vengeance and having a wonderful time chasing off the flocks of smaller sandhills and geese that also found the corn enticing. Later on, however, most of the whoopers walked disdainfully through generous supplies of corn to seek their natural food in the muddy bottoms of the ponds. By great luck, a splendid family group, those occupying the outstanding territory at Middle Pond, found whole yellow corn completely irresistible! For the remainder of the winter I was able to watch these birds at close range at any time I wished to do so; although it was usually necessary to creep into my blind in the early hours before they came in to feed from their night roost across the pond. As a result of this happy situation, I was able to provide both Roger Tory Peterson and Allan Cruickshank with a perfect setup for the fine photographs they secured of this family when they visited the refuge a few weeks later.

Of course the chief purpose of the bait-and-blind combination, from my point of view, was to observe, in detail, such important activities and developments as care, feeding, and weaning of the young, prenuptial dances of the adults, territorial defense, plumage changes, and a host of other manifestations in the daily life of the whooping crane. I have seldom known such high moments as those I spent perched quietly behind my burlap, with one of the biggest, rarest, and most wary birds in the world going about the business of everyday life only 150 feet away. I had to move about inside my shelter with the greatest caution and suppress every threatening cough or sneeze. Sometimes I sat there for ten hours at a stretch. It was worth it! I saw the whooping crane on terms that I had never dreamed possible and that few, if any, had ever experienced before me.

The fact that this Middle Family had taken over the best territory on the entire wintering grounds was an indication of the superiority of these two birds, especially of the vigor and boldness of the male. He was an unusually handsome specimen, with a fierce yellow eye, deep carmine skin on his noble crown, and a glistening black "mustache" across his lower face. His satiny plumage was superb, the lovely, plumelike tertials fluffing out over his tail with all the haughty male-ish grandeur of a seventeenth-century cavalier. And, indeed, except for the extreme solicitude he displayed toward his mate and offspring, his demeanor was nothing if not cavalier in itself. If another whooping crane from an adjoining area stepped over into what the Middle gentleman felt was his realm, his head went up and he sounded his thrilling challenge at once. *Ker-loo! Ker-lee-oo!* His mate joined in these calls, her less piercing tone following his by a fraction of a second, so that the two voices together produced vibrating, shrill, almost reedlike notes. The other whoopers, a full half mile or more away, usually sent back an answering challenge, but it was a halfhearted affair and mere bravado, for the next thing I saw was two white forms retreating through the tall grass and moving back into their own kingdom.

The pairs that were proudly rearing a youngster had stronger and far more assertive characteristics than those that had returned from the North emptyhanded, if that term is permissible with reference to a bird. The added stimulation of being responsible for the protection and general welfare of offspring seemed to call forth all of their powers and keep them at top pitch. At this time in its early life the young bird followed the female wherever she went, and it was she who fed it dainty morsels—a wonderful sight when it was almost as tall as she—and taught it eventually to probe the mud on its own. In her turn the female's behavior in most other matters patterned itself after that of the male, when and if the necessity for a temporary break in the endless feeding routine developed. Otherwise she and the young bird walked here and there, searching the pond for crabs, worms, fishes, or mud shrimps, while father, ever alert and constantly suspicious, raised his head every half minute or so to scan the horizon for signs of trespassers or other dangers.

Now and then a couple of hapless cranes would blunder so far across the line into Middle Family's territory that papa went after them in the same moment that he threw out his first shrill challenge. It was a sight to see! In early January, when the blue flowers of the salt-flat cranberry (*Lycium*) were in bloom, territorial frictions were at their peak, though the flowers had nothing to do with it. The cranes had been engaging in prenuptial dances since mid-December, and the bond between each well-established pair, while seemingly never a casual one, was in the process of being cemented anew. When the male sighted a violation of his boundaries he stood up as tall as he could stretch, his bill pointing straight upward, and turned loose an ear-shattering call. The female, head up, joined in, while the youngster, looking startled, was nevertheless poised and ready for anything. That young one learned about life very quickly. After the first call the male lowered his head and his entire body stiffened, the neck now held straight out and arched slightly. In another instant he was running forward for a take-off, the female and young right behind him.

With great flicking wingbeats, all three bore down on the intruders, who were gamely standing their ground perhaps 400 yards away. The male remained in the van, of course, flying straight in on target and coming to earth only a few yards away. As soon as he was grounded he went right for them, his long neck and heavy bill thrust out in front of him like a spear, his strides long and his wings beating to lend him further speed. The two trespassers had been standing very straight and tall, and when this animated spearhead was only a few feet from them they suddenly took flight. I have seen a defending male pursue such intruders more than a mile, pushing them through the air at their utmost speed. They always flew at a low altitude, the escaping bird twisting and turning, banking and swerving, and trying every trick in the book in an effort to shake off the relentless fury on his tail. I never saw actual contact or real battle. Somehow, in spite of all the challenging and aggressiveness, it is always avoided.

As already related, the dances begin in mid-December or a little thereafter. These spectacular performances mark the beginning of a new breeding cycle. With the immense size of the birds, this dance is one of the great dramas of the bird world. It may begin quite suddenly, as the family group is standing idly on a ridge of salt-flat grass, preening their feathers. The male bird turns, walks off into the shallow water, and stretches, raising his wings over his back, bending forward slightly as he does so. All at once he starts to dance, bowing toward the female, who now steps into the water beside him. Raising his satin-white wings with their jet-black tips to the fullest extent, he leaps high in the air, executing a half turn before landing. The female is now in the formalized attitude of a dancing crane, her neck arched, wings and plumes slightly raised, whole body stiff and yet graceful, like that of a ballerina. They begin by leaping together, but it is the male who leaps most often, in what appears to be a perfect frenzy of emotion. As they come down, springing lightly on their stiffened legs, both birds touch the surface with their bills, scooping water over themselves in a sweeping sidewise motion.

At the high point of their leap they throw their heads back, arching their necks so that the bills point skyward. The wings flap in a flowing, graceful rhythm. The legs are stiff and straight, so that they act like springs, sending the birds bouncing upward again and again like two people on pogo sticks. When they strike the ground at the end of a series of jumps, they run toward each other, nodding their heads very gravely and flapping their huge wings. Then more leaps. Once the male, in a tremendous spring, jumped clear over the female, turning almost completely around as he was coming down.

The climax is an exhausting series of bounding leaps, an almost frantic effort, and then, as suddenly as it began, the dance is over. On another occasion, I saw the male continue his leaps solo, bounding off across the pond for some distance, the female walking away as if she had had enough. Throughout these performances the young crane watches in a bewildered manner at first, and then resumes his feeding as if completely bored by the whole business.

As the winter season moves on, a definite change takes place in the relationship of parents and young. When the dances of the adults have become an almost daily occurrence, so that for certain periods in the day the pair are more or less preoccupied with them and with each other, it is time for the weaning of the youngster. By now the young crane has lost nearly all of the buff and rusty feathers of his extreme youth and from a distance appears entirely white and indistinguishable from an adult, although at close range you can see remnants of his immaturity. The proud regard of his parents, especially the tender care of the mother, has been such an unwavering flame that it must come as a decided shock to him when she abruptly turns on him one day and, with head lowered in the attacking posture, runs at him and sends him flapping off in frightened bewilderment. It is time to break the tie, to cut him loose from her apron! The youngster is driven off again and again, for he can't believe it's true. At length, accepting this new state of things, he sulks on his own pasture, finding his own tidbits, as he is now perfectly capable of doing.

Nevertheless, with this lesson learned, he is at length permitted to return to the family precincts, though on a different basis. And from time to time he must be reminded of his new status. For the day of departure draws near. You can see it in the restless movements of the birds themselves, and almost feel the urgency of it in the air. And when they take to the upper reaches at last, and wheel magnificently until they find the course, the young crane will journey with them. The busy winter will then be over, and with spring and the long voyage northward a new chapter is opened, and with it will come new scenes, new dangers, and new hopes.

*The Whooping Cranes fixed my attention and I,*
*an old hunter,*
*Told you their history, how they were nearing*
*extinction,*
*How years ago I had seen them blithely*
*winging their way*
*Against the steel blue heaven of South Dakota*
*And heard them trumpet in triumph when they had*
*conquered the sky.*

EUGENE MURPHEY *

# V : On the migration battlefront

When April comes to the Aransas salt flats, that tiny pinpoint of space in a big country where the last flock of whooping cranes winter, their preparations for departure are virtually completed. As early as the last of February or sometime in March a breakdown in the strict territorial setup may be noted. Pairs and families flew into areas outside their particular kingdoms more often, to feed in burns on the higher ground, for example, and once, in March, the Slough Family, after feeding on a burn a couple of miles from their usual abode, returned there by flapping several hundred feet into the air and soaring in wide circles and great sweeping spirals, as if testing the joys of flight that were soon to come. Again, at the end of my second winter, on April 17, as I was driving along East Shore Road near Carlos Field, I saw four whoopers circling and soaring at about 1,000 feet. I thought at once that I was about to witness an actual migration take-off, and indeed, one of the four birds kept pulling out of the circle and

* "The Whooping Crane."

moving off toward the north. But the others were not influenced by this and continued their gyrations, so that the rugged individualist had to turn and rejoin them. All were calling constantly and moving, still in an endless round of circles, toward Mullet Bay to the south. After a little, they spiraled downward and came to earth on the edge of the bay.

On that date (it was in 1948) twenty-four cranes had already departed. The four birds I had watched disappeared that same night or early the following morning.

Toward the end of my first season at Aransas I decided to leave ahead of the cranes and watch for them somewhere along the Platte River in Nebraska, the first major stopping place en route to Canada. Olaf would be on hand to record their departures from Texas, and it looked like a good opportunity to check the migatory movements in detail. A great deal had been written about their migrations, but much of it was either out-of-date or of questionable value. At that point I had not yet studied all the extensive literature on *Grus americana*, a vital step in the job at hand, but I had read enough to realize that our recorded knowledge regarding the whooping crane and its true status was nothing if not confused.

There were many reasons for this confusion, most of them rather interesting in their revelation of changing human values, of opinions geared to the times and sometimes sheer unabashed emotional enthusiasms. The early travelers, and even the early ornithologists, may be excused on the grounds of a general lack of information, but more recent writers repeated certain mistaken accounts verbatim and without questioning their accuracy. In this way a myth of whooping-crane abundance was built, and it was a woefully flimsy and entirely false structure. The earliest narrative was that of Richard Hakluyt, dated 1589, and the title alone is intriguing enough to admit it to immediate consideration: *The Principall Navigations Voiges Traffiques & Discoveries of the English Nation, Made by Sea or Over-land to the Remote and Farthest Distant Quarters of the Earth at any time within the compasse of these 1600 yeeres*. It seems that in the course of these "voiges" the inland waters off North Carolina were reached, and there "the party of Captain Philip Amadas" went ashore in July on Wokokon Island in Pamlico Sound (possibly the present Ocracoke Island?) and "having discharged their harquebas-shot, such a flocke of Cranes (the most part white) arose, with such a crye, re-doubled by many echoes, as if an armie of men had showted altogether." These could hardly have been whooping cranes, from the location, the date, and the nature of the description. "Cranes" could just as well have been herons or egrets, and the "crye" could just as well have been the combined voices of terns and skimmers, which were doubtless abundant in that region. Nevertheless, a number of authorities, beginning with Thomas Pennant in 1785, have thought they were whooping cranes, and some authors argue quite illogically in an effort to prove them so.

Other more recent observers, like the English botanist Thomas Nuttall who floated down the Mississippi in 1811, simply made an honest mistake in identification. Yet his description of a "mighty host" of whooping cranes passing over in migration has survived and has been widely copied and repeated. The fact is, the whooping crane did not follow the Mississippi flyway within historic times, and Nuttall's host was undoubtedly made up of lesser sandhill cranes, which are still an abundant species. Yet even the great Audubon failed to distinguish correctly between the young whooper and the sandhill crane, so a mere botanist can be forgiven.

For a time, even after they had been reduced in numbers by the guns and the farming activities of settlers, whooping cranes were enthusiastically pursued as game birds. An item printed in a periodical called *Sports Afield—A Journal for Gentlemen*, published in Denver in 1888, described the hunting around Grand County, Colorado, in April of that year: "Ducks and other water fowl are not as plentiful as they have been the seasons before. Cranes, though, are very numerous this season—some of them big white fellows. One was shot recently that measured 6 feet, 6 inches." This measurement probably referred to total length, from the tip of the bill to the tip of the toes, so this was an unusually large specimen. There are extant a number of narratives on the hunting of these birds, both for sport and for museum collections, all of them highly enthusiastic.

The museum ornithologists suddenly woke up to the fact that their collections were devoid of specimens of *Grus americana*. Spencer Fullerton Baird pointed out in 1858 that there were none at that time in the public museums of the United States. In the five or six decades that followed, this deficiency was corrected, but even so, in all the museums of the world, there are today less than 200 skins and skeletons. A greater number were doubtless either shot by meat hunters or killed indirectly, by settlers who broke up the nesting activities of potential parent cranes.

During the 1880s and 1890s there was a great rage for egg collecting, most of it with a scientific purpose, and the eggs of the whooping crane were among those sought after. They couldn't have been scarce, for an 1880 price list quoted them, in sets of two, at fifty cents each, and by 1890 this price had only gone up to two dollars. In North Dakota, Minnesota, and Iowa, where they were still breeding during the eighties, any nest that was found by an interested party was certain to be robbed. Yet egg collectors quite naturally rose up in wrath if anyone suggested that the practice of their scientific hobby contributed to the decimation of the species. In a way, they were right. They merely hastened an end that was foreshadowed by the draining of the first Iowa marsh and the turning of the first furrow in each of those fertile regions. Yet it is amusing to read, in an 1896 issue of the *Oölogist*, that the growing scarcity of many bird species was not considered a result of "egging," but of a combination of "hostile influences." The same writer goes on to say that in North Dakota within a comparatively few years it had grown difficult to find nests of the Canada goose, sandhill crane, whooping crane, trumpeter swan, etc. And he concludes with the elegant statement that "a high state of civilization and opulence of wild life are plainly antagonistic."

In the 1920s and the early 1930s, there was an astonishing state of confusion as to the abundance of the whooping crane, which could occur only in this amazing country of ours and in more or less recent years. Where else, except perhaps in England, would you find large numbers of private citizens, predominantly females, going afield to determinedly count birds, equipped with unbounded enthusiasm, a spotty knowledge of their subject, and inadequate glasses or no field glasses at all? Of course there has been a considerable improvement in field techniques and the over-all ability of bird watchers everywhere in more recent years, but at an earlier date such groups of well-meaning, eager "birders" were responsible for many erroneous and duplicated sight records of migrant whooping cranes that found their way into print and threw the entire picture of abundance completely out of kilter. Perhaps most of the errors were brought about as a result of the practice of accepting reports at second and even third hand, yet nearly all of the reports came from observers who honestly thought they had seen whooping cranes. In a year when some 100 or more migrants were accepted as the "official" figure for Nebraska alone, there were actually less than one-third of that number reported on the wintering grounds. Careful studies convince us that the wintering-ground records were for the most part quite accurate. On the other hand, a sincere interest in the welfare of the whooper was demonstrated by the amateur ornithologists and by hunters and other groups in various parts of the country where they could still be observed, either in migration or in their winter quarters, especially those that wintered in southwest Louisiana, and this interest kept alive a general awareness of the species' plight and a desire to "do something" to save it.

When I drove along the migration route into Oklahoma, Kansas, and Nebraska in March, 1947, I met and talked with all sorts of people who wanted to help. The publication of Andreas Feininger's photographs in *Life* helped a lot. It appeared that nearly everyone I met had seen this issue, and as a result they were all keyed up on the subject of whooping cranes. A really active interest, though, on the part of the general public was limited to those communities near major stopping places of the birds. At that time, centers of such interest were the towns of Jet and Cherokee, in Oklahoma, where Seth Low, then at the Salt Plains Refuge, had been spreading the gospel; the vicinity of Hoisington, Kansas, near the Cheyenne Bottoms, where U.S. Game Management Agent

Melvin Ramsey and State Game Protector Arthur Jones had been on the job; various towns on or near the Platte River in Nebraska, from Ogallala east to Grand Island (a distance of 190 miles); rural areas in North Dakota, especially in Oliver, Kidder, and Burke Counties; many communities in southern Saskatchewan, with Fred Bard in Regina as the hub; southeast Alberta, where the species often appeared in late summer or early fall, and various isolated posts northward toward Great Slave Lake. The town of Meadow Lake, Saskatchewan, where sight records had recently been reported and where we eventually stopped off during our work in that province, became another center of interest, and an important one.

When I reached North Platte, at the fork of the North and South Platte Rivers in Nebraska, a delegation of some twenty men was waiting for me at the Hotel Pawnee. They were a welcoming committee from the 1,000-member Lincoln County Sportsmen's Association, and were accompanied by Wilson Tout, editor of a local weekly, as well as author of *Lincoln County Birds* and a prominent member of the North Platte Bird Club. They had come to offer the services of their organizations, and during the five weeks I was in Nebraska their help was an invaluable asset. Since the record indicates that through the years more whoopers had been shot on the Platte River and elsewhere in Nebraska than anywhere else, the concern for the future of the species, as expressed by this outstanding group of sportsmen, was highly encouraging.

My chief purpose in stopping along the Platte was to check all reports of whooping cranes. Theoretically, the line of migration was thought to be almost a direct route from Aransas Refuge in Texas northward through west central Oklahoma and Kansas to a major stop somewhere on the Platte River, thence on into the Dakotas, Saskatchewan, and so on. The big question was *where* on the Platte I would be nearest to the present line of flight. Although North Platte lay close to the western edge of the "area of probability," the center of which was just to the west of Lexington, 60 miles farther east, I gambled that since recent records were closer to North Platte, this was an indication of the present trend and I made the Hotel Pawnee my headquarters. With the help of my new-found friends I then went about making as many useful contacts as possible. In the North Platte *Telegraph-Bulletin* for March 24, a long article by Jimmy Kirkman, the sports editor, appeared under the headline ALLEN HERE, AWAITS FLIGHT OF CRANE. After calling attention to the various birds that might be mistaken for a whooping crane and giving a description of the whooper itself, Kirkman said:

> So, if you see a bird that answers to the above description hurry to the nearest telephone, wherever you are, and call Robert Allen, ornithologist of the National Audubon Society, who is headquartering at the Hotel Pawnee in North Platte, awaiting just such an alarm. Allen doesn't care whether you are certain or not. He wants to investigate all possibilities. As quickly as he can, he will follow up the report by airplane and you will have helped out in an important work, for, you see, there are only 29 whooping cranes left in this world.

This was sticking my neck out, but it seemed the only way to be sure of receiving all reports, even if most of them would, on investigation, prove to be false alarms. Beginning with the very next day, March 25, and running through to April 21, a total of 144 birds were reported to me as whooping cranes (although I knew that the greatest possible number to make flight would be 25 and, as it later turned out, was actually only 23). These reports were phoned in or relayed to me in person, by telegram and by messenger, from a truck driver, an airplane pilot, a garage mechanic, a schoolboy, two businessmen, three farmers, one schoolteacher, and so on. All were investigated. They proved to be everything from white pelicans, snow geese, and little brown cranes to ring-billed gulls (two reports!).

I was out on the river roads each day, driving west as far as Ogallala or east to the vicinity of Grand Island and Hastings. It can be bitter cold in Nebraska in March and early April, and that year was no exception. It snowed on April 4, and again heavily on the seventh. Driving east toward Lexington, with no heater in my government-owned car, I had to run blind off the road every few miles and melt the ice that formed on the windshield by warming it with my bare hands. In spare moments I gave talks to the Lions Club, the North Platte Bird Club, and other groups. It was a busy five weeks.

Through the special interest of Joe DiNatali of radio station KODY (Buffalo Bill's ranch was on the outskirts of North Platte), a spot was given to whooping cranes during the noon news broadcast each day. Many people heard of my project on their radios who wouldn't have known of it otherwise. It was a casual, chatty presentation by the regular newscaster, beginning with some such opening remark as, "Well, let's see what the news is today on the whooping crane. I know that lots of you folks want to hear how many of these rare birds have left Texas and if any have shown up so far along the Platte. Well now, as of yesterday . . . ," etc. These broadcasts had just the right tone and attracted a lot of attention. They proved to be a tremendous help.

All this time, nearly 1,000 miles to the south, in Texas, Olaf was covering the entire mainland range so as to watch for departures. I kept in touch with him by telegraph. On April 7 the Dike Pair had disappeared, and on the ninth, the Middle Pair. It was like hearing of the departures of old friends. On April 11 he was unable to locate the Middle Family and the Bay Pair. Then, on April 14, all of them had evidently cleared out except for two "singles" that did not migrate. At his end, Olaf was in a sweat for fear he had merely overlooked some of the birds, and at my end I was in just as bad a sweat for fear I wouldn't be in the right place at the right time!

With some friends from North Platte, I drove late one afternoon up the river toward Hershey, where little brown cranes came in at dusk to roost on the willow-grown sandbars. After feeding all day in stubble fields for miles around, these smaller and far more abundant cranes fly by easy stages toward their roosting places. At 3:15 P.M. we saw several thousand settled in pastures and stubble some five miles west of North Platte. Thousands more were in the air, and the mingled sound of their gutteral voices could be heard at a considerable distance (I frequently heard them when I was in my hotel room as they were passing over the city). Some of the birds on the ground rested quietly; others picked around in the corn stubble looking for food. One large group was digging away at a manure heap. Others were dancing, leaping into the air with wings flapping. Their leap is light and buoyant, not as formalized nor as stiff and springy as that of the whooping crane. And individuals that seemed to have no special relationship to other birds in the flock performed as independent members of a group of dancers, but not as partners in an already established pair. According to Larry Walkinshaw of Battle Creek, who is the leading authority on the sandhill cranes, these birds may be observed leaping about like this at almost any time of the year. They seemed to me to be highly nervous, and as they leaped about they stabbed at each other with their sharp little bills and squabbled in an angry and irritated way. No whooping cranes were seen or heard among all these flocks, although they sometimes travel in company.

Later that same afternoon (April 4), we spotted a white bird with black wingtips soaring with a flock of 21 sandhills. It was a snow goose. Appropriately, it snowed that same night!

By the ninth, the Dike Pair and the Middle Pair were on their way. Today, we still don't know all the stopping places where the birds rest and feed en route, but from subsequent data it appears that they loaf along by easy stages and require from four days to a week to cover the 920 miles, more or less, from Aransas to the Platte River, a daily average of only 130 to 230 miles. Since they are strong fliers and can make close to 40 miles per hour over the ground in normal weather, it is logical that they should come to earth for feeding and resting at suitable retreats along the way rather than fly straight through. From our knowledge of their needs and the record, it seemed probable that among such retreats would be the Red River of the South, between Texas and Oklahoma, the salt plains near Cherokee, and the Cheyenne Bottoms in Kansas. I had driven through these and other places on the route on my own northward migration and I knew that at two of them—the Cherokee plains and the Cheyenne Bottoms—several observers would be doing their best to see whooping cranes. Seth Low reported a sight record of two whoopers on the salt plains on April 1 of the previous year, but he saw none in 1947. But these

Stephen F. Briggs

*The author and a Florida Bay compatriot, the man-o'-war bird, a visitor from the West Indies. This adult male displays the full extent of his bright scarlet throat pouch or gular sac.*

*The first week of February is a high point in the life cycle of the roseate spoonbills of Florida Bay. The young birds are then about seven weeks old and, in their soft pink and white plumage, are testing their wings in flight for the first time.*

*Young roseate spoonbills being fed by one of their parents, which share the duties of care and feeding during the first two months of their offsprings' life. Growth of the young is extremely rapid and they must be supplied with tremendous amounts of small fish, water insects, and crustaceans—their staff of life. A rare photograph of a rarely seen event.*

*Stephen F. Briggs*

*Stephen F. Briggs*

areas are extensive and difficult for one or two observers to cover from one end to the other. In spite of their conspicuous white plumage and great size, it is surprising how easily you can miss spotting two or three whooping cranes within a large area of wilderness of varied character and topography. They might hide in any one of these places for two or three days at a stretch without being reported. At any rate, on the ninth, which was too soon to expect any of them to reach the Platte, for by then I had had no reports of departures from Texas, I drove to Ogallala and talked with Loren Bunney, a state game warden and old hunter. He lived as a boy in Harlan County south of Holdrege, Nebraska, between the Republican and Platte Rivers. At the age of ten he started hunting, "some fifty years ago," and even at that time (around 1897) whooping cranes, he told me, were a rare sight, although his home was within the main migration pathway of that period. Now and then he saw one of "the big white ones" in a flock of sandhills, and sometimes, back in those days, a flock of 24 or 25 whoopers flying together. But as a rule they traveled in groups of 2, 4, or 6. He said that although his work took him up and down the length of the Platte, he had observed "very few white ones" in the past twenty years.

Late that afternoon, back at my headquarters, a message awaited me from a radio listener who reported "a white crane in a flock of sandhills two miles south and two miles west of Hershey." At 5:10 P.M. I had located the sandhill flock and, sure enough, there was a white bird among them. It was another snow goose!

The next day I received Olaf's wire advising that four of his flock had been missing since April 6 or 7. I sent telegrams at once to all of my contacts up and down the river and called up Charlie Craig, the announcer at station KODY, and asked him to flash the news over the air on his twelve-thirty broadcast of the eleventh. Our little army of observers was now alerted. From Eddie Brown in Kearney I had a return telegram advising that he and his wife were flying their light plane as far east as Great Bend every day. I had already arranged to fly the western segment with John Clinch, manager of the North Platte airport.

By April 11, nine cranes were in flight somewhere between

Aransas Refuge and the Platte River. Four of them had been en route since the sixth or seventh, or for as long as five days. Was it too soon to look for them? Not knowing the answer to that one, we looked anyway, flying carefully chosen routes and doing as much ground work as time permitted. No whoopers were seen and no authentic reports received. Then, on April 14, late in the day, Eddie Brown and his wife were flying downriver between Lexington and Kearney. Near Overton they saw three large white birds moving off toward the northwest. They were whooping cranes! That evening I received the good news by wire and later, in rare confirmation of a rare event, Eddie sent me some cuttings from a 16-mm moving-picture film that Mrs. Brown had taken of the birds. They were unquestionably whooping cranes.

As the only trio to leave the refuge prior to that date was the Middle Family, it was apparent that this particularly vigorous group had been "on the road" no more than four days.

On that same day, Olaf's communiqués indicated that the entire migrant flock of 23 birds was now on the way. Once again I alerted all cooperators, by personal conversation, telephone, radio broadcast, and telegrams. For five agonizing days nothing happened, although several false leads were run down. Then, at ten minutes of eight on the morning of April 19, I had a telephone call from Lee Jensen, the state conservation officer at North Platte. He was excited. "Get out to Earl Mather's farm near the diversion dam," he told me. "Earl just called in to report 5 whooping cranes on his place. Looks like the real thing!" I was in my car in less than a minute and racing east along Route 30. Finding Mather's farm, I skidded into the driveway. A quiet-looking woman came out on the porch of the small farmhouse, drying her hands on her apron. She knew what I was looking for without my telling her. "Earl's out behind the barn on the edge of the stubble field," she said. "Those birds just flew south toward the river and he's looking for them." I thanked her and hurried for the barn. "We heard about them over the radio," she shouted after me. I nodded, breaking into a trot and yanking my binoculars out of their case. In another minute I met Earl Mathers, walking back from the stubble field and looking unhappy. He described the five birds accurately and said he had never seen any like them before. "Heard about it over the radio," he said proudly. "Always listen to the twelve-thirty news." I suggested we walk down to the river, which was close by. There, from the high bank, we counted 124 white pelicans and my hopes plummeted into my boots. "Mr. Mathers," I said sternly, "you must have seen white pelicans." "Mr. Allen," said he, drawing himself up with considerable dignity, "they were not these pelicans here. I've told you what they looked like and I'm sure they were the birds you're after." He closed his mouth like a trap and stared at me. "All right, Mr. Mathers," I replied. "I'm sure you're right. I'll get over to the airport right away and search for them from the air. Better chance of finding them again than beating through these willow thickets." Thanking both him and his wife profusely and promising to let them know what luck I had, I drove like a madman for the airport.

When we were in the air we located the Mather place and from there began a systematic search of the South Platte, toward which the birds had evidently flown. Suddenly, while still some distance off, I saw them, five white spots against the gray brush and brown sand and water of the river bottom. We had been aloft only ten minutes. The pilot, Eaton, swung over their position at less than 100 feet altitude, almost stalling the light plane so that I could take pictures. I snapped my Contax several times and then we circled back again at a higher altitude to look them over more critically. They were apparently a pair and a family group of three, traveling together. The young bird in the family group still showed a faint but unmistakable tinge of rust on his head. Only one of the three youngsters on the refuge the winter before still showed at this date even this much rust color anywhere in its plumage. Without a doubt the trio was the North Family, which had disappeared from Aransas between the eleventh and the fourteenth. The other pair I could not identify, but knowing their habits and relationships so well, I assumed they must be the Slough Pair, who lived on the adjacent territory and had disappeared during the same period.

On the previous day a pilot at the airport near the Cheyenne Bottoms, in Kansas, had seen three birds that were evidently whooping cranes. Others were observed near Washburn, North Dakota, on April 23 by Harry Jones, and a few days later near

North Portal, close to the Canadian line, by Joe Hill. Then the tiny legion dropped from sight in the vast region of northwest Canada. Where they were bound for remained at that time, and for some time to come, a mystery as baffling as any that has faced the ornithological world in modern times.

These whooping cranes that nest in northwest Canada and winter on what is now the Aransas Refuge in Texas have been our chief concern in recent years, but there were other population groups in times past, and they had their separate migration routes. Not a great deal is known about them, but from what we have learned of the original breeding sites and wintering locations it is not too difficult to trace the paths that lay between. For example, back in 1722 Mark Catesby obtained the skin of a whooping crane from an Indian in South Carolina, and in that period the species was said to occur on that coast and probably on the Georgia and Florida coasts as well. They were also reported later from the southernmost shores of New Jersey. If these were wintering birds it seems likely that they migrated across the Appalachians from somewhere around Illinois, the nearest known breeding place, and there are records for logical areas in between, including the report of Audubon and Wilson from the vicinity of Louisville, Kentucky, on March 20, 1810.

Other whooping cranes must have come south to the Gulf Coast of Louisiana from nesting grounds in Manitoba, Minnesota, Iowa, and Illinois, while those breeding farther to the north and west, in North Dakota, Saskatchewan, Alberta, and the Northwest Territories, journeyed by their separate routes to wintering locations along the Texas coast, from the region of Galveston all the way to Brownsville and to the vicinity of Matamoras on the Mexican side. There were also still other whooping cranes that joined the great flights of sandhills into the high plateau country of Old Mexico. There are records from the region southeast of Guadalajara and close to Lago de Chapala, where the elevation exceeds 3,000 feet. But it is clear that the largest wintering flocks preferred sea level along the Gulf Coast from the Rio Grande Delta Plain to southwest Louisiana, including the highly favored tall-grass prairies of the latter region.

We may picture these original flyways as extending all the way from the deltas of the Mackenzie and Anderson Rivers above the Arctic Circle to the southern extremes of west central Mexico near the Pacific, southwest Louisiana, and the extreme northeast coast of Florida. But the greatest width as a solid migration highway was the diagonal stretch from southern Alberta to northern Illinois, a distance of nearly 1,500 miles. This diagonal marked the approximate southern limit of breeding and the line of departure for the several flyways. At the Gulf Coast these main flyways narrowed to the 500-mile stretch between the Rio Grande Delta on the west and Marsh Island, Louisiana, on the east.

Compared with this broad migration highway of the past, the thin line that is followed by these birds today is a sad but impressive commentary on their present condition. The reduction, gradual at first, gathered speed toward the end of the last century and has kept on at a rapid rate down to very recent years. So far as our own country is concerned, you can draw a straight line north and south across the six states of North and South Dakota, Nebraska, Kansas, Oklahoma, and Texas, and if you begin this line close to Portal, North Dakota, at the International Boundary and terminate it at Austwell, Texas, some 1,500 miles to the south, you will come very close to describing the present migration route. Actually the pathway isn't a perfectly straight line, but it doesn't deviate more than 50 miles in any direction from the route you have drawn.

As a migratory species the whooping crane was last reliably reported in adjacent states in the following years:

| | | | |
|---|---|---|---|
| Indiana | 1881 | Arkansas | 1914 |
| Michigan | 1882 | Minnesota | 1917 |
| Wisconsin | 1884 | Montana | 1918 |
| Illinois | 1891 | Louisiana | 1935 |
| Mississippi | 1902 | New Mexico | 1938 |
| Iowa | 1911 | Colorado | 1941 |
| Missouri | 1913 | Wyoming | 1945 |

None have been reported from these states since.

When the present campaign to save the whooping crane began,

with the establishment of Aransas Refuge in 1937, the only migratory flock left was this same one that survives today. All of the others had disappeared and the surviving group had been reduced by April, 1939, to only 18 birds. Another flock survived at that time in Louisiana, but they were nonmigratory in their habits and numbered only 13 birds. The entire Louisiana group has since been extirpated, a tragedy that has been described elsewhere.* The fortunes of the wintering flock in Texas have seesawed up and down during the seventeen years of which we have detailed records. Their numbers, as of April in each of these years, plummeted to an all time low of only 15 individuals in 1942, but reached an encouraging April high of 33 in 1950 (actually 34 was the high of November, 1949, but one bird was lost over the winter). The average has been 24 whooping cranes. Once we had learned the situation on the wintering grounds, there remained two other spheres of interest: the nesting region somewhere in Canada and the migration highway in between. In the beginning we knew very little about either. It has been a long pull, but we are now much further ahead with our knowledge of all three areas. The migration route can now be traced on a map almost from town to town, and the importance of this knowledge to our efforts at preventing the shooting of these great birds during their hazardous flight should be perfectly obvious.

I have already told something of my early experiences along the migration route. From that time on the situation showed a steady improvement through the fall flight of 1949. We estimated that in the years 1945–1949 only 7 seven whooping cranes were lost, while the over-all gains amounted to a clean 12. Then something went haywire. It seems unbelievable, but in spite of the great amount of public good will that had been generated during the first years of our campaign, there were still many people who took an entirely different view. It is not often that we see or hear an outright expression of this alien attitude, but several incredible samples have been sent to me. One was a letter from a distraught farmer in Saskatchewan. He told of certain of his neighbors who

* See *The Whooping Crane*, Research Report No. 3, National Audubon Society, N. Y., 1952.

were outspoken in their opinion that all this fuss about the whooping crane was a lot of nonsense. They proposed that the best way to put a stop to it would be to kill the few birds that remain and then forget the whole thing, thus saving the taxpayers a lot of money and, they implied, making them much happier about life in general. They likewise announced their intention of using their guns at every opportunity to promote such results. Another letter, addressed to the editor of a leading newspaper, objected to the space that had been given to the whooping crane in a recent editorial. It went on: "...As you may judge from the foregoing I myself do not give a whoop for the whooping crane. From what I have observed and read he is a dim-witted gawk of a bird whose pate has become more or less addled in the course of time until now he is not quite sharp enough mentally to be up to the fundamentals of procreation. This in a world where stupidity is nothing unusual is nevertheless pretty dumb and to my thinking deserves everyone's acquiescence to the idea that as far as extinction is concerned the sooner the better.... Don't you think in all honesty that our children's children's children will respect our memory more if we forego the expenditure of whatever monies are being spent to preserve these birds and leave them—these kids unborn—just ever so little of a bank balance with which to face the exigencies of that world of tomorrow?"

We are very willing to agree that stupidity is not unusual in this world of ours, although we will hold back from giving any direct examples. I would also suggest that there are other things of value that we might leave our children's children's children besides a bank balance. But apparently this gentleman has never heard of them.

As for the Saskatchewan farmers who want to see the whooping cranes disposed of, they are an active threat, very real and quite possibly dangerous. When things began to go haywire with our migrating whoopers it was their kind that stood behind the guns. The facts are startling. Beginning with the departure of the flock for the North in April, 1950, and carrying them through the remainder of that year and all of 1951 and 1952—a total of six round trips over the migration route—24 whooping cranes were lost! This frightful toll represented 45 per cent of all whooping cranes that had died or been killed since the year 1938.

As late as 1952 we still did not know the exact location or nature of the breeding grounds, but we knew the migration route pretty well. It was our conclusion that most of these losses were taking place along this route, chiefly in the fall, with some possibility of stray, nonbreeding birds getting mixed up with people like our Saskatchewan farmer friends in late summer, prior to the fall flight. The autumn migration route becomes dangerous as soon as it reaches the limit of northern settlement in Alberta and Saskatchewan. There are a few potential danger points farther to the north, on the shores of Great Slave Lake and along the Slave, Peace, and Athabaska Rivers perhaps, but local conditions are such that we do not worry too much about them. The real threat begins as soon as the birds have passed to the south of the Beaver River in west central Saskatchewan. From that point on across the well-populated prairies to Rice Lake west of Saskatoon, Swift Current, Weyburn, and other towns and villages in that province, and on into North Dakota, the possibility of danger is constant.

Actually, the whooping cranes have no greater army of friends anywhere than in Saskatchewan, thanks to the general appreciation of nature by most of the residents, and to the splendid work of such outstanding citizens as Fred Bard, the director of the Provincial Museum in Regina. But it takes only one man or boy with one gun to kill one or more whooping cranes. At Rice Lake, for example, where the birds frequently come to earth, the protective attitude of the general public has been reported by items in the Saskatoon *Star-Phoenix*. When whoopers were observed on Rice Lake, which is 20 miles away, a reporter rushed to the scene. His photograph of two of the birds appeared next day on the front page, under a headline in red ink: STAR-PHOENIX PHOTOGRAPHS RAREST BIRD IN WORLD,WHOOPING CRANE. Almost one-half of the front page was taken up by the story that followed. A second item, two days later, told how "hundreds of Saskatonians" visited the lake over the weekend to see the birds, and related that requests had been received from papers all across Canada seeking more details and pictures.

During the fall migration four years later the *Leader-Post*, in Regina, carried a front-page story, with three photographs of a whooping crane that had been injured, perhaps by gunshot, east of Weyburn. This bird was cared for by a local veterinarian, who amputated the left wing and placed the left leg in a cast. The bird was then loaded into a U.S. Fish and Wildlife plane, which happened to be on hand, and transported to Texas, but it died en route.

The editor of the Toronto *Globe and Mail* wrote:

> We doubt if the existence of whooping cranes makes the slightest difference to the balance of nature or to the destiny of man. But it's comforting to think that there are still people who can take a profound interest in such things as the nesting habits of the whooping crane, the diet of the porpoise, the locomobility of the snail or the hereditary peculiarities of the fruit fly. It helps maintain and fortify whatever sanity remains.

No doubt very few people read Thoreau any more. Above all Thoreau sought for and found reality in nature. Among men, as Norman Foerster once wrote, "he found manifold evasion and deceit covering the reality," and this sent him to nature, which is artless. Today we might not agree altogether with Thoreau's estimate of his fellow men, but we do agree with those who believe that he found values in nature that should be known and reckoned with by all men of sense and good will. Sanity, sincerity, artlessness, reality—if these can be more than mere words to us, then they can be the keys to something very good and eminently worthwhile. Even more worthwhile, in the long run perhaps, than a bank balance—but there I am afraid not everyone will agree!

As of early 1953, with the whooping-crane flock alarmingly reduced in numbers in spite of all our previous efforts, the National Audubon Society inaugurated a new campaign aimed at reaching everyone living along the 2,000-mile migration route from central Saskatchewan to Aransas Refuge. In the first week of September, as the whoopers were preparing to take off on their long journey, a special news release was sent to newspapers all over the country. Public service announcements were mailed to TV and radio stations within states on either side of the route and to many others. Pictures of whooping cranes and mats for newspaper use were distributed and movie film and stills made available for TV showing (some networks showed the full ten-minute film to TV audiences as far away as Florida). State game commissions ran feature stories in their regular periodicals, and some states, Nebraska for example, carried pictures and a "Don't Shoot This Bird!" warning on the back cover of their state game laws, or on the backs of hunting licenses. Texas alerted their game wardens along the route and got out special publicity. An Audubon educational leaflet was printed and distributed to school children. Civic groups, local Audubon Societies, garden clubs, sportsmen's organizations, Scout and Campfire groups, farm clubs, and many others responded with widespread publicity advertising the urgency of the situation and asking for caution among all those who went afield with a gun.

As a result, for the first time since 1949 and for only the fifth year on record, the flock came out of Canada and crossed the United States to its sanctuary in Texas without a single loss. Our reaction, quite naturally, was one of elation and vast relief, but we knew that this was not really a victory, but only a temporary truce. Actually, the battle had just begun.

*. . . Send down*
*Thy trumpet note—it seems*
*The voice of hope and dauntless will,*
*And breaks the spell of dreams.*

HAMLIN GARLAND *

# VI : Northern search

In 1945, with a major war still in progress, a start was made in the vital task of locating the Northern breeding grounds of the whooping crane. Fred Bard, in Regina, agreed to take on this job, but he could only do so on a part-time basis. This was in April, when the cranes were already migrating northward. There had been a lot of discussion back and forth as to the most likely search areas and the best methods of search. Ground search, with cars and canoes, would be slow and difficult in that vast country, while airplane charters would be expensive. Yet search by aircraft seemed the only method that offered any hope of success.

Bard went to Edmonton in June, following arrangements that had been made for assistance from the U.S. Air Force. However, the commanding general was unable to authorize flights over northern Saskatchewan, where Bard was particularly interested in searching. Finally, in an Army transport plane he was flown to Watson Lake, Yukon Territory, where he boarded a PBY and

* *The Herald Crane.*

flew next day to Dease Lake, British Columbia, over mountains and passes at 5,000 to 7,000 feet.

Following reports of whooping cranes in Alberta, an area in that province was searched by Bob Smith of the U.S. Fish and Wildlife Service. No whoopers were seen. Then, with Fred Bard, Smith drove 1,000 miles by car, and in a chartered plane looked over Campbell Lake, near Nipawin, Saskatchewan, from where other reports had come. No whoopers were seen.

This disposed of the two "hottest" rumors then available!

With Sewall Pettingill taking over the search job, the task was resumed in May of 1946. Dr. Terris Moore piloted his own light plane and Pettingill was the observer. A considerable area was covered in northern Saskatchewan, and on north to the marshes of Lake Claire and the western tip of Lake Athabaska. As Smith and I were to do later, Sewall came amazingly close to the actual nesting grounds. Other search was made farther to the south and east, both on the ground and by aircraft with Bob Smith at the controls. No whoopers were observed. It was Pettingill's estimate that by aircraft alone he searched some 15,000 square miles of country.

In planning the 1947 search, Fred Bard and I believed that we were close to the right line of migration, although we had no idea whether or not the cranes made unexpected right-angled turns to east or west. Although Pettingill had covered the "best" areas in 1946, we felt that some of this region ought to be searched again, since no observers could be expected to see every corner of so vast a territory on any one series of flights.

On April 26 my family joined me in North Platte and the following day we took up the chase, only vaguely anticipating the many difficulties that were in store for us. Arriving in Regina on May 1, we met Bard at the Provincial Museum and held a council of war. As a result of Fred's excellent publicity job, reports of migrant whooping cranes had been pouring in since the previous spring. These had been carefully sifted, and by plotting on a map those that were considered authentic, we had a valuable picture of the big birds' movements through the settled portions of Saskatchewan. It seemed more than merely interesting that if you drew a straight line from Aransas Refuge to Regina it passed directly through North Platte! Observations had been made of whooping cranes passing over Regina proper, and others had been seen close to that city. It appeared, however, that the migrants fan out once they reach the short-grass prairie and aspen parkland zone that extends from the International Boundary near the Manitoba line northwestward across southern Saskatchewan. Before it became an important wheat-farming area this region was an outstanding whooping-crane breeding ground. The last nesting of the species observed by anyone had been two breeding pairs found near Kerrobert, Saskatchewan, in 1922. Since then the population that survives has been hatching its chicks in the unknown wilderness farther to the north. But the prairie-parkland region is familiar ground to them from an ecological standpoint. As a species they are still at home there, except for the isolation factor needed for nesting, and as they move on north it is not surprising that they spread out over this ancient realm of their ancestors.

From the vicinity of Regina, the trend of their migration seemed to be in a north-northwesterly direction, toward the marshes of Lake Claire in Alberta, toward the wet lands south of Great Slave Lake, toward heaven only knew where. It was Fred's conclusion that we should eliminate potential territory close at hand before searching farther afield. I agreed with this and decided to base somewhere along the line of flight on the northern rim of settlement. I could undertake a certain amount of search by car and canoe, but the logical method was to use aircraft. Arrangements had already been made with our partners, the U.S. Fish and Wildlife Service, and early in June I was expecting to be joined by Bob Smith, who was assigned to waterfowl surveys in that area and was equipped with a Grumman "Widgeon." Meanwhile, the next move for me was a base of operations somewhere in west central Saskatchewan.

We landed in Meadow Lake on May 11, after roaming over a considerable area en route. In every town and hamlet we met people who wanted to know the latest news about the whooping crane. They knew who we were on sight! Our cavalcade consisted of a station wagon with the name of the National Audubon Society on its panels, a small trailer loaded with camping gear, and a sedan with the U.S. Government shield gleaming conspicuously on each side. The station wagon had a Texas license plate and the government car had the official U.S. plates fore and aft. We needed no banner to announce our mission, for these good people were so well informed and so keenly aware of the whooping-crane situation that they spotted us at once.

Meadow Lake is on the edge of "the boosh," to use the local pronunciation, and at that time had many of the aspects of a frontier town—the muddy, unpaved streets, one-story frame buildings, primitive hotel accommodations, and a cheerful, friendly populace. We made friends at once with Jim Barnett, the District Game Superintendent, and met the members of his field staff. Maps were poured over, migration reports discussed, and a great deal of speculating indulged in. Mrs. Barnett, as a schoolteacher, was greatly interested in our two children, then nine and fourteen. What were we doing about their schooling? I felt that as a teacher she considered this question more important than the location of the whooping crane's nesting grounds. My wife explained that like many American families wandering over the face of the globe with small children in tow, we kept up their studies by correspondence with a private school at home. She sat them down each morning after breakfast—in hotel rooms, roadside cabins, the back seats of automobiles, and, later on, in tents in the bush—and heard their lessons. They loved it and not only kept up with their normal studies, but were usually ahead of the average students in their respective grades when they returned at last to a more settled existence.

After my talks with Jim Barnett and his crew, I decided on Flotten Lake for our base camp. At that time, Flotten, 45 miles north of Meadow Lake, was the outer limit of travel by car in Saskatchewan. It is situated at latitude 54°37′ north, longitude 108°29′ west, in a mixed woodland region of the so-called Boreal Forest. In other words, "the boosh." More important, it had a virtually uninhabited shoreline, deep water for landing our plane, and no resident Indians to complicate matters. And it lay as close to the outermost edge or jumping-off place on the migration route of the whoopers as you could have decided on without calling in a debating society.

On May 13, in a light rain, we pulled up to the south shore of the lake and pitched our tents. There was still ice on the surface, but it was just beginning to break. In open water Holboell's grebes were courting. Late in the afternoon we watched a flock of eight whistling swans flying north across the lake. Two young fellows working with the Department of Natural Resources came to call, bringing us a mess of jackfish for our supper. After an 8 o'clock sunset, the air temperature dropped to one degree above freezing and the loud, wailing voices of the red-necked grebes could be heard through the night.

During the next week we were practically immobilized by a period of stormy weather. There were strong northerly winds and considerable rain and hail. At one point we broke camp and moved farther along the lake to a more sheltered site where there was some protection from the wind. One day there was a regular gale from the northeast. It rained in a heavy downpour, with a series of hard squalls in the afternoon and a great deal of hail. Our big problem was to keep a supply of dry firewood on hand, and Bobby and I hauled in all that could be stacked under cover. Both tents were jammed with half-wet logs, on the cots, under the cots, and on the ground in between.

There were many birds to be seen. On the fourteenth a flock of about fifty western grebes settled on the lake. These grebes nested in a colony on the north end of Flotten, while the Holboell's variety built their fragile structures among the bulrush at the southeast end, close to our camp. The common loon also retired to nesting sites on the far side of the lake, where we later discovered their lovely olive-gray eggs while searching for a beaver colony. Each of these voices was added to the nightly chorus, and we soon became so accustomed to them that we couldn't have slept if they had stopped. On May 16 we heard the first song of the little ruby-crowned kinglet, which was evidently planning to nest in the tall spruce trees near camp. They were quite numerous in that location and their loud, clear, warbling song, delivered from the very top of a spruce, soon became as characteristic of our Flotten camp as the cries of the grebes and the loons.

On the twenty-first, in spite of the condition of the roads following several days of rain, we headed back to the settlement. We were nearly out of groceries. I had had no word from Bob Smith and it was essential that I make some arrangement for a supply of gasoline if we were to fly out of Flotten during early June. Those first days at Flotten had been unforgettable. In its own way, the spell of stormy weather had made our camp life interesting and exciting, so that we cherished the most ordinary things. To be able to sit quietly for a moment instead of chopping firewood, to put on a pair of dry woolen socks, nicely warm from hanging in front of the fire, to lean back at sundown, after a hot supper, watching the embers in the open hearth and listening to the many voices on the lake—these were simple pleasures that we enjoyed to the utmost. There were moments when I almost wished we might stay right there, undisturbed and forgotten.

We found our way to the settlement and sent out and received the necessary messages. The local agent for Imperial Oil agreed to set up a 1,000-gallon tank on the shore of the lake and send up a tank truck to fill it. I talked with an endless stream of "old-timers" who recalled having seen whooping cranes, most of them in bygone years, although two seemingly reliable reports placed our birds near Meadow Lake in May, 1946, and on the preceding April 20, just one month before our arrival. Each of these old-timers had his own idea of just where they were nesting, and I went over maps with them until I was dizzy. First this location seemed to be favored, then that one. One old man thought that the Muskeg River was undoubtedly the place, while another liked any part of the area to the west of Lost Lake. The practical difficulty was that these men were limited by pack-horse distances and they knew little of the country in summer beyond 30 airline miles from the hills north of Flotten. On the other hand, with our plane we would cover that entire region in an hour's time and then, like the cranes themselves, spread out over limitless distances. At that time we had only a hazy notion of the type of country we could expect to find our birds inhabiting. In spite of past performance and the nature of former breeding sites elsewhere, no one knew for certain where to look for them and what types of areas to bypass.

As we were leaving Meadow Lake for our return to Flotten, one of our new friends came trotting up to the car with several strawberry plants. Would we mind running off the road a few miles and delivering these plants to Dave Lachausseur on Waterhen Lake? I had met Dave, a huge French-Canadian trader and a jolly, voluble, and interesting character. It would be interesting to visit the Indian village where his trading post was located. We reached the Waterhen River, clattered across the rough plank bridge and, finding the right turning, set off down a narrow woodland road. After a little, the road dropped off toward the river again, but at this point there seemed no way across. On the far shore, however, we saw a number of Indians standing around, and after I had shouted to them that we wanted to cross they laid some heavy planks over to our side and, with some difficulty, I managed to drive over. Clear of the other side, we were soon on a trail that was so far from being a road that I began to fear we would never make it through to the trading post. The chief problem was to avoid a stump on the port side and, at the same time, miss hanging up on another stump that was hidden from view on the starboard side. We never found out the secret of this and before long were jammed between two stumps, one of which was caught solidly beneath our rear end. At this juncture along came my friend Dave, full of apologies for the stumps, which were his property. After getting on hands and knees to inspect the situation beneath our car, he stood with his back to the heavy vehicle, clamped huge paws under the rear bumper, gave several deep grunts, made ferocious grimaces and, to our utter astonishment, lifted the car free of the stump! We couldn't believe our eyes. Getting clear of the second stump was mere child's play, and soon we were through the woods and at Dave's place on Waterhen Lake.

It was now getting close to the end of May, but the temperature was still just above freezing at night. On the twenty-fifth a small flock of little brown cranes flew over, obviously migrating northward. In that latitude there was now only some four hours of darkness, and we were often up at three in the morning to watch the magnificent sunrises. Two days later, after an extremely cold night, there was an early morning hailstorm followed by snow. The air temperature dropped to 26°F. Until the aircraft arrived there was nothing more that we could do. We put in the days exploring the vicinity of the lake. With the Department boys and Pete, who operated a mink ranch nearby and was our only near neighbor, I walked around the east side of Flotten and off in the foothills beyond the north end as far as Salt Creek. We found the tracks of deer and black bear as well as sign in the form of browsed willow tips and droppings. Pete said that the moose winter in that area but leave in late February or March for muskegs 20 or 30 miles farther north, returning to the Salt Creek region in the fall. We walked through heavy thickets of birch, alder, aspen, and willow over a large tract that had once been a spruce forest. The spruce had been destroyed by a great forest fire shortly after this part of Saskatchewan was opened for settlement following World War I. Back at the lake shore we came across an abandoned Indian camp and saw a "sweating lodge," which is the Cree version of a Turkish bath. It consists of several saplings that are stuck in the ground and bent to form a low framework, over which a hide or piece of canvas is thrown. A number of stones are then heated and placed inside the lodge. When cold water is dropped on the stones they send off clouds of steam, to the delight of the Indian crouching inside. There was also a Cree bath brush lying nearby, a bunch of twigs and coarse grasses lashed together at one end with bark fibers.

On our recent visit to Meadow Lake I had met Lefty McLeod and Cliff Lebey, who fly for the Department and who assured me they would drop by for a visit. Within a few days we heard an aircraft approaching, and shortly a little biplane on floats had appeared, coming in for a landing. They taxied up to our beach and we helped them pull the craft ashore tailfirst and secure lines from each wingtip to convenient trees. They were real bush pilots and had a great store of information about the surrounding country. Lefty, in his fringed caribou jacket and with felt hat always at a jaunty angle, was the talker, and with long experience in that region he was extremely interesting. He said that the lakes just to the north of us and at a higher elevation—Primrose, Canoe, Keely, etc.—were now clear of ice for the first time (this was May 28). We made coffee and also fed them the first corn bread they had ever eaten—with syrup. They declared it better than the local "bannock," which is a Scottish johnnycake made of white flour. Evelyn promised to cook a batch every time they landed at Flotten, as long as our corn meal held out. We had the two young biologists from the Department as our guests for supper that evening and sat late around our fire, talking and listening to the night. They were leaving next day for another assignment. A few weeks later their canoe turned over in a deep lake farther to the south and one of them, who was wearing rubber hip boots, was drowned. The news of this tragedy was the saddest experience of our entire summer.

June brought with it gnats and mosquitoes, and the first Sunday visitors from "outside." Our little interlude of wilderness camping was at an end. It also brought a welcome rise in the thermometer. The birds at Flotten were in full voice: chipping sparrows, white-throats, juncos, all trilling for dear life. And the big loons were now at the peak of their vocal efforts. We thought this wild and tremulous call the most beautiful sound on the lake. Bobby went ashore on Baldy Island on June 3 and found two duck nests, one evidently a mallard's and the other a widgeon's. The females were still laying. On this day the temperature climbed into the 70s for the first time and Evelyn boiled clothes with a vengeance, for it was perfect drying weather. The sudden warmth also brought other changes. The mosquitoes increased, a whole colony of large black ants swarmed out of a dead spruce stump, and butterflies appeared to flit about in the sunshine. All at once it was summer, or something very much like it.

In the afternoon Lefty McLeod dropped out of the sky for coffee and corn bread and to tell me there was no message from Bob Smith. On the sixth, he came in again with a letter from Smith and another from Larry Walkinshaw, who was searching possible whooping-crane areas farther east and south. Smith wrote that he would reach Flotten that day or the next. As the afternoon wore on, we climbed the hill west of camp to watch for him. At four-thirty we heard the whine of his two engines and in another moment his fast little amphibian appeared, circling low over the lake. Now we could get down to business.

It was another couple of days before Imperial Oil delivered the 1,000-gallon tank and filled it for us. Meanwhile, McLeod offered to lend Bob enough gasoline and oil to get us started. From this point on, from June 8 until June 26, we flew almost constantly, covering with painstaking care a vast area in west central Saskatchewan, northeastern Alberta, and around Great Slave Lake in Northwest Territories. The search area was limited by certain features of terrain and habitat. On the east is the edge of the Pre-Cambrian Shield, which knifes across western Canada from the east side of Lake Winnipeg to Lake Athabaska, Great Slave Lake, Great Bear Lake, and the Arctic coast at Darnley Bay. Within this rocky region to the east there may be uranium and gold and other precious ores and metals, but the lakes are deep, there are no marshes, and it is no place to look for whooping cranes. To the west the limiting feature is a combination of forests, muskegs, and, from Camsell Bend on the Mackenzie River northward, mountains. We did not expect to find our birds in forests or in muskegs or in mountains. This left us with a roughly hourglass-shaped area extending from Candle Lake on the east to Primrose Lake on the west in Saskatchewan, narrowing around Lake Claire in northeast Alberta and spreading out again to take in the western end of Great Slave Lake, including Wood Buffalo Park, the Slave River aspen parklands, and Mills Lake near the head of the Mackenzie. It would be difficult to estimate the square miles involved, but the distance from Candle Lake to Mills Lake is over 700 miles. In the three weeks that followed, we spent over 55 hours in the air and logged nearly 6,000 miles—all of it within this area. As far as we went, no possibility was overlooked.

On the first day we searched out the entire Lost Lake region—the Muskeg River, the Martineau River, and Primrose Lake, as well as muskegs east of Primrose and north of the 18th baseline. It is a forest area, with some scattered muskegs. The only extensive marsh is a strip of phragmites and bulrush along the north shore of Primrose. The muskegs in all this part of Canada, we soon learned, are usually of two types. One type is rimmed with spongy-looking sphagnum and small tamaracks; the other has meadowlike borders with grass and, rarely, marshy corners. Most muskegs are of the sphagnum type and appear almost sterile. There is more life in the meadow type, and we inspected all of them we came across.

By June 16 we had searched all possibilities in Saskatchewan except a few lake areas near Prince Albert. We pulled out of our Flotten base, leaving my family to the tender mercies of the wilderness for the next ten days while we continued the search into Alberta and Northwest Territories. Eliminating lakes and marshes in the provinces was relatively easy. For the most part, it can be said that within those areas where we did find a suitable marsh there was a logging camp nearby or an Indian village or other human activity. No sign of whooping cranes and no hope for them in such circumstances. The marshes around Lake Claire and Chipewyan are a splendid habitat, but the local Indian population can penetrate every corner of these areas in summer by boat and canoe. The same is apparently true of certain parts of Wood Buffalo Park, particularly near the Peace and the Slave Rivers. This is not meant to imply that the whooping crane has been destroyed by the Indian population, for that is not the case by any means. It is very possible that whoopers nesting or attempting to nest in some of these areas in the past have been disturbed and possibly killed by Indians, but these were probably isolated cases and those particular whooping-crane populations may never have been very abundant. The real damage was done years ago in Illinois, Minnesota, Iowa, and North Dakota and in southern Manitoba and Saskatchewan and east central Alberta. And if these prosperous, well-populated farming and resort areas were to be converted from wilderness to their present state, then there was no way of preventing the destruction of the whooping cranes. They are a real, dyed-in-the-wool wilderness species, and in these circumstances they could not continue to exist. Those that survive are a small remnant that still finds an irreproachable wilderness in which to nest and a protected semiwilderness in which to pass the winter. Our job was to locate that lost nesting ground, but in that second summer of search (for Pettingill and Moore had been over some of this ground before us) we failed to find them. There were traces as far north as Hay River and Pine Point on the south shore of Great Slave, but Smith and I saw no whooping cranes. Not until seven years later were we to know how close we had come to them on that first attempt!

Nevertheless they were there, somewhere in that vast wilderness. For they returned to Aransas in the fall, bringing six new young birds with them. And the 25 birds we had counted in Texas in April were now 31. In their lost and secret place they had wrought magic, and we began to think that perhaps things might be just as well off as they were. Still we felt we must continue the search. The North is being developed rapidly. Airplane travel is changing the picture, and soon every corner will be explored for ores, for oil, for timber, for fish resources, for anything and everything that man can use. This little legion must be found, and provisions made to safeguard its future.

Having missed our birds in the region south of Great Slave Lake in 1947, we next cast our eyes still farther north, toward the relatively narrow strip of lowlands between Great Slave and Great Bear, and on to the river deltas of the Arctic coast. In April of 1948, a flock of 28 whooping cranes left Texas for the breeding grounds, 2 birds remaining on the refuge through the summer and another having been lost there in March. According to plan I joined Bob Smith in Canada early in June.

We left the airport at Regina, the capital city of Saskatchewan, on the third, stopping off that night at Prince Albert, where at Gordon Lund's we had our first real taste of the North in the form of caribou tongue sandwiches. Next day we flew into Alberta and low over Watchusk and Gordon Lakes, where forest fires were burning so fiercely that the great pall of smoke forced us to land on the airstrip near Fort McMurray. The nearest settlement is Waterways, some miles away on the Clearwater River near its junction with the Athabaska, and we eventually found a car that would take us there over the muddy road, although the fare that he charged placed the Indian driver in the highwayman class.

In the morning, in spite of a thick haze of smoke, we took off and followed the Athabaska toward Lake Claire, beyond Fort Chipewyan on Lake Athabaska, and on to our destination at Fort Smith, beyond the Slave River rapids. En route we ran sample duck counts over the 800 square miles of the Lake Claire marshes and the 500 square miles of the Athabaska delta. In the Lake Claire marshes we flew over scattered bands of the greatest wild herd of bison that remains on the North American continent. It was a magnificent sight, these huge animals roaming at large and under primitive conditions. We saw two big buffalo wolves trotting along on the rear flank of one herd, the nearest group of cows and calves apparently paying no attention to them. After all, in a completely wild state the wolves have always been there, and so are simply an accepted and integral part of the scenery.

After a pleasant night at Fort Smith, we set out rather late the following morning, because of a localized drizzle. But Signals reported a 4,000-foot overcast at the eastern end of Great Slave Lake, and clear at Hay River, so we took off and at one o'clock that afternoon we landed on the airstrip at Hay River and had lunch in the dusty and then only mildly booming settlement. We were anxious to move on and decided to continue as far as Fort Simpson, down the Mackenzie River at the mouth of the Liard. This would put us on into new territory for both of us. By three-thirty we were over the head of the Mackenzie, which stretched off into illimitable distances. As we flew on we could see, up ahead of us, vast mountain ranges and jagged peaks, blanketed in clouds. Beyond Jean Marie River we left the main stream and dove in low, over muskegs and forests of tamarack and spruce, to see what ducks might be nesting on the shallow lakes of that area. Then on to the Simpson strip, where we put down at five-thirty. We were now on our way into the real North. Another day of flying and we would be close to the Arctic Circle.

Next morning we were again late getting off the ground, as the airstrip is six miles up the Liard River from the settlement and we had come downstream the evening before in a freight canoe paddled by a crew of Indians. So, in the morning, we had to work our way upstream against the current. Fortunately the game warden with whom we had stayed was equipped with an outboard motor for his light canoe and was good enough to carry us up to the landing. We were airborne before noon and an hour and a half later were beyond Wrigley, with the Franklin Mountains to our right and the rugged Mackenzie Range to our left. Far off in the northwest, on the borders of Yukon Territory, we could see high peaks covered with snow. Shortly we could make out the westernmost arm of Great Bear Lake, and then we were approaching the airstrip at Norman Wells. As we came in to a landing we noted deep snow patches on the Carcajou and Norman ranges close on either side of us. It was raining lightly and was chilly, but we found snug quarters at the Imperial Oil Company's camp. And that night we slept soundly in spite of the daylight that now did not end with the day.

The following morning, the eighth of June and the sixth day out from Regina, we awoke to the disappointment of a low ceiling, a high wind, and a considerably lower temperature. We waited around, Bob talking shop with Sandy Tweed, a Canadian Pacific Airlines pilot with wide experience in that part of the North. By 2 P.M. Aklavik reported that the ceiling had lifted to 3,000 feet, so we got off the ground and headed out on the last lap. It was still overcast at Norman Wells, and before an hour had passed we ran into fog and rain. At 3,000 feet the outside temperature was 36°F. Staring through the dripping windshield, Bob remarked that the weather up there would be difficult to estimate. "This is where weather, as we know it, is made," he said. In a wet fog, and with an unbroken wilderness beneath us, we skimmed across the Arctic Circle and felt no different from the way we had before. Absolutely painless incident! The time was close to 3:30 P.M.

Beneath us some of the smaller lakes were still frozen over and the whole panorama was bleak and cold-looking. We lost the first batch of fog and then ran on into another and thicker bank. At 5 P.M. we were over Arctic Red River. Ahead, to the west, lay the snow-topped Richardson Mountains and directly before us, immense and ill-defined, stretched the vast delta of the Mackenzie. Bob brought the little amphib down close to the main stream, where we skimmed along over great islands of rotting ice that were moving swiftly for the open sea farther north. Breakup had started on the twenty-ninth of May but, as we learned later, the rampaging ice had jammed in the Pokiak and Peel, close to Aklavik, causing a serious flood which had only just subsided. Now West Channel off the town was clear, however, and Bob brought the plane in for a water landing in midstream, setting her down against the rush of the muddy current. We had reached our first goal.

An old friend who had come in to Aklavik some years before from the Yukon told us to remember above all things that the first impression one makes is particularly important in these Arctic outposts. "They see so few strangers," Johnny had said, "that they note very carefully everything you do and say and never forget any of it. Be sure and make a good first impression or you'll be sunk." I thought of this advice as we taxied toward the black mud of the shore, where several men were waiting to greet us. When close in, I crawled to the nose, released the hatch, and then stood up in the bow with a coil of rope all ready to throw to the men on the bank. Bob nosed her all the way in and I managed to get an end of my line ashore. Two of the men held fast to the line and Bob shut off his engines. After that no one moved. Bob sat where he was, looking about him with a tired but well-pleased smile, I stood foolishly in the nose and the four men, saying nothing, stood expectantly on the bank. Well, I thought, we must make a good first impression and I guess the next move is up to me. Obviously, the thing to do was to go ashore, shake each of these good fellows by the hand by way of greeting, and then see to the business of securing our aircraft. I stood up on the nose and, grinning cheerfully at our new friends, leaped for the bank. I made it all right, smack into that black, silty mud, hip-deep. With exclamations of dismay, three of the men ran off for logs and planks which they threw down across the mud so as to reach me. With their assistance I was then hauled out, a sorry sight. What a first impression!

The four men were Bill Carson, the Hudson's Bay manager, the Imperial Oil agent, the local game warden, and Ward Stevens, then engaged in a muskrat study in the delta and later Game

Superintendent for the Territories. We found the people who live in outposts like Aklavik are among the most cheerful, the most friendly, and the most helpful human beings on the face of the earth.

We learned that most of the Indians and Huskies (as the Eskimos are called in that region) were out in the delta hunting muskrats. The season would end on the tenth of June and then they would come trooping in, by boat and canoe, until the summer population of a thousand or more natives had assembled. Then, they told us, the sunlit nights would resound to the beat and the chanting voices of the drum dance, not to mention the incessant howling of the sled dogs, the whine of outboard motors, and the blare of the mechanical phonograph at the North Star Inn, a native gathering place. Now all was relatively tranquil and if we tacked a blanket across our bedroom window, to keep out the midnight sun, we might catch up on our sleep before the great disembarking.

Next morning we talked with Mr. Roberts of Imperial Oil and learned that the recent flood had carried his entire stock of gasoline drums downstream, hundreds of them. He hadn't so much as a gallon of the 87-octane we would need to begin our survey flights over the delta. Inspector Kirk of the R.C.M.P., who was a dead ringer for Leslie Howard, told us he was planning to take the big police boat downriver to look for the "steels," as the drums are called, and would let us know if he found any with our number on them. Meanwhile, a barge was reportedly on its way from Norman Wells with a new supply. But until gas arrived, we were quite effectively grounded.

We visited that afternoon with the R.C.M.P., and they invited us to go upriver with two of their men on a round of trappers' camps. We jumped at the chance, of course, and that evening joined Phalen and McKinnon and went with them aboard the police launch.

The Mackenzie Delta is about 150 miles in straight-line length, from Separation Point to the extreme northern projection of Richard's Island near Hansen Harbor. It varies in width from 40 miles at Aklavik, to more than 50 at Reindeer Station and a mere 18 miles across the tip of Richard's Island west of Kugmallit Bay, on the Beaufort Sea. At Separation Point, where the delta begins, the main channel forms three branches. These unite again a little beyond and the main stream flows on as far as Reindeer Station, then breaks off toward the west as Middle Channel, and the main river goes on north, around the foot of the Caribou Hills to Kugmallit Bay and the sea. Meanwhile, as the delta lands flatten out, the onrushing stream breaks through its banks on every hand to form a thousand small channels, a network of rivulets, tortuous and intricate, but all ending eventually in the sea. Throughout this pattern, there are thousands of tiny lakes formed by the ever-changing whims of the delta, as channels shift their courses and new banks are thrown up or old ones destroyed. There are two main types of habitat, the wooded delta, which is the upstream portion and covers some 3,600 square miles, and the treeless delta near the coast, covering about 1,600 square miles. In the wooded portion, spruce, fir, and willow grow along the banks, while the treeless area has only a few small willows and is chiefly a region of broad meadows and wide mud flats.

The entire delta region except the north end, toward the open sea, is enclosed by mountains or hills. To the west are the Richardson Mountains, rising to peaks of over 6,000 feet, while the eastern boundary is formed by the Caribou Hills, 500 feet in height, and the adjacent upland tundra, a high and gently rolling area of formidable aspect. Our first view of this whole vast panorama from the air had been bewildering, but that evening, in the police boat, we saw the narrow, winding channels, the shallow, tree-lined lakes, and the muddy banks at close range, and their character was soon familiar to us. At one camp we went ashore. The men were still off somewhere gathering pelts, but a fat and very jolly Loucheux or Kutchin woman, known as Elizabeth, was hard at work washing clothes, assisted by a couple of shy children. She was dressed in a series of loose garments known as "summer parkas," cut from light cotton material and worn one over another, and she had caribou-hide mukluks on her feet. The washing machine was a surprise. It was an old-fashioned manual affair operated by hand and it probably had a long and interesting history. Elizabeth, nearly overcome with giggles, kept working the handle back and forth, vigorously, all the time we were in the camp. There was a tent, quite comfortably rigged, and all around were the stretched and drying pelts of muskrats. To one side the naked carcasses were heaped, to be carried back to the settlement and fed to the sled dogs. The Mackenzie 'rats have a thick, dark fur that was selling that spring for as much as $2.25 each at the Bay in Aklavik and bringing nearly twice that in Edmonton. Some of the camps would take a thousand or more pelts during the brief open season, so such comparative luxuries as primitive washing machines, up-to-date battery radio sets, and ice cream and movies at the settlement are entirely within the scope of these pleasant natives. In protecting the trapping rights of the natives of these territories, the Canadian government has done an admirable thing. The Loucheux and Husky populations of that region are not merely self-sufficient; many of them are relatively prosperous, with property and resources beyond the ability of most natives. Most of the well-to-do Eskimos that we met, however, had made their wealth from Arctic fox furs, which are trapped during the long, dark winter months when they are prime. Incidentally, few muskrats are trapped in the delta, but are shot in the head with a .22-caliber rifle bullet. We soon learned how expert some of the natives are at this type of hunting. Bob wanted a native-made parka and Bill Carson recommended a local seamstress, a very pretty young Indian girl who lived upstream on the Peel. Word was sent out and a day or so later she appeared, with tape measure and material. Bill explained that she had been out hunting and that the night before, in ten or twelve hours' time, with her little peashooter, had slain a black bear and more than 200 muskrats. We were much impressed, especially as she was as shy and as full of feminine giggles as old Elizabeth.

The gasoline barge arrived on the fourteenth. It came to anchor in the channel early in the day and required until evening to unload, adding more confusion to the already crowded waterfront. We sat on empty oil drums and watched. There were many birds to be seen right in the town or close to the outskirts. Bold black ravens hopped about on the snow patches close to houses and native tents, looking for scraps of garbage. Little flocks of short-billed gulls trotted along the beach on similar errands. Once we saw a group of six whistling swans flying swiftly northward along the far side of West Channel, and both the pomarine and long-tailed jaegers were observed close to shore. In the evening the "winnowing song" of the Wilson's snipe was frequently heard along the banks, both toward the Pokiak and upstream along the Peel. They must breed in the wooded portion of the delta in great numbers. An article in the *Canadian Field Naturalist* on the birds of the delta by A.E. Porsild gave many of the Eskimo names for birds. We were not only much entertained by them, but they proved helpful in discussing birds with the natives. There was no name for the whooping crane, but one of the older Eskimos, Douglas Oniak, had told Porsild that he had seen the big white birds with the black wingtips many years ago in that region.

Now that our fuel had arrived we needed only good weather to begin our work. But a cold rain and poor visibility kept us grounded until the sixteenth, when we finally took off and skimmed out across the wide delta. Beyond the Caribou Hills, in the direction of the Eskimo Lakes, where we had hoped we might find whooping cranes, the visibility was poor. It was not until the following day that flying conditions improved to such an extent that we were able to have our first look at the tundra near the Eskimo Lakes. To our dismay, most of the lakes were still completely frozen and, with its higher elevation and the total absence of the warming effect of the great body of water flowing down the river, this entire upland tundra area was weeks behind the delta in shaking off the icy hand of winter. We saw a good many ducks and geese, however, as well as whistling swans, willow ptarmigan, and little brown cranes, but no sign of whooping cranes. The Beaufort Sea was a solid expanse of ice, right to the shore. The small coastal settlements of Kittigazuit and Tuktuk were completely frozen in and looked like the Arctic stations that they are. Yet it was quite mild, the outside temperature at a 100-foot altitude along the coast being 28°F. on the eighteenth of June.

During this period, until the end of June, we logged nearly

forty-four hours of flying time, much of it running low level transects that gave us an excellent picture of both the species and the approximate numbers of waterfowl and certain other birds in a number of habitats from the Mackenzie Delta as far as Anderson River, more than 200 miles east of Aklavik. We estimated a population in this vast region of 369,000 ducks of several species, 21,000 geese of three species, 2,300 black brant, and 16,000 whistling swans. Little brown cranes numbered about 3,200, but not one whooping crane was observed, although we looked with special care at some excellent country lying between the Anderson and the Kugaluk. Now and then a huge Barren Ground grizzly bear, *Ursus richardsoni,* would be observed, bumbling about over the tundra, but we saw only a few representatives of this dwindling race, and counted more trophy skins around Aklavik than live animals in the wilds. The word *Aklavik* is the Eskimo name for the Barren Ground grizzly.

We also made a couple of side trips, including one into the Yukon. It was the second of July, and the first clear morning in some days. After breakfast, Bob cocked an appraising eye at the heavens and "allowed as how" we might hop over to Old Crow and be back in time for supper. "You mean," I stammered, "Old Crow, on the other side of those mountains? In the Yukon?" "Yep," said Bob, "Old Crow." We were already strolling along the riverbank, on our way to the airplane, and by 11:45 we were off the water and heading south over the delta. No time to worry about such details as what the weather might be doing in the mountains or on the other side of the divide. Not much time to worry about anything. South of Aklavik the Rat River comes pouring out of the mountains from up around McDougall Pass and empties into Husky Channel, a branch of the Peel, downstream from Fort McPherson. The Scots certainly have left their mark on that North Country. Sir John Richardson, in whose honor the mountains themselves were named, was born in Dumfries and was a product of the University of Edinburgh and the Royal Navy. I don't know if there are any monuments to Sir John around Dumfries but there are several in North America, including a number of birds with which his name has long been associated, notably the little Richardson's goose, as well as a race of the grizzly bear, and, of course, the mountain range. This last is quite a monument. As we reached and identified the rushing torrent of the Rat River and as Bob pulled our little amphib around so that its blunt nose was headed directly toward them, the mountains rose before us in all their hard and craggy aloofness. The river tumbles down a great gash in the rocky slopes, and the width and character of this opening didn't look exactly hospitable. Bob flew in fairly low so as to keep out of the uncertain and drafty altitudes of the summits and we skimmed over broad alpinelike meadows, high on the face of the lower slopes. On one of these a light-colored mountain sheep stared at us without moving, as staunch as the rocks about him. Then the pass narrowed and the sides grew steep until we were flying through a winding canyon, with the river a thin torrent 1,000 feet beneath us. Far above, we could make out scudding clouds and mist around the peaks, but in the lower altitudes the sun was shining and the visibility good. Now and then the air was a little rough and we struck both updrafts and downdrafts, but nothing unusual or alarming.

On the Yukon side of the mountains we found ourselves over the upper reaches of the Bell, which joins the Porcupine and flows on into the Yukon River above Yukon Flats. The canyons of the Bell twist and turn every which way, so that we were constantly banking around great steep walls of rock and slipping this way and that to keep as near the middle of the cut as possible. But the weather remained clear and fairly calm, so that we had no trouble getting through.

The settlement at Old Crow is a Loucheux village of log huts. We could see them crowded together along the edge of a high bank overlooking the Porcupine, which makes its start here at the junction of the Old Crow and the Bell. But we headed off across the flats to the north, for we wanted to get this chore out of the way before trying to land at the settlement. It is an entrancing region and appealed to me at once as having a sort of "lost world" character. No wonder the Loucheux speak of themselves as "The People," as if they lived in a separate universe inhabited by no one else. It is true, of course, that many primitive tribes have this same illusion, but doubtless few tribal environments are so perfectly isolated, both physically and culturally, as the remote basin of the Old Crow. We estimated that it covers about 2,000 square miles, a really tremendous region. Although surrounded by steep and furrowed mountains that rise to shoulders, spurs, slopes, ridges, and peaks of sedimentary Mesozoic rocks, the basin itself is considerably less than 1,000 feet in elevation and is almost perfectly flat. The habitat is transitional in character, with areas of spruce as well as extensive barren lands. There are many shallow, rectangular-shaped, sedge-rimmed lakes and ponds, and in them we found the highest density of waterfowl that we came across all summer. These consisted of scoters, baldpates, and scaup in great numbers and smaller numbers of pintails, golden-eyes, old squaws, and canvasbacks. Our estimate of the total duck population was 112,400 for all species, an impressive figure that was based on a calculated density of 56.2 ducks per square mile. There were also some 4,800 Canada geese and perhaps 100 little brown cranes; but not one whooping crane.

According to Cpl. E. A. Kirk of the R.C.M.P. detachment at Old Crow, mosses and other typical tundra plants abound on the treeless stretches. On the shores of many of the lakes, great piles of rotted vegetation and silt are piled 10 and 20 feet high. Through the length of the plain, meandering in elaborate oxbows and long, winding loops, flows the Old Crow River, entrenched from 60 to 125 feet below the level of the valley proper. We saw very few natives in all that vast and rugged wilderness.

When our sample waterfowl transects had been run, we turned back to the vicinity of the settlement, partly because we were curious to see the capital of the Loucheux and partly because we wanted to talk with Corporal Kirk, the only white man living permanently in that part of the Yukon. The level of the river was above normal depth—fortunately for us, as it turned out—and as we swung in low over its surface it appeared to be racing along at a record clip. No place to land a fast little Grumman, ordinarily. But Smith didn't hesitate for more than half a second and in we came, landing with a great splash and bouncing a couple of times before the aircraft decided to act like a large-winged fish

Stephen F. Briggs

*The midmorning nap, an important health factor for young spoonbills.*

*Whooping cranes march toward an Aransas Refuge watering place.*

John J. Lynch

*Right: A whooping-crane family group on their Texas wintering territory. This scene is at Middle Pond on the Aransas National Wildlife Refuge.*

Lawrence H. Walkinshaw

*Left: Even the wildest of birds become gentle and cooperative when skillfully handled in captivity. "Pete" and "Jo" being fed special delicacies in the original Aransas Refuge enclosure.*

*Right: Her dignity is a natural heritage, and "Josephine," the female of the captive whooping cranes, is completely unaware of her fame, or of the hopes and prayers that have gone her way.*

*Below: A great deal of luck was needed to get this aerial photograph of five migrant whooping cranes on a sandbar in the Platte River in Nebraska. The date was April 19, 1947.*

Robert P. Allen

*Robert P. Allen*

*Robert P. Allen*

*Robert P. Allen*

*Tea with the Copper Eskimos during Northern whooping-crane search.*

*A Florida swamp buggy solved our transport problem on Inagua.*

*Benjamin Franklin Brown*

and push hard against the stiff current toward shore. As usual, a crowd of Indians was lined up on the pebbly beach, and after a miss or two I reached them with an end of rope. Quite a pull was required, but they stuck at it and soon we were heaved in along the shore and safely tied up. Corporal Kirk, a stocky, quiet chap, was on hand and, after greeting us, he remarked somewhat casually that it was a lucky thing for us the river had been high. "If it had been a foot or so lower, I guess you'd have hit those stakes out there," he said. Stakes? It seemed that there were several rows of wooden stakes in the river where we had landed. The Indians used them when setting their nets to catch fish. A little less water and they'd have caught *us!* Bob grinned, wiping the palm of his hand across his face in a characteristic gesture, which seemed to say, "They might have caught us, but they didn't!"

With Kirk and the local shaman we walked into the village, and, over a cup of tea with the constable, discussed the area we had just flown over. As we were making ready to leave, a young Loucheux girl shyly approached Kirk and, after some words we didn't understand, handed him a small envelope. With a broad smile he turned it over to us, a love letter destined for Aklavik—so far, far away for this dark-skinned maiden and her swain, but a mere hop, skip, and a jump for us and our magic carpet. For we would be back at Mrs. McNeice's table in time for supper! Or so we hoped.

We got off in something of a hurry, for it was obvious that the mist in the mountains was turning to rain. And if we ran into rain on our way back through those passes it might be a bit uncomfortable. We were a good eight or ten minutes off the water and deep in the narrow canyons of the Bell when the first rain caught us. As it streaked suddenly across the Plexiglas of the windshield we looked up and saw a black mass of wind-swept clouds directly above us. Below us was the twisting course of the river, roaring swiftly downgrade, and on each side, hemming us in, rose the steep, inflexible walls of the canyon. In another moment the full force of the gale struck us, bouncing us around like a ping-pong ball and cutting visibility to zero. Immediately, Bob did the only thing that could possibly save us. He dove straight for the river, still dimly discernible beneath us, and leveled off less than 100 feet above its tumbling cataracts. Then, using the white water of falls and rapids as a guide, he jockeyed the plane along, his eyes nearly bugging out of his head with the strain of watching the water below, the steep walls close on either side and the ever-present danger of an invisible, sheer flank of rock dead ahead.

Never did that little craft seem to have such speed! In close quarters like that her 110 miles per hour gave us the sensation of riding an unguided missile up a blind alley. It was a nightmare! Ahead we could see absolutely nothing, and the only way Bob steered her around the abrupt, wholly unpredictable turns in the canyon was by watching the trend of the stream below us and exercising a rare and admirable judgment. The squall didn't slacken until we were nearly through the course of the Bell, then it cleared enough to see us safely over the descending Rat. But it was rough going all the way and we didn't relax until we came out into the clear warm air of the upper Mackenzie delta. Bob sat back with an audible sigh, and when I looked at him I saw the beads of sweat that covered his face.

That was but the start of our second summer of search. There were other areas to be looked at and our hopes were still high. The North is a big country, and we weren't licked yet.

*. . . Wild and wide are my borders,*
*stern as death is my sway,*
*And I wait for the men who will*
*win me—and I will not be won in a day.*
ROBERT W. SERVICE *

# VII : Arctic adventures—the search continued

Even in summer, when, except for the mosquitoes, you can be comfortable in the sunshine out-of-doors twenty-four hours of the day, there aren't too many diversions around an Arctic outpost like Aklavik. We were waiting for the arrival of the gasoline barge so that we could begin our survey flights over the surrounding country. We discovered most of the diversions in the first two or three days we were there and then repeated them, mixing them up as to sequence just to make it more interesting. We could join the Eskimo and Loucheux families that crowded nightly into the movie theater, but of course there were only the five pictures, and after we'd seen each of them two or three times their entertainment value wasn't worth the one-dollar admission price. Besides, unless you came an hour ahead of time you had to sit on the floor, right up against the screen. Once a week there was homemade ice cream at the hotel. There was the North Star Inn, where they sold root beer that they made themselves, and where there

* *The Law of the Yukon.*

was a jukebox, the only one in the settlement. They had a couple of Bing Crosby records, and the rest were mostly hillbilly or cowboy tunes, which the natives go for in a big way. But three or four evenings of this was enough. You could walk downstream as far as the Anglican church and upstream as far as a low bank where there were some Indians living in tents, before the mud got to your knees, but you had to walk pretty slow to kill an hour over this route, so we didn't depend on it for steady recreation. It was more fun to stick around the beach just below the C.P.A. landing and watch the natives who were always coming and going by boat and canoe.

The radio station, operated by the Canadian Army's Corps of Signals, installed a little 100-watt long-wave transmitter after the war. Naturally, there was a big boom in battery radio sales right away, and shortly, no matter how remote or how primitive and cheerless in other respects, no native trapper's camp was complete without one. Phonograph records were the standard program material, but thanks to "Red" McLeod's patience and special interest, the natives contributed some of the most colorful and most entertaining broadcasts with their own Eskimo or Kutchin singing and drum music. Red found them eager to perform before a mike, once they got the hang of it.

We heard an amusing story about the first effort to broadcast church services on Sundays. As in many Northern outposts there are two hard-working churches in Aklavik, the Anglican and the Catholic, and they are great rivals for the natives' favor. When McLeod first decided to put Sunday services on the air he quite naturally offered an hour to each of the churches. The Anglican priest, a bustling, energetic Canadian with thoroughly modern ideas, accepted at once, but the good father from the rival church, an old-country Frenchman with a beard as long as his cassock, refused to participate on the grounds that it would be undignified and improper in every way. The Anglican father laboriously prepared sermons in the Eskimo lingo every Sunday and dutifully delivered them over the hitherto unblessed Arctic air. He even assembled his native choir, and the good old Anglican hymns, sung in the native tongue, of course, were also sent out over the subzero air waves. One Sabbath, as was his way, the Catholic father left his flock in charge of one of the brothers and, hitching up his dogs, mushed out across the thick river ice to visit those of his flock who were established in trapping camps in the hinterland. Imagine his chagrin when, on arriving at the first camp, he found everyone harking intently to the enterprising voice of his Anglican rival! In the next camp it was the same, and in the next. The magic of the radio, out there in the Arctic wilderness, was such a rare and absorbing delight that the enraptured natives scarcely gave the poor father-in-the-flesh a passing glance. In great haste he backtracked to the settlement, and thereafter his voice likewise broke upon the Sabbath stillness, within the confines of his allotted time, of course, which was the hour that followed the Anglican service. Courtesy of the Canadian Army.

The mission schools were still in session, and one of the teachers at the Anglican School asked me to give a bird talk to the children. There were 112 youngsters, Eskimos and Loucheux Indians, ranging in age from six to sixteen, and they were assembled in one of the classrooms under the practiced supervision of Miss Law and Miss Harrington. They had already heard about our search for the lost nesting grounds of the whooping crane and were quite excited about it. There were a lot of bird pictures on the walls and several childish drawings of birds on the blackboard, including two or three free representations of whooping cranes. I learned that Mary Harrington, a highly capable artist, had particularly encouraged these efforts. Without benefit of slides or other illustrations, which were quite unnecessary after all this advance billing, I talked about the cranes, the mystery of their nesting place, and the reasons for our search. In the plump and handsome faces before me there was an almost electric attention. This was something they could understand, and I could feel the eagerness with which they drank in every word, and see the quickness of their imaginations in the dark slant of their bright little eyes. When I asked for questions at the end of the talk half the hands were in the air at once. They wanted to know a hundred things about the crane and its habits. They were especially interested in hearing about the Texas coast, more than 3,000 miles away to the south, where the surviving whoopers winter, and they laughed in amazement and disbelief when I described for them a land where it seldom snowed and where we shivered with cold when the thermometer stood at thirty degrees *above* zero.

After we started flying out across the broad delta of the Mackenzie and on over the wilderness of the tundra, these children watched anxiously for our return from each day's flight. When we had tied up our little amphibian to the riverbank and were walking toward our quarters, several of the boys would come running up to ask if we had found the whooping cranes. The first few times we replied in the negative they showed keen disappointment, but interest and hope were still alive in their faces. Then it became an old story, and we saw them looking at us a little differently. We had let them down and we were no longer heroes. Soon they stopped running out to greet us, and then they scarcely looked at us if we passed them on the road. Our own disappointment at not locating the whoopers that summer was bad enough, but the silent treatment we received from those native children was the bitterest pill we had to swallow. We would slink back from the landing as if we had just been caught kicking a dog. Both of us had moments at that time when we felt that we were complete failures and might as well give up the whole thing. It was a very humbling experience.

We were soon so busy with our job of estimating waterfowl populations that we were able, by degrees, to salvage a certain amount of self-respect. It also helped to take it out on that dangerous lord of the tundra, the Barren Ground grizzly, which we were able to do with practically no risk to our own necks. The first bears that we saw were a pair that must have come down to the delta to fish after breakup. We found them far out on the flat, almost treeless region that comprises Ellice Island, facing Mackenzie Bay. They were in a bunch of willows and we saw them as soon as they started running, for the silt that still clung to the branches had dried to a powder, and as the great beasts fled pell-mell through the slender trees the dust flew from their flanks in clouds. It wasn't until we met other bears as we flew low over the open tundra that the idea of swooping down and talking to them occurred to us. Actually, I think this was Bob Smith's idea. We had been working over the delta country rather industriously and were branching out to cover the adjacent region eastward over the upland tundra and northeastward to the islands off the coast and the lonely mud flats of the coastal tundra toward Cape Dalhousie. We had found snow geese and black brant nesting on islands at the outer extremity of the delta, and even ptarmigan on some of the larger islands that were extensive enough to boast the rolling upland habitat. On the twenty-second of June it was warmer, with a southerly wind and a pleasantly hazy sky. Off the coast near Tuktuk and in the western end of the Eskimo Lakes the ice showed definite signs of breaking. As we skimmed low over the mossy, uneven surface of the tundra, we spotted a whistling swan sitting on her eggs on the very top of a little hill. And down the slope to one side, beyond the vision of the swan, a great lumbering grizzly was moving, his tremendous head lolling from side to side. He was climbing directly toward the swan. At the same moment the grizzly heard our engines, and we saw him look up with an expression of surprise and annoyance. Bob banked the plane as rapidly as safety permitted and came back directly toward the bear. The beast had turned and was now running downgrade at a tremendous rate. Bob flew within 150 feet of him, banked the plane so as to give him a direct look at the huge animal, and when we had him exactly on our beam, Bob turned his head toward him and yelled, "Run, you big fat slob! Run, you blankety-blank so-and-so!" The bear ran, and kept on running after we had pulled up and were far above and beyond him. Bob, grinning broadly and with his good spirits completely restored, turned to me and said, "I always wanted to cuss out a grizzly bear. Notice how surprised he looked? No one ever talked to him like that before!"

By the twenty-fifth, the ice had broken up enough to allow us to make tentative water landings on some of the deeper tundra lakes. We landed at about 69 north and close to 132 west, beyond the tree limit between the western extremity of the Eskimo Lakes and Urquhart Lake and some 90 airline miles northeast of Aklavik. We waded ashore through the icy water and, for the first time, saw the beauty of the tundra at close hand. The crocuses were in bloom and the ground birch was heavy with catkins. Robins, which nest north to the limit of trees, were there, and so were tree sparrows, fox sparrows, yellow warblers, and other harbingers of the Arctic spring. We walked over the thickly bedded reindeer moss, picking the blossoms of the Labrador tea and searching for early tundra flowers. Longspurs flew up in front of us and in the next hour we had found the nests of the white-fronted goose and whistling swan, and seen many other tundra birds: Hudsonian curlews, old-squaw ducks, two kinds of jaegers, and several different shore birds. Bob, who is an indefatigable fisherman, tried casting with a shiny chrome spoon as a lure. At first the big trout, who had certainly never seen anything like this, lay there in the cold blue depths and stared suspiciously without making a move to rise to the lure. Then curiosity and habit overcame this initial distrust and one regular granddaddy of a trout grabbed the spoon and after a good fight was landed. The fate of this first trout should have been a warning to the others, but it didn't work out that way and Bob soon had a mess to carry back as a welcome change from reindeer meat. It seemed quite possible that these trout had never seen any kind of man before, and I suggested to Bob that perhaps he had taken advantage of their primeval innocence. At which he simply passed the platter in my direction and I helped myself to another one.

In July, with undaunted hope, we scouted the muddy delta of the Anderson River not far from the long-abandoned site of old Fort Anderson where, in the early 1860s, Roderick Ross MacFarlane had observed migrant whooping cranes each spring and fall. We saw no whoopers, but there were sizable colonies of snow geese and black brant, so we decided to try and find a safe stretch of water for landing to investigate the area on the ground. It is a remote region on an untenanted part of the Arctic coast, 200 miles east of Aklavik and nearly 400 miles west of the little settlement at Coppermine. There is a great deal of wilderness—and nothing but wilderness—in between. When the R.C.M.P. learned of our plans they insisted that we borrow from them a heavy-caliber Winchester. They argued that if we were attacked and killed by a wandering grizzly it would just make a lot of trouble and extra paper work for them. We gladly accepted the rifle.

A trial landing was made on the Anderson delta on July 13. It is a good-sized stream that rises to the north of Great Bear Lake and flows on northward, jogging west to join the Carnwath and so on north again to Wood Bay and the sea. The delta is hemmed in by upland tundra on the west and high bluffs to the east, and is not very extensive. As the river reaches its terminus close to the bay two channels are formed, but several islands intervene at this point, so that there are actually four channels when the Anderson finally empties into Wood Bay. On the widest of these, between the two largest islands, Bob decided he would find enough water to land. He skimmed low over it once, came around a second time, and put her down without difficulty. We anchored and waded ashore. To the west of the channel we found an island suitable for camping. Later we learned that at low tide our channel was so narrow and shallow that either a landing or a take-off would be impossible. At low water the amphibian lay flat in the soft mud of the bottom, literally high and dry.

When we returned to "the Real Neglek Island," as we called it, after the Eskimo name for the black brant, we had to wade ashore again, in cold, waist-deep water, carrying our camping outfit and supplies on our heads. There was no timber and not enough driftwood along the beaches to supply firewood. Cooking had to be done on a small G.I.-type gasoline pressure stove, a highly efficient, one-burner affair. We found a dry place for the tent and in less than an hour we were established and supper was steaming in the pot. We stayed several days in this lonely spot, investigating the bird colonies on the adjacent islands and exploring the edge of the nearby tundra. They were wonderful days after the exacting routine of constant flying. Ordinarily only Eskimos would visit such a location, and even these people would not show up there very often. Nevertheless, we saw the tracks of three pairs of mukluk-shod feet in the mud at the brant colony and guessed that a party of natives had raided the nests not long before to obtain the eggs or young geese, as is their practice all along that coast. But throughout our stay we saw no other signs of human beings.

On a high bluff along the east bank was a small house, occupied during the trapping season, as we learned later, by Malcom McNab, but it was empty during our visit to the delta. In winter all travel would be by dogteam on the sea ice or along the length of the icebound Eskimo Lakes. There is a winter trading post at Stanton, just beyond the mouth of the Anderson to the east, and others at Maitland Point and Cape Bathurst, but in summer we had the entire region to ourselves. Except by airplane, summer travel in those regions is difficult and unprofitable.

The blank brant numbered around 1,200 and the snow geese something like 700. Both had young in various stages of growth. We also found several pairs of glaucous gulls with downy young, and when we picked up the little ones to photograph them the adults dived on us with a fierceness and a tenacity I have seen in no other bird. We also observed two parasitic jaegers hunting together, one in the dark and the other in the light color phase. Among other birds noted were several Sabine's gulls, a species that neither of us had seen until our first flights over the flat coastal tundra on the outer Dalhousie peninsula. Here they appear to nest, along with king eiders, old squaws, scoters, and occasional snowy owls.

When flying over the tundra to the east, near Liverpool Bay, we had seen grizzlies, but fortunately none appeared along the Anderson during our stay, and the fact that we were camping on an island provided us with a natural moat within which we slumbered peacefully. We did see scattered caribou on the tundra bordering the west shore, and several times one of the huge tundra wolves (*Canis tundrarum*) that inhabit that region called on us. Each time we retired this wolf left a circle of tracks in the mud around our tent. The imprint of his huge forepaw was wider across than the palm of my hand. But he never bothered us, and we caught a fleeting glimpse of him only once. How such a big animal could conceal himself so successfully on an island less than two square miles in extent, and almost without cover, was one of the mysteries of the entire summer.

Before leaving our camp on the Anderson I tried to obtain photographs of the "real neglek" on its eggs. We had found one isolated nest in which the clutch had not yet hatched, and near it we set up a makeshift blind. Since we had no regular blind with us, it was necessary to lash an old piece of burlap sacking between the emergency paddles from the aircraft, so as to form a kind of screen, and then hold this upright with several guy lines tied to the tough little sprigs of Arctic willow. When this contraption was in place, we retired so as to permit the neglek to get used to its appearance and proximity. At length we returned. I crouched behind the screen with a camera and, after a moment, Bob ostentatiously walked away.

The "real neglek" had been watching this performance from the beach close by, running up and down in her peculiarly tilted fashion, head forward and gait erratic. When Smith had retreated to some distance, the bird showed signs of wanting to get back on her eggs, but evidently wasn't at all happy about the screen. With much twisting and turning of her short neck she ran up and down, trying to satisfy herself that all was well. Finally she grew bold enough to work her way back to the nest. Then, just before deciding to settle down on her clutch, she ran a little toward me and to one side, craning her neck so as to peer behind the screen. For a brief moment the real neglek and I looked into each other's eyes. Immediately, she ran back to the nest again, her plump body tilted over in a starboard list, with her neck arched forward. Then, still dissatisfied, she trotted on to the other side and peered at me from that direction. I sat perfectly still, of course, and again looked briefly into her anxious eyes. Back she ran to the nest and then came around once again to the other side of the screen. This could have continued all afternoon, but after a little I took pity on her and gave it up as a bad job. If you had ever gazed into the eyes of a real neglek you would understand my emotions. There was no further choice in the matter. I pulled down the screen, rolled it around the paddles, and hightailed it out of there. And she returned, at her own one-sided gallop, to that beautiful downy nest and the eggs that were of such concern to her. And the world—or that small, rather bare but highly interesting portion of it in which this little drama transpired—revolved on an even keel again.

Toward mid-July the weather at Aklavik became really summery. On the thirteenth, in the shade back of McNeice's kitchen, the thermometer showed 87°F. As we flew to various nearby areas that required further checking we noted a number of fires near the northern limit of tree growth. It seemed certain that no people were in these remote territories and that such fires had been started by the electric storms that were of almost daily occurrence. Several reports of whooping cranes trickled in from regions farther south, and some of these came back to us by radio from wildlife officials in Fort Smith, Ottawa, and Washington. Up to this point we had observed no sign of the big white birds and we would very shortly be pulling out for the last leg of our survey, with only one potential region not looked at.

The last days at Aklavik were pleasant ones, as all of them had been. We had made a host of new friends, among them some of the finest people we had ever met.

The morning of the twentieth of July saw an overcast sky and a definite coolness in the air. A little past noon the wind sprang up out of the northwest and started to blow. It blew great guns. We were busy most of the afternoon tying down the airplane and keeping a close watch on it. For three days it continued, with very heavy rain most of the time. The level of the river climbed rapidly, cutting away the bank in great chunks, so that we had to shift the position of our craft constantly. In the meantime, Carman Pearson had flown his small float plane to the herders' camp on Richards Island, 120 miles north, to pick up the wife of one of the Lap reindeer herders, who was expecting a baby, and bring her to the doctor in Aklavik. When the storm was over Carman came flying back alone. He had been grounded by the blow at Kittigazuit and could go no farther. During the height of the storm the sixteen-year-old wife had given birth to twins. And both of them boys! Since they were born almost in the middle of a reindeer herd, and smack in the middle of a storm, we hoped they would be named Donner and Blitzen, but probably this was asking too much.

On the twenty-third, the weather having improved, though still a trifle "scruffy" upriver, we said our last farewells and, at three-thirty in the afternoon, got off the water and headed for Norman Wells, beyond Fort Good Hope. There we were again grounded by unfavorable weather. Our object was to reach the coast again at Coppermine, on Coronation Gulf, a straight-line distance of nearly 500 miles east from Aklavik, but more in the neighborhood of 700 miles the way we would go. This meant flying across Great Bear Lake, where we could probably find gas at an active airstrip on the southern end of McTavish Arm. From there we could take off across country until we found the Coppermine River, and then it ought to be easy to follow it all the way to its mouth on the coast.

Finally, on Sunday, July 25, the weather reports were good, except for a 22-mile wind along the coast. We took off and were soon approaching Keith Arm of Great Bear Lake, the site of Franklin's winter quarters, 1825–1826. It was from here that Franklin and Back journeyed to the mouth of the Mackenzie and west to Return Reef in their effort to reach Point Barrow, where they hoped to meet Beechey and the H.M.S. *Blossom.* And in that same summer of 1826, Richardson and Kendall went from here to Coppermine by boat, returning all the way to Fort Franklin on foot!

After obtaining a drum of 100-octane gas from some Royal Canadian Air Force lads at Eldorado, we hit the air again and skirted the east side of McTavish Arm to Hornby Bay at the northern tip, then headed for the September and Coppermine Mountains in the distance. Soon we were over the river itself, with the long reach of the Dismal Lakes off on our port side and the Septembers almost beneath us. High above the Coppermine Mountains we were flying at 2,700 feet above sea level and could see Coronation Gulf off in the distance. By 4:40 P.M. we were on the water and had taxied in to an anchorage just off the sandy beach and close to the Company's boat. With the help of D'Arcy Munro, the Bay factor, we were soon ashore and enjoying the hospitality of D'Arcy's comfortable quarters. Before supper was over we had met nearly all the whites in the settlement, Dick Connick and the other R.C.M.P. boys, Canon Webster and his charming family, and the Transport people. We also were visited by a troop of Eskimos who marched up to the door and started in without ceremony. D'Arcy intercepted them and sent them away after exchanging a few words in their own tongue. It seemed that they were merely reviving a recently established routine that in the last few years had followed the arrival of an airplane, which, even in 1948, was a rare event at Coppermine. Each native was carrying in his hands a piece of crude copper, just as he had picked it up in the vicinity of the settlement. They wanted to trade them to us for dollars! Very enterprising people. After sending the Eskimos off, with assurances that we would be delighted to trade with them (though in a very small way!) later on, we sat and talked until far past midnight.

Over the next two days we were busy flying, going west within sight of Darnley Bay and Cape Parry, where the Melville Mountains rise close above the sea, and then east, over the rugged musk-ox country to Bathurst Inlet. This coast constitutes an important segment of the Northwest Passage. Dolphin and Union Strait, which we flew over in passing between Victoria Island and the mainland, was first seen by Richardson (in 1826) and named after the two boats of his party. And through these same waters passed Amundsen in the *Gjoa* on the first east-to-west voyage all the way through (1905). The tundra between the Melville Mountains and Coronation Gulf is very beautiful, but almost lifeless compared with that we had worked on farther west between the Mackenzie and the Anderson. A few scattered pairs of whistling swans outnumbered everything else. We saw one tundra wolf, almost white in color, and, near the shore, some glaucous gulls and old-squaw ducks. The river mouths are narrow and choked with gravel. On the tundra proper there are many outcroppings of limestone rock and scattered areas on which many loose rocks are strewn helter-skelter across the rolling slopes. To the east we flew over some of the roughest country we had ever seen. From Stapylton Bay to Tree River are massive flows of basaltic lava, superimposed over the limestone. The slope of these lava flows is toward the north, with sheer cliffs to the south, some of them magnificent, like illustrations by Gustave Doré. Beyond Tree River the region is a solid floor of sterile-looking, Pre-Cambrian rock, barren and extremely rugged. In some of this area small herds of musk ox survive, but we saw none of them. Waterfowl were almost nonexistent. At Coppermine, Dick Connick had an Eskimo hunter show us his hunting arrows, similar to those used to kill musk ox, although it is forbidden by law to kill them in any manner. Originally the points were carved from bone or walrus ivory, but all of these had been ground from old files or knives. One was double-headed for impaling birds like ptarmigan. As for protection of the musk ox, Dick told us that he had come across a party of natives who had just killed two of the rare Bovidae. They had used spears and clubs and, although they knew it was frowned upon—in fact contrary to the white man's law—nevertheless they were dancing around in great glee, grinning like schoolboys and quite proud of themselves. "What could I do?" Dick said. "They pay no attention to words, and I can't fine them because they have no money or throw them in jail because we have no jail. The thing's impossible!" So they go on killing a musk ox or two now and then. However, if there are any number of the animals in that terrible country we saw to the east of Coppermine they should survive indefinitely. It would be a wonder if even a Barren Ground Eskimo could find his way very far through that rocky purgatory and survive.

These Copper Eskimos are quite different from those we had come to know at Aklavik. They are caribou and seal hunters, and more primitive than any natives we observed anywhere in the North. Few of them knew any English, or at least they were unwilling to try it on us. Many were living in caribou-skin tents, including one stout old woman who sat on some hides thrown on the ground in her open doorway, bare to the waist and unabashedly boiling tea water. There was also at least one old-type sod house, like a winter igloo in shape and made of squares of sod cut from the grassy slopes. It was abandoned, and a bleached set of moose antlers lay on the roof. Sled dogs were tethered in long rows near the beach or back toward the hills, big, vicious brutes much like those we had seen at Aklavik. The natives were friendly and whenever we walked near one of their tents they asked us to have tea with them. At first we thought they were attempting to sing the well known air from *The Mikado,* for they would shout, in their high-pitched voices, "Tea-too-wit! Tea-too-wit!" Or, "Tea-too-wichy!," as it sounded on occasion. We soon learned that "Tea-too-wichy!" means "Tea is ready!" To sit around and drink tea and talk—a favorite pastime of these simple people—is to engage in a "Tea-too-wit." Even the stout old party without a shirt sang out a cheerful "Tea-too-wichy!" at us, but her skin tent had such a high odor, even from twenty feet away, that we declined, as politely as possible.

We also learned the way in which these Eskimos have economized their language with regard to such frequently used and important words as yes and no. For "yes" they open the eyes very wide, raise the eyebrows and wrinkle the nose. For "no" they utter a sharp, nasal "i-h!" or "i-ih!," slurred slightly but actually only one syllable. Very effective.

On the twenty-eighth, in spite of a light rain and overcast, we loaded our gear aboard and prepared to take off on our return flight. To all intents and purposes our summer's work was completed, although we still wanted to have a look at some possible whooping-crane territory between Great Bear and Great Slave Lakes. We gave Canon Webster a flight plan that he said he would try and have radioed on ahead (it never got through!) and took off at three o'clock for Eldorado and Yellowknife.

One hour later, as we were approaching McTavish Arm, the rain increased, with strong gusts of wind from the southeast. Visibility grew rapidly worse. In another few minutes we were completely blanked out—no vision at all. The mist and rain swirled around us and we hurtled along, blind as bats and far worse off, because we had no sonar such as bats are equipped with. Suddenly, as we were beginning to sweat with apprehension, a hole in the mist opened up quite unaccountably and there below us lay an open bay. We had a momentary view of a wooded shoreline and saw in a flash a few figures that were unmistakably Indians standing on a high bank in front of some rude tents. Then we were skimming along close to the water, which was as rough as the open sea, watching for a chance to put down. In a little bay, behind the protection of a small island, we had our chance.

Bob brought her down neatly, and with a sigh of relief we taxied into calm water and anchored. Later, when it was obvious that we would have to stay down until the weather lifted, we lowered the wheels, moved in close to shore, and ran long ropes in to some trees on the bank. Although it was rocky and uninviting we had no choice. After checking our maps we decided that we were down in the entrance to Hunter Bay, Great Bear Lake, having landed first in Western Channel inside of Achook Island. The Indians, probably Dogribs, were nowhere in sight and we estimated that their camp must be nearly 10 miles away on another bay.

Toward evening the wind dropped off and veered to the southwest. Fog set in, and with it a steady, drizzling rain. We were short of rations but still had some tea, Scotch oatmeal, and pilot biscuits. Bob, the imperturbable angler, tried one of his chrome spoons off a big rock at the tip of the island and landed two good-sized trout. When we had eaten, we lay down inside the airplane on top of our duffle. Our mutual feeling was that it could have been much worse.

Around midnight the wind shifted to the northeast and blew a gale. With this shift in wind direction we were now on the exposed face of the island and in real trouble. The aircraft was being pounded on the rocky shore and there was no way that we could move. In fact, there was only one thing that could be done. Jumping into the waist-deep, icy water, each of us grabbed hold of a wingtip and held her off as best we could. The rain was heavy now and stung our wet hides. We were soon blue with cold and thoroughly miserable. Even an hour of this would have been bad, but we had to hang on for the next sixteen hours! There was no chance for any sort of relief and no opportunity to eat or even smoke. All we could do was hang on, numb with exhaustion and cold.

At three-thirty the next afternoon the wind dropped slightly. The aircraft had taken some severe pounding but was far from being wrecked. An hour later the wind backed up, counterclockwise, into the northwest, giving us the protection of the north tip of the island. What a relief! We managed to cook some oatmeal and after eating it we lay down and slept for a solid fourteen hours. The rain continued and the air temperature dropped to 41°F.

The next day was the thirtieth of July. The wind stayed in the northwest and blew hard, but after some hot tea we were quite comfortable. Examining the airplane, we found that the tire on the starboard wheel was flat and the condition of the hydraulic retracting gear doubtful. No other damage of any consequence. Taking the ax, we cut some long poles to use in getting our craft afloat and clear of the island in case the wind dropped sufficiently.

It was nearly five in the afternoon when the sun broke through momentarily. At six-thirty the wind showed signs of moderating and we had hopes of getting away. Finally, around nine o'clock the wind dropped perceptibly and we prepared to move. Two things worried us: our battery had not been charging when we left Coppermine fifty-four hours previously and the wheels might be jammed. We would be unable to get off the water unless the wheels came up. There was one way to settle it. We poled into the clear, the engines started without any difficulty, and after a few doubtful seconds the wheels came up. In another minute we were racing across the surface, and then we were airborn and on our way. In forty minutes we had reached Eldorado. Wading ashore from a sheltered anchorage, we were met by a Canadian Air Force captain who soon had us fed and bedded down in the officers' quarters. We relaxed in style.

There was a lot more, of course, but after Hunter Bay all of it was somewhat in the nature of anticlimax. As far as that summer was concerned, Smith and I had had it. We searched to the south of Lac la Martre but saw no sign of whooping cranes. It was as if they flew North each spring and vanished from the face of the earth.

*. . . We believe that the best chance of the whooping crane's survival in the wild is through their production of young in the wild . . . We are for keeping the wild and captive supplies separate.*

JOHN H. BAKER *

# VIII : Rusty

For centuries, in various parts of the world, cranes of many different species have been kept in captivity in zoological gardens, private aviaries, and on the grounds of expensive and well-manicured estates. They are gentle, handsome, and highly decorative. Compared with many other birds they adapt themselves to such an existence quite well. A number of species of cranes breed successfully in captivity, notably the gigantic saras crane from India, the common crane of Eurasia, the white-necked crane of Mongolia and Manchuria, the demoiselle crane of Eurasia and North Africa, and our own sandhill crane. Although there have been a good many whooping cranes held in a captive state through the years, none had ever nested successfully. When the Whooping Crane Project was getting under way in 1945, it was learned that there were two injured birds of this rare species in captivity, one in a private enclosure in Nebraska and another in the New Orleans

* *Audubon Magazine* (1956).

Zoo. If these two birds were male and female, they might pair off if brought together under the right circumstances.

It should be understood at once that the primary object of our investigation was to provide for the future survival of the whooping crane in a wild state. Anything less than that would be only as a last desperate resort, in so far as the wild population was concerned. On this subject of wild, free-flying birds versus birds that are caged, or pinioned, or restrained in some other way, there are two very definite schools of thought, one as adamant as the other. You remember the words sung by Private Willis in the opening scene of Act II of *Iolanthe*— "... every boy and every gal that's born into the world alive is either a little Liberal or else a little Conservative!" It's something like that in this situation, and there's really no use explaining one's position because no one is going to change it, neither you nor the other fellow. Yet, there is much to be said on both sides. Public zoos, for example, are of immense educational value, which increases in proportion to the intelligence and knowledge with which they are run. And people who keep birds in captivity may learn a great many things about them that will be unknown to the field ornithologist, though there are, admittedly, few Jean Delacours and few Konrad Lorenzes, more's the pity. Those who work in the field of plain, simple, and unadorned wildlife conservation, on the other hand, generally adhere to certain common ideals, even though some of these may seem foolish and others may be more and more unattainable as time goes by. Basically, considering the main object in view, these ideals are sound—even in the face of a rapidly changing world and of increasing pressures against the very results the wildlife conservationist may be seeking. Perhaps their basic soundness actually increases as materialism increases, if that is what is happening. In any event, it is clear that the conservationist wants to keep as many wilderness habitats intact as can be wrested from the forces of evil and preserved in an inviolate condition. He also wants the flora and fauna within these representative areas as completely undisturbed as possible.

Regardless of personal feelings and deathless convictions on the subject, we had to face the question of how best to utilize the two captive cranes. All of us were in agreement that nothing would be lost, so far as the survival of the wilderness race was concerned, by bringing those two birds together, if this could be arranged. I visited both the Gothenburg Gun Club in Nebraska and the zoo in New Orleans and, in addition to looking the two cranes over carefully, I discussed with those in charge the ideas that we had in mind. As a result of the cooperation of Jack Kennedy and other members of the Nebraska club, their bird was made available to us. George Vierheller of the St. Louis Zoo very generously agreed to send a truck out to Nebraska for it, and to keep it in St. Louis long enough to look it over and bring it into condition for the eventual trip to New Orleans, where George Douglass, in charge of the zoo there, was quite delighted at the prospect of bringing the two birds together. All this was accomplished, and at length the pair of them were placed in the same enclosure—for by astonishingly good luck, as it turned out, the Nebraska bird was actually a male and the New Orleans bird a female. This was early in 1948.

While the Nebraska bird was still living in its original pen near Gothenburg, I had looked up its history. The *Lincoln County Tribune* for June 11, 1936, contained this item:

> Brady, Neb., June 10 (Special to *The Tribune*).
>
> A large white Heron was sighted by the Henry George girls while riding their bicycles Friday and returning to the house with the news, Mr. George took the car and drove the Heron for a mile into a 5-foot wire netting fence where it was caught. It had been shot and one wing and its eye were injured. It easily looked over the fence. It was turned over to the Gothenburg sanctuary where it was let loose.

Some "Heron," that could "easily" look over a five-foot fence! The date, too, was hard to understand, for the average spring-migration date in recent years for Nebraska has been close to mid-April, though there were a few records for May. Yet this actually was a whooping crane and in this ignoble manner he became a flightless, one-eyed captive. When removed from the Gothenburg enclosure he was thus no less than a dozen years old, quite possibly—if appearances meant anything—much older. There he had reigned in solitary splendor, for he never became friendly with his human captors nor did he consort with the lesser sandhill cranes or the ducks and geese within the same pen, except to make occasional raids on the eggs of captive Canada geese that nested in the area. Partly because of these raids, and partly as a result of his aloof, one-eyed, male demeanor, he had been known as "Old Devil." Later on, when we were momentarily in doubt as to his sex, Bud Keefer renamed him "Petunia," with the proviso that it would be shortened to "Pete" if he turned out to be a male. So "Pete" he eventually became.

The female bird had been in the New Orleans Zoo since late in 1940, or something less than eight years when Pete arrived. As we reconstructed her personal history, she was apparently one of the small Louisiana resident flock that had lived in the marshes near White Lake (theoretically, as a species, since the Pleistocene!). In the late summer of 1940 heavy rains had flooded this marsh and the 13 birds that comprised the whooping-crane population had been forced to seek higher ground. When the waters fell to their normal depths, only 6 cranes returned. This individual had been wounded by a farmer in Evangeline Parish, far from their usual haunts, and carried to the zoo where she was nursed back to health.

In discussing the subject with various people and looking into the literature, I came across several interesting and even significant stories about captive whooping cranes. One had been winged on Grand Prairie, in Dunklin County, Missouri, many years ago (the last Missouri record was for 1913, but this bird may have been shot as early as 1860), and kept as a pet by a Dr. Cook of Cottonplant, and later by his widow, for a period of more than thirty years. A juvenile female had died in the Frankfurt, Germany, Zoological Gardens in 1871, an adult had died in the Jardin des Plantes in Paris in 1872, another adult in the Philadelphia Zoo about 1892, another in the Central Park Zoo in New York in 1898, and so on through a long and somehow rather futile list. Many years ago several captive whooping cranes were kept at the Mexican Hacienda El Molino "as one of the attractions of the place." There is no record of their attempting to nest. The Duchess of Bedford kept eleven species of cranes on her estate in England (*circa* 1907), and four species nested successfully. Among those that made no attempt to nest was the whooping crane. Also in England, Lord Lilford had a captive female that was purchased in 1892. She lived at Lilford Hall for forty years. For a number of years she laid infertile eggs, sometimes sharing the same nest with a female Manchurian crane, who was also an egg-layer. Even after the whooper ceased to lay she guarded and brooded the infertile clutch of the Manchurian female.

In 1913, the Bronx Zoo had one captive whooping crane, and the energetic Dr. Hornaday advertised widely for a mate for this bird, hoping that they might breed and thus help to save the species from extinction. Nothing came of the project. The last time I talked with the late Edward Avery McIlhenny at Avery Island, Louisiana, was in December, 1946. He told me that in the early 1880s his father had taken him to prairies near Avery Island to hunt prairie chickens. There were at that early date only five houses in the hamlet on the Vermilion River now known as Abbeville (now the principle town in a parish of over 40,000 people), and not a fence post had been set up from there to the Sabine River, 100 miles to the west. Whooping cranes were still relatively abundant, and they shot them on the prairies as well as around Avery Island. As a boy he had kept several "wing-tipped" whoopers, and they were great pets. However, they developed an unfortunate habit of catching his mother's young chickens and eating them, so he had to get rid of them. Apparently they never nested, or "Mr. Ned" would certainly have told me about it.

There are other records of captive whoopers, but the most sympathetic story is that of S. W. Oliver, who kept one as a boy in what is now Walworth County, South Dakota, but was a part of Dakota Territory in the fall of 1885, when these events took place. This is close to the Missouri River, and the whoopers came through on migration in some numbers in those days. However, it was a rare occurrence for them to stop off, and when six alighted in a nearby field Mr. Oliver and his brother stalked them and brought down two with their shotguns. One adult bird was killed outright, but the young one, still in the buff plumage, was only slightly injured and so was taken home and kept as a pet. It was named "Bill" after a tall, gangly neighbor boy, and became a regular member of the family. Bill was so delightful, in fact, that he won over the Olivers completely, and from that time on they never killed another whooping crane.

More than sixty years later, in 1948, Mr. Oliver by the merest chance picked up a year old copy of *Life* containing the photographs of whooping cranes and the brief account of their situation mentioned earlier. As he wrote me, "... it stirred up memories that had long lain dormant of my beautiful pet Bill, and it made me feel blue as I read there were only 29 left ..." So he sat down and wrote a simple and charming narrative of his experience, which was subsequently published in *Audubon Magazine*. The editor sent me the manuscript asking that I read it and return it with my comments. This is what I wrote:

> The story of Bill is a remarkable and touching one. I have watched many "Bills" among the family groups of whooping cranes that spend the winter on Aransas Refuge in Texas and I can vouch for Mr. Oliver's accuracy. The very manner in which he was named, after an awkward and gangling neighbor boy, reveals an intimate knowledge and understanding of the whooper during his first winter. The way Bill had of walking to the sloughs where he fed, instead of flying, is typical of the species. His "talking" notes are those that pass between the members of a wild family. The "dance" that Mr. Oliver tells about—Bill and Oliver, Sr., participating—describes steps and figures that are in fact the famous and often wrongly described dance of the whooping crane. ... I would not quarrel with Mr. Oliver's interpretation of Bill's behavior—*enjoyment, love, thinking* may not be the right words technically, but you and I know what is meant and Bill's response to tender care, his complete loss of fear and his obvious attachment to the Oliver "family group" is completely understandable in any terms. It is significant that Bill was killed, quite thoughtlessly and need-

lessly, by a boy "from the East." Mr. Oliver writes me that he hadn't worried about Bill because he did not foresee a boy from the East out with a gun, "a boy who had never seen a crane, goose or duck before." I imagine that these are the fellows who have killed most of our lost whooping cranes. They are without knowledge, without understanding and without purpose. Now we are without Bill and nearly all of his kind. Mr. Oliver's story will convince you that we are much poorer because of this loss. Much poorer than most of us seem to know.

Yet, in spite of the appealing nature of these birds in captivity, our object cannot be to acquire a pen full of "Bills." No matter how attractive and interesting they can be under such circumstances, they are not whooping cranes in the fullest sense. Their wild spirit and fierce nature tamed, their majestic flight denied, the thrilling drama and mystery of their annual migrations abruptly stemmed—these things cannot be permitted. Of course, the two injured birds already in our hands were another matter altogether. If they were capable of boosting the stock of living whoopers by a single unit it would be well worth our trouble. And theirs too, I felt, for the life we planned for them would be infinitely better than the solitary and even stifled existence they had been leading. Whatever happened, they would at least have one day in the sun!

In the fall of 1948, with the consent and cooperation of George Douglass in New Orleans, the two cranes were carried by truck to Texas. Careful plans had been made for their reception at Aransas Refuge. We had selected a tract of 150 acres of brackish marsh that approximated a typical winter territory, and that adjoined, for good measure, a fresh-water cattail marsh that was biotically similar to the whoopers' wilderness nesting habitat. A sturdy nine-foot wire fence surrounded the entire tract. The location was an isolated one, yet was within a few minutes, by car, of refuge headquarters. The birds were taken first to the San Antonio Zoo, where Fred Stark, who has had remarkable success in breeding animals of many kinds in captivity, including certain cranes, was ready to look after them following their long journey. Finally, in October, they were released in the Aransas enclosure. With a deep sigh all around we left them, except for systematic observations, and turned to other matters.

One important feature of the new enclosure, in our opinion, was the fact that it provided a variety and an abundance of natural foods, as well as plenty of elbowroom. There were blue crabs, mud shrimps, marine worms, and other habitual food items in the ponds and on the shorelines of the brackish sector, and frogs, snakes, insects, and other palatable items in the fresh-water part. In addition, a ration of whole yellow corn was provided, certain amounts of it soaked in wheat germ oil.

In December, the two birds performed a prenuptial dance. In March and April of 1949, they danced frequently. Then, late in April, a marked change in their usual behavior was noted. When the daily ration of corn was given them they usually came striding up to the fence to receive it. When Bud Keefer went to the fence on April 27, only the female (Josephine, which, it will be noted, is also a conveniently bisexual name!) came up for corn. Pete remained hidden in the cattails. On the following day this behavior was reversed, and on the twenty-ninth it was definitely observed that Pete was crouching in the cattails while Jo came out for corn.

On April 30, Bud investigated and discovered a nest containing a single egg. A second egg appeared May 1.

I was at my home in Florida when these exciting events transpired, but as soon as I could manage to get away I left for Texas, arriving at Aransas on May 12, which was believed to be the thirteenth day of incubation for the first of the two eggs. The big question was—were the eggs fertile? Pete, as we knew, was then at least fourteen years old, and probably older, while Jo was no less than ten. Both had been in solitary captivity for many years. No one knew what to expect.

I established a hard and fast routine. The boys had erected an observation tower overlooking the nest area, and in this I passed each day, arriving before daylight every morning and staying until after dark. One thing was certain: whether the eggs hatched or not, here was a unique opportunity to watch the nesting behavior of the whooping crane, perhaps the only opportunity anyone would have. From the all too few descriptions in the literature of wild nestings, we knew something of the general classification of the nesting site and the appearance of the nest and eggs. The record showed that they had been nesting in Grant County, Minnesota, in 1876; Franklin County, Iowa, in 1882; Hancock County Iowa, in 1894 (the last U.S. nesting on record); and Saskatchewan in 1922, the last observed nesting anywhere. There were also other locations, less adequately described. As to the nest-side behavior of the cranes themselves we knew nothing at all, except the way in which they had conducted themselves when disturbed and, in some of the older narratives, the way they had behaved when shot at! Here, then, was a real opportunity to learn something entirely new about a rare species.

This first Aransas nest was a flat mound constructed chiefly out of salt-flat grass, with some strands of cattail leaves and sea oxeye (*Borrichia frutescens*). When we measured it some time later it had an outside diameter of 180 by 184 centimeters (about 5 feet 10 inches by 6 feet). The extreme height was 25.4 centimeters (about 10 inches). It was well hidden in a dense growth of narrow-leaved cattail, and more or less surrounded by water that varied from 30 centimeters (about 12 inches) on April 30 to only 1 or 2 inches by May 23.

A careful record was kept of the minute-to-minute activities of both Pete and Jo. They took turns at incubating, and at first there were usually six nest reliefs during the daylight hours. As the weather grew warmer these reliefs increased until they averaged between seven and eight through the day. Pete was a very good partner and actually spent more time on the eggs during the day than Jo, averaging two hours at a spell to her one and one-half hours. Over-all, Pete assumed more than 70 per cent of diurnal incubation duties. Larry Walkinshaw found that a male sandhill crane was on the eggs nearly 63 per cent of one morning period during which such observations were possible. We were unable to watch them at night, but it is believed that the female does most of the night brooding while the male stands guard.

The incubating bird was so well hidden when sitting on the nest that had we not known just where to look, and had the advantage of a 20-foot tower only 150 feet away, plus a 19.5x spotting scope, it would have been the greatest kind of luck to have seen her at all. I thought of our long hours and days of searching for the nesting grounds of the wild pairs in the North, and wondered how closely we might have passed them by without spotting them! When away from the immediate proximity of the nest the non-setting member of the pair may be quite conspicuous, but not necessarily so. It depends on whether this bird is resting, feeding, or defending the nesting territory.

The nest-relief ceremony is not spectacular, as with colonial species like the egrets or herons. I should say it is simply matter-of-fact. When relief was delayed or overdue, the brooding bird stood on the nest or even walked off, leaving the eggs momentarily unattended. In such case the other bird was usually close at hand, and immediately walked up and took over. As a rule, the incubating and free periods seemed to be arranged in an orderly and easily managed sequence, so that the business of hatching the eggs is an amazingly efficient one. Although, generally speaking, the incubation phase may be a weary and even boring routine, it is not without drama and an occasional flare of emotion. One evening at dusk (7:10 P.M.), the male was on the eggs, when the female was seen to raise her wings suddenly and jab violently at some object hidden from view in the cattails. The male sat like a graven image. A few minutes passed and then Jo sounded an alarm note, startlingly loud on the quiet evening air, and with wings held partly open, ran toward something in back of the nest. Pete remained immobile. In another moment we saw a white-tailed deer retreating rapidly, with Josephine in hot pursuit. Pete stayed perfectly quiet throughout the encounter. This doe had given birth to twin fawns in the shelter of a small, dry, wooded clump close by, and the cranes were kept busy running her off throughout their tenure.

As a general thing the birds were quiet through the incubation period, calling only when deer invaded their nesting area, or when large birds flew over or otherwise disturbed them. Once they whooped loud and challenging protests at an army bomber flying over, even though it was quite high. More often than not it was the guard bird that did the calling, but both birds sometimes called together, usually when a turkey vulture, Ward's heron, or caracara flew over, close to the nest. This call seemed to be both a warning and a challenge, and it also seemed to be a way of relieving the tension of comparative inactivity. To remember this particular call I wrote down symbols indicating one double note that swooped (or "whooped") on a downward scale, followed by a more rapid series of four triple notes, punctuated in the middle.

When one of the birds took over at the nest it carefully placed a foot on each side of the eggs, then lowered itself to a sitting position, wriggling or twisting slightly to get the eggs settled properly against the brood patches. Sometimes it stood up again at once then tried a second time. Less frequently, a third and fourth attempt were necessary. In rising, especially after a long time setting, it often had to make quite an effort to pull itself up, for it rises entirely by muscular action and control, without pushing with the bill as, for example, the incubating flamingo does. The incubating bird frequently reached under its breast feathers to touch the eggs lightly, perhaps to move them a little. When turning or rolling the eggs it usually stood, but sometimes it sat "on its elbows," as it were, and, reaching under its breast, moved the eggs slightly.

The bird that was relieved at the nest often showed real pleasure at its release. Both Pete and Jo exhibited this reaction. Once Jo stepped off the mound and Pete took over, turning around and around on the nest in a standing position and touching the eggs briefly with his bill before sitting down. Jo stood for a moment and then went running and skipping off toward the open marsh, her wings flapping gaily. Another time she walked as far as the nearest salt pond and, standing on the bank, did a wonderful little dance—apparently through sheer exuberance—twirling and leaping around and around, dipping her body low, wings extended, and then leaping sideways as if seeing how cunning she could be. Usually the free bird started feeding very soon after being relieved. On May 18, I noted two species of small, semi-aquatic mollusks, the usual grass shrimps, several spiders, a number of small frogs, and miscellaneous crickets, grasshoppers, bees, and flies in the salt-flat grass close to the brackish-water pond. In the rain pools here and there the water boatmen were numerous. For more substantial fare the cranes walked farther out on the salt marsh where blue crabs were the chief item sought. Once Jo went to the salt pond and fed quietly with several foot-poking snowy egrets. After she had fed for some four or five minutes she stood very straight, stared at the snowies as if seeing them for the first time, and then ran toward them belligerently, so that they flew off. One day when Pete was probing around on the higher ground, where painted buntings were singing beautifully from the mesquite brush, he came on a large rattlesnake, half coiled on a patch of bare ground. Pete walked up to him and started dancing up and down, wings flapping. Around and around the snake he went, the reptile's head turning slowly to watch him. After a few minutes Pete broke the impasse by suddenly walking off. On another occasion, however, he attacked a large cottonmouth moccasin, beat it to death by stabbing furiously at its head, and then proceeded to swallow it entire, which was a tall order and must have required fully ten minutes to accomplish.

In addition to feeding, the guard bird spent a lot of time coping with real or imaginary dangers. Most of this consisted of chasing off other birds, especially American egrets, snowy egrets, Ward's herons, Louisiana herons, and roseate spoonbills. Pete was devoted to this particular duty and wouldn't tolerate these birds within several hundred yards of the nest. I saw him chase the larger egrets as far as the north end of the salt pond, which was nearly a mile away. Once, when he was getting all set to run off a group of egrets, a Ward's heron came flying over and settled in the water nearby. Pete immediately turned to face this more formidable, but actually disinterested and altogether harmless intruder. He gave several war whoops, strutted stiffly and with elaborate dignity, lowered his spearlike head and charged, running forward with great strides and flapping his wings rapidly. He fairly skipped across the water and was very close to being airborne. The poor heron, glaring at this juggernaut with an expression of dismay, as well he might, waited until what seemed the last minute and then flew. With only one good wing, Pete usually ended the chase at this point, slowing and shortening his stride, using his wings as a brake, arching his neck until it looked like that of a swan, and coming to a rather abrupt but wholly dignified halt. I couldn't avoid thinking of Don Quixote charging the sheep. At times he and Pete even looked alike! His mate, a younger bird and in finer plumage, always seemed clean and neat, but Pete, from so much chasing through the mud and water was usually dirty and ruffled-looking. Often, after a series of exhausting chases, he walked back to the vicinity of the nest dripping wet, and almost black underneath from the splashing mud. He was a game old warrior and did the best he could.

Unfortunately, it was not good enough. For several days both birds had acted strangely, poking unnecessarily around the eggs and getting on and off the nest more frequently than usual. Once on the nest they stood up and sat down again in a restless routine. Then, on the twenty-fourth day of incubation, both birds left the nest together for the first time since incubation had begun, walked blithely toward the open meadow, and danced. They then retired to the salt flats. Investigation revealed that the eggs had been smashed, quite clearly by the birds themselves. On examination, it seemed evident that they had been infertile.

All this proved to be too much for Pete, who was last seen alive on the following July 21. Early the next morning loud calls were heard from the enclosure, so loud that Russell, the clerk at headquarters, roused from his bed to listen. Getting dressed, he awoke Julian Howard, who had succeeded Bud Keefer as refuge manager, and together they went to the enclosure. It was Jo who had been calling, standing alone on the open salt flats. Nearby they found old Pete. He was lying on his back in shallow water, and he was very dead.

Julian's immediate reaction to this tragedy was to attempt the capture of "Crip," a whooper with an injured wing who had been living by himself on the wintering marsh since he was first observed by Olaf and myself in February, 1947. When this undertaking had been approved a posse was organized and, in due course, Crip was captured and placed in the enclosure with the widowed Josephine. These two splendid birds became more than friends at once and, after the usual period of prenuptial dancing, they mated, built their nest (this time out on the open salt flat), and arranged to deposit therein a single egg. This was in April, 1950, incubation apparently getting under way on the morning of the twenty-second. As it proceeded, word was relayed to me at my home, and when the day of reckoning drew near I again hit the road for Texas, reaching Aransas on May 23.

The very next day there was a marked change in the behavior of the pair. Josephine took over the job of brooding shortly after 10 A.M., and from then on scarcely moved. This was estimated to be the thirty-second day of incubation, and we guessed that she could then both see and hear the chick, for the egg must have already pipped. We scarcely slept that night. Early on the twenty-fifth we climbed the tower and waited impatiently for the light to increase enough so that we could see what had happened. From the behavior of both parents it seemed certain that the miracle we had been hoping for had actually taken place. They both stood alongside the nest, giving rapt attention to something that lay hidden in the shallow depression of grass and leaves in the center of the mound. Throughout that day we took turns at watching through the telescope, but were unable to confirm without any question that the object in the nest was a chick. We couldn't actually *see* it! The following day, which was May 26, at a few minutes past six-thirty in the morning, I saw him. He was so tiny I could scarcely believe my eyes, but there he was, a rusty-colored, downy little thing, moving about on the nest on wobbly legs and being dutifully cared for by both parents. The miracle *had* happened! "Rusty," the first whooping crane ever hatched in captivity, had entered the world at an unknown hour during the night of May 24–25. Officially, we called it May 25. The only previous hatching date then on record (in Saskatchewan) had been May 29.

On the third day of his brief existence, Rusty was out of the nest, as a young whooping crane more than forty-eight hours old is supposed to be. He was very active. As Crip leaned over to feed him, I saw Rusty trot across his father's big feet, running with the tottering friskiness of all small precocial birds. Then he

*Stephen F. Briggs*

*A section of the great Horse Cay flamingo colony on Inagua in 1952.*

*Flamingo nest mounds in Venezuela, deserted after raid by fishermen.*

*Mr. & Mrs. Wm. H. Phelps, Jr.*

*The long, hot days of incubation—some thirty of them—are a period of tedium for flamingos and for observers alike. Many displacement activities relieve the monotony, and a "seventh-inning stretch" is one of these.*

Stephen F. Briggs

*Flamingos feeding on "mud," which may be very rich in an organic content of various bacteria, algae, diatoms, protozoans, molluscs, and marine worms.*

Stephen F. B

*A crèche of young flamingos, now very gooselike in their gray down, and highly vulnerable to all enemies, natural and unnatural.*

Stephen F. Briggs

came trotting back again, between the towering columns of Crip's long legs, and stopping, he looked up. We were too far away to hear it, but no doubt he was uttering the "strange piping whistle" that Bradshaw heard when he saw the young whooper at the last Saskatchewan nest. Then Crip bent over with a soft and graceful tenderness, and finding the tiny mouth with the tip of his great bill, fed him. In all my experience with birds, this was the most wonderful, and the most moving scene I have ever witnessed. Everett Beaty, who was with me on the tower, now had a good look at Rusty, much to my relief, as things turned out.

On the afternoon of Rusty's third day the parents wandered some yards from the nest, and from the way they stepped, looking down and evidently feeding him from time to time, the little fellow must have been running along at their feet. Our position was more than 200 yards from the nest, and even with a powerful telescope we could not follow Rusty's progress beyond that point, as the growth of sea oxeye was so heavy and of such height that he was completely hidden. It was at this juncture that we first began to feel concern for his safety.

That same afternoon we saw turkey vultures soaring close to the cranes, and once a caracara flew into the area and settled for some moments on an open stretch of ground, apparently watching them. Julian brought us his small-bore rifle, which was equipped with a telescopic sight, and we kept it close at hand. Toward dusk we heard the parent cranes call, and saw several raccoons running along over the salt flats not far from the nest. One of the boys took the rifle and walked up along the west side of the enclosure fence, but the 'coons had disappeared.

That night the weather changed abruptly, and at dawn there was a high wind and a cold, biting rain. Anxiously we peered through the half-light to where the nest was located. Both of the old birds seemed to be there, one of them crouched on the nest as if brooding the chick. As daylight advanced they remained in this position and then, to our consternation, the brooding bird stood, and the pair started off in a leisurely manner toward the far corner of the enclosure. We could not see Rusty and didn't know if he was running along beside them or not. The tension grew. What had happened to Rusty? A lone vulture appeared, skulking about in the oxeye clumps some distance beyond the nest. The two cranes continued to move off until they were a quarter of a mile north of the nest. Julian had installed an old army-type, battery-operated field telephone on the tower, and I rang him up and told him my fears. When he had joined me the two of us entered the enclosure. Crip and Jo seemed hardly to notice us. For more than an hour we searched through the mud and grass for Rusty. We never found him! All that remained was the empty nest, soggy in the rain, a few pieces of broken eggshell, and, in every patch of mud, the unmistakable tracks of raccoons. Rusty had vanished.

Thus ended, for the time being, our efforts to produce whooping cranes in captivity. Other attempts have been made since, with tragic and heartbreaking results. Meanwhile, the wild flock, migrating to the Canadian breeding grounds on schedule, has hatched and reared a total of 25 young whoopers since Rusty's loss. It seems clear that we must make these wild birds our chief concern. In their continuing ability to return each fall with young lies the whooping crane's only real hope of survival.

*. . . To sea, bound for an unknown island, and to seek for buried treasures!*

R. L. STEVENSON *

# IX : I learn of flamingos and hurricanes

Our continued failure to find the whooping crane's breeding grounds—in 1946 and 1947, and again, after such high hopes, in 1948—had been, collectively, a bitter blow. Along with many others, I had put a lot into it, both physically and emotionally, and taken nothing out but disappointment and frustration. Nor had it helped matters much when, in November, 1947, I came down with tularemia, as a result of handling an infected jack rabbit that was being used as crab bait during our studies of those important crustaceans in the Aransas wintering ponds. The new streptomycin drug helped greatly, but it took many weeks to get my strength back. The blank that we drew at the end of our 1948 search had added even more fuel to the smoldering fires of my general distress.

Back at home in Florida I had begun work on a monograph of *Grus americana*, a tough enough job under the best of circumstances, and even before this chore was completed I started putting

* *Treasure Island.*

together plans for a new study project—a full-scale investigation of the status of the American flamingo. We had been concerned about the flamingo situation for some time, particularly in the Bahamas, and Paul Zahl's reports from Andros were anything but reassuring. The National Audubon Society had been the pioneer agency in efforts to obtain protection for these birds in the Bahamas, in 1905, and again in both the Bahamas and Cuba in the period 1922–1933. The Wild Birds Protection Act, which is the basic wildlife conservation law in the Bahamas, had been a direct result of Frank M. Chapman's flamingo resolution at the first meeting of the Audubon Board of Directors, held in New York on January 30, 1905. And the establishment of the National Flamingo Refuge in Cuba in 1933 was the outcome of Dr. T. Gilbert Pearson's work in that country over the years. But something more had to be done, and soon! The great Andros Island colonies in the Bahamas, famous the world over, were reported to be completely deserted following raids and other disturbances, including "buzzing" by both military and civilian aircraft. It was John Baker's conviction that a thorough investigation of conditions over the entire range of *Phoenicopterus ruber* was in order. And this was to be my next job.

It was at this juncture, in December, 1949, that I first met Stephen F. Briggs of Milwaukee, and Naples, Florida. Steve had been taking enough time off from his many business affairs to give considerable attention to bird photography. It is always of interest to learn how these things come about. Steve is a genius with gadgets. As a boy on a farm in South Dakota—which was still Indian Territory when he was born there—he was the local expert on the new horseless carriages. Before he was old enough to vote he had taken a neighbor's steam-propelled vehicle apart and put it together again, successfully. A born inventor, he has improvised countless mechanical devices, and holds more than 500 patents. One day, when he was working in his lab on an improved carburetor, there was an explosion and Steve's hands—the sensitive hands that are the natural gift of artists, surgeons, and mechanical geniuses—were badly burned. When they had healed, the fingers remained stiff and unresponsive, and their owner, utterly depressed, felt that from here on life would have very little to offer him.

It was his wife's idea to buy him a camera and get him interested in photography. Bea gave him his first Leica, which can become quite a complicated gadget when all of the accessories are added, and, since they were living in Florida in the winter, photographing birds was simply the next logical step. This year, at an age when most men are giving up golf as too strenuous, Steve Briggs is on his way across half the Pacific to Midway Island to photograph the albatrosses!

We began our many pleasant days in the field together in Florida Bay, not far from my home. Steve wanted most of all to get pictures of the roseate spoonbills, and he is still so fascinated by the pink birds that he continues to return for more almost every season. When he heard about my projected work with the flamingos he proposed at once that we join forces. Thus it was that in early May of 1950, with Charlie Brookfield, we made a preliminary investigation in Yucatán, flying nonstop from Miami in a DC-3. Little seemed to be known about the Yucatán flamingos at that time, and it was an exceptional opportunity. It was likewise one of the few bright spots in a year that was otherwise a difficult one for me. We located the main flock still gathered in their winter quarters in the Ria de Celestun, and in the old city of Mérida we met Joaquin Roche, who has been of so much assistance to us since in connection with our flamingo studies and protection program in his country.

It was just after our return from Yucatán that word reached me of the imminent possibility of a hatching in the whooping-crane enclosure on Aransas Refuge. I hurried to Texas and remained there until after the tragic loss of little Rusty.

Troubles have a way of coming all together. I can recall rather vividly the growing and quite unreasonable aches and pains that had been plaguing me during this period. A specialist in New York said they came from "a slipped disk" and plastered a very uncomfortable cast on my neck, which I threw overboard the first time I had to turn my head to count whooping cranes from an airplane. Finally, in October, I left the annual meeting of the

American Ornithologists' Union in Minneapolis literally writhing with pain, and came home to Florida a very wretched man. When I could get to a doctor I learned the unhappy truth: I was suffering from Strümpell-Marie disease—rheumatoid spondylitis—an arthritic condition resulting in large part, perhaps, from a deficiency in the adrenal gland. A heavy layer of calcium had been forming over the ligaments about my spine, and the pain came chiefly from pressure on major nerves.

I came home and tried not to think of the possibility that I would be a bedridden cripple, perhaps for many years. There seemed little hope of anything else. For three or four years, I was told, the pain would be a constant, twenty-four-hour tenant. Then the spine would be completely calcified and gradually the pain would be relieved. But by that time I would be bent over in worse shape than Old Black Joe. Meanwhile I could take about thirty aspirin tablets a day and try to be cheerful. What a prospect! Cortisone was just coming on the market in 1950 and before the year was out I was subjected, somewhat experimentally, to large doses. This was before cortisone was synthesized, and it was expensive and difficult to obtain. Fortunately, I proved to be one of those lucky people who can take cortisone without injurious side effects, and the results were miraculous. In less than a month I was on my feet and, although still pretty stiff, I was able to search for ivory-bills in the Apalachicola River swamps with Jim Tanner. By March I was well enough to join Steve and Bea Briggs on our first trip to the flamingo colony at Inagua, a visit that is described in another chapter. And then, in May, as the next step in our new investigation, I journeyed once more to the Bahamas, this time alone, so as to undertake a thorough search of the old flamingo nesting grounds on Andros Island.

In Nassau, with the help of Elgin Forsyth, I made arrangements to charter the twenty-one-foot sloop *Alert*, along with the services of her builder, owner, and skipper, an Andros native named McPhee, and his sometime mate, cook, and jack-before-the-mast, Herby. McPhee was recommended to me as a leading citizen in the Negro settlement at Mangrove Cay, Andros. He was said to be a man of parts and an excellent seaman. I liked him from the first moment I saw him, and my respect for him grew as our voyage to Andros progressed. We eventually anchored in the mouth of Grassy Creek, made famous a half century ago by Frank M. Chapman as the natural gateway to the great flamingo cities of South Andros. For several days we trudged over the wild interior of that deserted region, finding the remains of old flamingo nest mounds and much else of interest, but only twelve rather sad-looking flamingos. McPhee proved to be an excellent guide. We did a thorough job of scouting, and returned, finally, to Mangrove Cay settlement. We reached the settlement at midday on Sunday, May 13, chatted with Mr. Darville, the commissioner, and with his permission sent a radiogram to Nassau, advising that we would be in the following day. With that we were on our way.

I have never supposed that the fact it was the thirteenth had anything to do with it. Of more importance, perhaps, was the deceptively fine weather, in which we were not undeceived by the pleasant people at the government weather station and, above all, by the knowledge that we were homeward bound. I have been a homeward bounder many times, from long voyages and short ones, and there is always an accompanying exhilaration that has no counterpart—for me, at least. It isn't that you are glad to see the trip over and done with, or anything like that, it is simply that you have another job under your belt, and you can look forward to relating all the fantastic things that happened to you, and to getting cleared away for the next one. In spite of our dismal failure to find an active flamingo colony on Andros Island (truthfully we had very little hope of finding one, to begin with), I see that my notes—little, unimportant paragraphs jotted down hastily through all of that bright Sunday—have a light tone that seems hardly in keeping with the results of our expedition. This I now put down merely to a touch of homeward-bound fever. It was a few minutes past two in the afternoon when we came back aboard the *Alert*, anchored off Mangrove Cay, picked up the hook, and set out for Nassau, on the neighboring island of New Providence. My notes relate that there was "a spanking breeze, as the saying goes." The jubilant tone is unmistakable.

McPhee, at the tiller, showed no premonition of the danger that lay ahead, and Herby, dreaming of the rum he would be able to buy next day, was in a pleasant torpor—his version of the homeward-bound fever. Both are good sailors, as good as any in the Bahamas, and it seems certain that they had no suspicion of trouble.

At Middle Bight Cay we crossed into the Tongue of the Ocean, dipping easily from the green and brown shallows behind the reef into the dark, intense blue waters that drop off precipitously to depths of as much as 1,000 fathoms. It was then that Herby roused himself long enough to predict that, if the breeze held, we would make the bank below Southwest Reef, to the south of New Providence, by nine o'clock that same night.

It was about three that afternoon when we heard the first thunder, off in the west. We could see some angry-looking clouds building up, but they seemed safely far off, and they appeared to be moving along the length of Andros, offering no threat to our passage across the Tongue. After a little we could see a couple of heavy squalls breaking over the island beyond and behind us. Our lazy thoughts scarcely troubled to estimate which settlements, on the coast we were leaving, might now be getting a drenching. We were completely unconcerned. Within an hour all this had changed. The southeast breeze increased until we were skimming along like a racing yacht. Then it lulled momentarily and set in from the northwest. Within minutes a squall appeared, bearing down on us suddenly from the north. As it struck, in great drops that slapped hard against bare skin, Herby let go the jib and, with the same movement, lowered the big weather-stained mainsail to the deck. We sat shivering in the sudden chill, grinning foolishly at our goose flesh and wet through. However, it was still nothing but a rain squall, and we were far from worried.

The first squall was followed by another, and this one, more severe than the first, either lasted longer or was overhauled by a third and a fourth in such rapid succession that their beginnings and endings were indistinguishable. The wind picked up steadily as the day wore on, and it was nearly dark before a lull occurred. The sky was low and leaden, and angry clouds, heavy and sullen with moisture, went racing by overhead. Against the wild pattern of equally leaden seas, mixed flocks of Audubon's shearwaters and noddy and sooty terns chattered amiably as they flew by or hovered close to the surface. By this time our little company was less cheerful.

As darkness closed around us, McPhee, less certain now of what lay ahead, suggested to Herby that he try his hand at boiling some tea. With a troubled glance at the sky to windward and another at the reefed mainsail, Herby lurched aft, where McPhee and I crouched uncomfortably on the open deck, and crawled, mumbling to himself, into the tiny cabin. "Ah'll make you tea aw right," he called, "but it's strong coffee for Herby, strong an' bittah." With the easy skill of long practice he primed and lit the battered Primus, somehow keeping the pan of water in its place and the whole thing in operation, although the tiny sloop was rolling and pitching in a distressing manner. I suspect that the use of a Primus stove was an innovation introduced aboard the *Alert* by the well-known Andros commissioner, Elgin Forsyth, since retired. Forsyth, long an advocate of this particular cooking device, often chartered McPhee and Herby's craft for official voyages to the scattered settlements of his dark-skinned charges along the southeast Andros coast. The usual Bahamian cookstove, of the maritime variety, consists of a rough box of sand in which the native buttonwood is burned to a glowing bed of coals. So the use of a Primus brought the *Alert* up a notch or two; she was hardly in the yacht class, but unquestionably she was superior to the ordinary Mangrove Cay vessel.

As night and foul weather settled around us, I soon learned that the modernizing process had not extended to the navigation department. The native Bahamians, especially some of the blacks, are expert boatmen and amazingly good rule-of-thumb navigators. However, their skill and knowledge is like that of old river pilots I have met elsewhere: all in their heads. As the storm grew more intense, and our position more alarming in the darkness, I observed McPhee consulting his compass rather frequently. This compass was, in itself, a discouraging piece of equipment, and Lord Kelvin himself would have scornfully disowned it. The wood box in which, in its best days, it had been suspended was now held together in a haphazard way by bits of string tied round and round its exterior. In spite of this makeshift repair job, the various parts of the box kept slipping out of alignment, so that the compass dropped, unsupported, into the bottom. It seemed to me a hopeless instrument under the circumstances, but McPhee had a way of fixing it on the unsteady deck, clamped loosely between his large bare feet, that must have worked, for he went on consulting it and called out every shift in the direction of the wind. Reefed down and forced to luff up into the wind every five minutes, besides drifting badly as we were, it appeared that any attempt to set a course and stick to it would be impossible, but McPhee continued to make all the headway he could, and seemed to believe we had a chance of at least crossing the deep waters of the Tongue sometime during the night, even though far south of our goal.

The wind had been veering about between northwest and north, then it moved closer to northeast and shrieked down on us with a voice that was a steady and ominous roar. Herby, having served us our tea, along with some cold and soggy remains of johnnycake, our only meal for many hours, now wrapped both arms around the mast so as to be handy to the halyards. As a particularly vicious gust arose, McPhee would shout almost before it struck us and down would come the big tattered mainsail, Herby yanking at the stubborn hoops like a madman. Then, at a word from McPhee, he would haul it partway up again, just sufficient canvas to keep our head toward the wind. The typical Bahamian sail has no reef points, but is reefed by passing a tricing line under the foot of the sail and hauling at it through a block that is secured to the mast below its head, thus lifting the sail and forming a big V-shaped opening in its middle. This simple device reduces the amount of sail area in a hurry.

The night advanced and our little company settled down to a cold, wet, and comfortless routine. McPhee squatted on his heels at the tiller, steadied himself by means of a hand on the sheet. Herby clung to the mast, his worn yachting cap twisted on his close-cropped head so that the visor fell over one ear. And I stood in the partly open hatchway, a hand against the straining boom. As each crisis arrived—and every succeeding squall seemed trying to engulf us—it was met by a flurry of wild shouts and clumsy activity. In spite of everything, McPhee managed to prevent the sloop from falling off and wallowing broadside. The seas were now of respectable size, although, in the utter darkness, we had to judge them by the lift and surge of the vessel rather than by sight. It rained tons of water in a heavy, unrestrained manner, as if poured out of a gigantic tub squarely on top of us. Once, utterly tired and on the thin edge of seasickness, I dropped inside the low cabin and stretched out on a bunk. Semi-enclosed as it was, the heaving and worrying of the tiny craft seemed even more pronounced than on deck. I rolled hard against the inside of the planking, then teetered on the opposite edge of the bunk. The clatter and banging on deck, the high-pitched, completely unintelligible shouts of my black companions, and the moaning shriek of wind and sea—no one could rest in that. After a few minutes I pulled myself to the hatchway again. Herby had crawled aft for a moment to consult with the skipper. It was a shouted consultation, although they were clinging to each other for support. Few of the words were clear to me, and at one point McPhee, apparently sensing this, said, loud and clear and directly in my face, "You'll forgive it if we use our own words at such a time. It is easier." I understood then that the phrases I was unable to follow were pure African, words held to by these transplanted people for more than 150 years.

There was worse in store for us. It may have been close to midnight when a series of violent and erratic squalls had us aching and exhausted, too weary and uncomfortable to care that we were so wet and cold. Already it seemed like the longest night I had ever experienced. In the midst of one usually severe gust, McPhee and Herby began shouting more excitedly than at any time since the gale began. For the first time that night I began to feel real alarm, for McPhee, who had remained a perfect rock of calmness, was now quite obviously disturbed. He had had his dark face almost inside the dilapidated compass and, as he looked up and shouted, there was surprise and disbelief and a definite note of anguish in his voice. Herby, staring at McPhee with round eyes, began moaning in a strange, piping sort of tone, thin and strained, with an intelligible phrase only here and there. Most of it was, "Sabe us, oh Lord above! God in Heaben, sabe us, sabe us!" The rest was a repeated "Lord! Lord! Lord!" over and over again in a low monotone. What McPhee had said was that the wind now showed signs of swinging into a counterclockwise pattern. This might be more than a gale, bad as that was; it could be a hurricane! We now found the means for lashing ourselves to the craft as best we could.

At about this juncture we saw the first waterspout. There was enough of a break overhead, a small thin spot, appearing suddenly and then gone again, to enable us to make out a towering pillar of water close off our starboard beam. McPhee said he had seen others trying to form; now here was one of the brutes nearly alongside us. This first one slid on by, a great black mass of clouds at its head, glowering like a mad thing, but there were many more in its wake. I suppose that everyone who, in his lifetime, has spent considerable time at sea gets to wondering if he will end in a watery grave. I know that I thought then, "Yes, Ishmael, the same fate may be thine."

Toward morning we were still afloat, and McPhee, whose eyes were phenomenal, picked out the flash of the Tower light at Nassau, which can be seen at least 18 miles at sea. Somehow we had made that distance.

As it grew light we could see the angry water around us. And the waterspouts. Not that we had a very good chance of avoiding them, if it came to that. Like the lone Negro in the dismasted sloop of Winslow Homer's water color, we could only stare vacantly at disaster and hope that our luck held out. Through the last hours of the night Herby had been singing hymns. There was no stopping him. Being the type that goes on lengthy binges and then, in his remorse, swears off the Demon Rum forever and takes up with the church for a period, his repertoire was considerable and well memorized. McPhee and I had to put up with it, along with the rest of our troubles. Once, during a lull, McPhee leaned close to me, and with a laugh in his deep voice, said,

"When we git t' Nassaw he'll head for th' fust rumshop!" The words of the hymns, in Herby's wheezy tenor, offered little comfort. *Crossing the Bar* seemed like the last straw. What a foolish, unprepared way to die, I thought, out here in these strange waters, in a boat with nothing but a torn, patched-up sail, in this day of efficient marine engines. With two men I scarcely know, and who probably don't care if I die or not. And, worst of all, in an unpredicted hurricane, at the wrong time of year. Who ever heard of a hurricane in mid-May?

At dawn, the wind and the heaving seas increased to such an extent that we finally had to drop all canvas to the deck and turn the sloop loose. She fell into the long rolling seas broadside, riding the gray slopes like a wounded duck and fighting the tops of the combers fretfully, the water breaking across her from rail to rail. There was nothing more that we could do. In the gray light the men's faces were taut and old-looking. Herby, mercifully, had stopped his singing. His usually bland features were an utter blank, drained of all intelligent expression. McPhee, still alert, like his stout little vessel, watched the approach of every big wave. I knew what he was watching for, and I wondered vaguely what we would do at the last minute. We counted as many as four waterspouts in sight at one time, two of them dangerously near.

In an odd way at that stage of the experience, I was actually enjoying the freedom of our uncontrolled movement. It was a seascape to remember. Against a sky that was tearing itself apart with frenzy, surrounded by a changing series of backdrops, dark and violent and forbidding, our naked mast careening at crazy angles, the loose halyards flapping and singing in the wind, we rolled and wallowed, pitched, lurched, bucked, dipped, shuddered and, with it all, swept along toward whatever lay in store for us, like a royal barge that must hasten to get there before all the rest. And we were still afloat.

By midmorning a lull aroused us enough to hoist the jib and a small corner of the mainsail. McPhee, looking grimmer than ever, loosed the sheet and let the sloop ride just a trifle off the wind, so that the breaking seas were on our starboard quarter rather than dead astern. Now we went forward with some purpose. Herby, his yachting cap jaunty instead of dejected, hummed gay and wordless tunes, peering ahead cheerfully from his station in the bows. McPhee said nothing, but tended strictly to business. When the sloop struggled to the top of an especially big wave, he had to fight with the helm to keep her steady. She tended to yaw at such times, and again, the boom would lift as if wanting to jibe. Once, at a moment like this, the boom leaped suddenly and lifted away from the mast, the mainsail billowing forward in the wind and dragging overboard. The boom went completely over, hanging there at a crazy angle and straining heavily against the boiling water and the wild rush of the vessel. It was all the three of us could do to haul it back aboard, McPhee very nearly losing his hold and going into the sea himself.

Calculating a strong westerly drift, McPhee now proposed that we try and sail her toward a recognizable landmark. As once again we approached Andros, we faced a new danger—the long reef that runs along the eastern perimeter of that island. Unless we came on the reef at a point where there was a known channel, we would certainly pile up against the sharp coral rocks and our adventure would be over in a matter of minutes. For my part, I had no idea where we were, by this time, but McPhee, with admirable composure under the circumstances and more than a little sea sense, seemed to have his bearings. About ten o'clock he asked Herby to shinny up the mast and look for High Cay, a great rocky cliff on a small island that forms a part of the Andros reef southeast of Fresh Creek. Herby clambered aloft, his bare feet using the hoops as steps, and, swaying there, thirty feet above us, one arm hugging the masthead and his free hand grasping the main halyards, he gazed long at the horizon. With a shout of "no lan', nuthin' but watah!" he slid back to the deck. From time to time he went aloft again and, handing over the tiller, McPhee took his turn. Finally, at close to 11 A.M., McPhee yelled from aloft, "High Cay, off to starboard!" It was like being born again.

Soon we could see the gray looming face of our landmark from the deck, and shortly after that, as if floating, dim and misty but unmistakable along the rim of the sea, the tops of tall pine trees on the main island itself. The reef was now in view as well, black rock jutting out here and there, but mostly it was a leaping, ragged wall of white water, churning and surging and breaking itself furiously against the hard barrier of dead and living coral. McPhee altered our course now, bringing the wind full astern. We raced up the slope of long rollers, poised, balanced on the crests, and then, as they broke, we held on for dear life, while the clutching sea swirled around our feet and legs before rushing angrily overboard. We were heading now for a narrow break in the reef just to the south of Green Cay, a channel that Herby claimed to know "like the pa'm of my han'." As we swept headlong and irretrievably toward it, McPhee questioned the degree of Herby's knowledge regarding the exact lay of the channel, and the latter began a long recital of the endless number of vessels he had conned through this particular opening. McPhee interrupted to remind him of his own uncle, "bes' seaman on Andros," who had lost his two-masted schooner, his crew, and his life trying to cross through this same reef just above Green Cay, and Herby abruptly stopped talking and took over the business of directing the course.

Small flocks of sooty terns now joined us, swooping and fluttering all about us, their voices more cheerful than they had sounded on the open Tongue some hours before. The reef was now just ahead of our lifting bows, and for the life of me I could see no sign of a channel. Alongside the mast, Herby was waving his long, loose-limbed arms this way and that, starboard a little, now port, now starboard again, his eyes, under half-closed lids, searching the foam, the wide sheets of dashing spray, and the turmoil of seething waters for the outlines of the opening. In another moment the sloop was in the very middle of this jarring turbulence and I waited to hear the crunch and splinter of our thin hull. But Herby had picked the right spot and before we could get our breath we were through, and racing into the shallow waters beyond.

McPhee jibed her and in another instant the *Alert* was trembling in the shelter of Green Cay. Down came the mainsail, and Herby was clearing the anchor line. Soon we were riding serenely on our anchor, and boiling water for tea, with strong coffee for Herby. By two o'clock both boys were laid out on their bunk,

McPhee with his wooly head against the soles of Herby's feet, and Herby with his now decapped head against McPhee's feet. They slept soundly like that for the next fifteen hours.

The storm had overtaken us on Sunday, the thirteenth. It was the following Thursday, May 17, when we finally reached Nassau. After what we had been through, the trip back could only be described as "an uneventful voyage." As soon as we were anchored off the old sponge dock and our business concluded, Herby, his yachting cap tipped over one ear, at its rakish best, mumbled his good-bys and ambled off into the waterfront crowd. McPhee looked after his long lean figure as one would at a child who has passed beyond the age of parental restraint. "Rum," he said bitterly, "th' cheapes' an' th' mostes' he can drink." I shook hands with McPhee and we didn't make anything of it, but he knew, and I knew, that his skill had saved our lives. There was only one thing I wanted just then, anyway. I followed Herby ashore, my legs a little unsteady when they reached the paving. I thought that I might have a small dram myself.

That unusual May hurricane, of which we had entered the distant southerly fringe, came roaring out of the Atlantic toward Hatteras, veered almost due south and, completely unannounced, swept on straight for Abaco, the Tongue of the Ocean, and Andros Island just beyond. As reconstructed by a surprised weather bureau, it swerved in a great westerly loop just before striking Abaco, kept swinging all the way around until it was heading east, and then went roaring off into the open Atlantic where it had been spawned. The sudden and completely unaccountable swerve to the west and the reversal of course that followed unquestionably saved us from a cold, lonely, and very wet grave. As stout as she was the *Alert* could never have survived the full blast of the hurricane, not even with the imperturbable McPhee at the tiller.

So far as the flamingos were concerned, our little expedition had brought back only negative information, and although it is against such a fabric that we see the true worth of more positive data, empty results bring with them empty hearts and a sense of disappointment. Nevertheless even with McPhee's skill we had more than our share of luck on that voyage.

It seems quite possible that hurricanes always have been a definite factor in the periodic reduction of flamingo flocks inhabiting certain vulnerable areas in the Bahamas and West Indies. Our American species, *Phoenicopterus ruber*, has continued to live close to the sea, on lands that may be frequently submerged during storms, whereas the other flamingos of the world have been able to move inland to higher altitudes. Our species is the only one seriously reduced in numbers at this time, except perhaps the rare James's flamingo of the high Andes, which may never have been very abundant. And, although man has been chiefly responsible for the destruction of flamingo populations in the West Indies, these unnatural losses serve to emphasize and render more serious the toll that may be taken from time to time by such natural forces as hurricanes.

In his reports to the colonial secretary in Nassau, 1922–1936, Elgin Forsyth, who, as commissioner at Andros, was also in charge of flamingo protection for the Bahamas government, presented a vivid picture of the destruction wrought by such storms. In 1925, after four years of rigid protection, the Andros flamingo colonies were again prospering, the main flock nesting in that year on Jack Fisher's Sound building up to an estimated 3,000 mounds. In September, 1926; August, 1928; September, 1928; and September, 1929, four hurricanes struck Andros Island. The 1926 storm hit at a time when the adult flamingos were dropping their flight feathers and the new crop of young were just learning to fly by their own efforts. The losses were so heavy that no colony was formed the following year. In 1928 a small group nested, but the young were virtually wiped out by the storm of August 6. When the September storm struck, one of the most violent of the century, the adult birds were again flightless as a result of the molt. In October, Forsyth and his men could find only 25 flamingos on all of Andros, although many of those that had survived doubtless did so by fleeing to Cuba and elsewhere. In 1929, such birds as returned were again dispersed or killed by the storm of September 26. It was not until 1935 and 1936 that the Andros flock recovered to some extent from these disasters.

Another prospect in that first year of our study was the small colony said to be nesting somewhere on the west side of Great Abaco Island, in an extensive and little-known region called "The Marls." With Forsyth I made two trips into this area and thus got to know it at first hand, as well as other things with the Abaco label stamped indelibly upon them. One of these was the mail boat. Although for some inexplicable reason she is named after a pirate who was hanged in the autumn of 1718 high on Charleston's Execution Dock, there is nothing swashbuckling about her. On the contrary. Like most of the boats that make scheduled runs among the Out Islands of the Bahamas, she has the appearance of having been rebuilt out of something that must have been a great deal trimmer to begin with, but not sufficiently capacious as to passenger accommodations, a shortcoming that had been corrected with a vengeance. And, from the crowd that was gathered in the pier shed a half hour before sailing time, every cubic foot of space was going to be needed.

At Government House in Nassau, Sir Robert Neville, then governor of the colony, and as such patron of the newly formed Society for the Protection of the Flamingo, had expressed keen interest in our plans. I reminded him of an earlier governor, Sir Henry Blake, who had been the first to describe this Abaco colony, following his visit of June, 1887, when there were a good many more flamingos in the area than we would be likely to see.

With our arms full of duffle and a box of groceries (for we had been warned that the shops of Abaco, though surprisingly numerous, are not overstocked), we clambered aboard and a few minutes later, at 5 P.M., the whistle blew, the lines were let go, and with much shouting and waving we were on our way. It is astonishing the number of people that travel on these out-island boats. The decks fairly swarmed. To cut expenses, Forsyth and I booked the least promising accommodations, as it was only an overnight run. These turned out to be a sort of after forecastle next to the steering engine, where double tiers of bunks had been built in against the hull on one side and the steering-engine housing on the other. Excess baggage, including her own, had been piled helter-skelter in the passage, so that one could scarcely climb through. It was a regular obstacle course. From overhead, strings of dried fish and conchs were suspended, swaying like extraordinary pendulums, and the fulsome emanations from these, mingled with the sweet scent of several bunches of overripe bananas, had me feeling uncomfortably dizzy before we were out of the harbor. Forsyth, an old campaigner in his native Bahamas, was quite used to such surroundings and was taking it all in stride, but he made no objections to joining me on deck, where the air and the view were a decided improvement.

Once clear of Nassau and on our course for the southern tip of Great Abaco, 50 miles to the north across the deep waters of New Providence Channel, the supper bell was heard. One look below decks showed us that others, more familiar with procedure aboard this particular boat, had anticipated the call. The two long tables were lined solidly with people who, from the way they were digging in, must have been counting on the announcement of this meal since breakfast. Others stood about, waiting for an empty place. The cook, a red-faced gentleman wearing a large, once white apron and a cheap felt hat pulled down over his ears, pointed a large cooking spoon in our direction and, in the high-pitched, singsong, slightly Cockney speech of the true Abaconian, said, "Ga-on deck 'f'you like, A'll call you fer nex' servin'." Together with a few of the others who were unseated, we gratefully retreated to the deck.

We were now well at sea and chugging along at full clip, the smell from the diesel engine swirling around us in the brisk easterly breeze before flying off to leeward and losing itself over the sea. Finding a bench not too far from the companionway, we made ourselves comfortable and sat there talking and smoking. Once the red face of the cook, hat still in place, appeared out of the gloom below. With a negative nod in answer to our no doubt expectant glances, he mumbled something like "A few women is still at it, wa-ont be long na-ow," and ducked out of sight. After a while it began to grow dark and finally, in the middle of one of Forsyth's delightful yarns about Andros Island, I suddenly remembered that we still hadn't had our suppers. Excusing myself, I popped down the ladder and was astounded to find the tables empty. In the galley the cook was wiping his large fisherman's hands on his apron and glaring at the sink, where several bulky pots were sloshing around in greasy-looking water. He seemed thoroughly aggrieved when I asked, rather pointedly, about supper. "Supper?" he said, as if he had never heard of such a thing in his life. "Why, supper's been gone mor'n a 'alf 'our aga-o." And then, just in case I might be entertaining any further ideas on the subject, he added, with a scornful snort, "Everything's et up!" Since our box of groceries was packed away with the rest of the freight, we climbed into our bunks supperless, deciding that the old hulk had been well named after all.

At ten the next morning we anchored off Hopetown in a steady downpour of rain. The captain made his home here and so here we remained until late afternoon, a slight hitch in the schedule that had not been mentioned at the shipping office. Breakfast had come and gone, and eventually lunch. By dint of careful planning and considerable maneuvering, we managed to find seats at the first table. The tea was both hot and strong, but we should have stopped with that. The remainder of both meals consisted of a bowl of water in which some kind of fish had been boiled. After examining the meager bones that reposed at the bottom, and to which a few strips of dark meat still clung, we suspected that they had been members of the ubiquitous jack family. At lunch a few potatoes were added, halved and boiled without removing their jackets. From their peculiar flavor it was all too apparent that they had been rescued from a surplus Florida crop that had been immersed in kerosene, as a means of removing them from a glutted market. Kerosene has an unmistakable, lingering, and most unpleasant taste! We swore that on our next voyage aboard this unmentionable craft we would stuff our pockets with something that was at least palatable.

It was just getting dark when we were at length put ashore at Marsh Harbour, where we were to meet Rodney Roberts and his sloop, the *Ramona R.* This was on a Wednesday evening, the twenty-seventh of June. On inquiry we learned that, not unexpectedly, Rodney was off along the coast somewhere, no one was quite certain exactly where, but probably at a small island where he had a "farm." We found an empty room at Rodney, Jr.'s, and settled down to wait. Thursday and Friday came and went, but no sign of the *Ramona R.* Then, on Saturday morning, a sail appeared beyond the small cays outside the harbor, and after a few minutes Forsyth pronounced it to be Rodney's boat. He knew her by her rig, and also by the obvious need for new patches here and there on the big mains'l. Rodney, a jaunty yachting cap on his graying head, a briar in his teeth, and bare of foot, was soon alongside, holding up some choice-looking melons for our approval and grinning broadly. "Rodney, you scamp," shouted Forsyth, "do you know we've been waiting here for more than two days?" "I'm not even sure what day i'tis-s," said Rodney, unabashed, "but I must say, Mr. Forsyth, you couldn't 'ave waited in a nicer place, now, could you?" "You see," grumbled Forsyth, turning to me with a twinkle in his eye, "sheer blarney, just as I warned you." Rodney took no notice, being occupied in cutting up a melon for us to sample. It was delicious.

That evening we set sail, taking with us young Rodney and an effusive colored gentleman from the nearby Negro settlement of Murphytown, which had been built by the government on a high bluff so as to be out of reach of hurricane waves. Cameron Happy Montour was a one-time flamingo watchman for the local commissioner, and he had recommended himself to us as the local expert on these birds and as an experienced pilot for our passage through the intricacies of The Marls. It had not been mentioned that he was also a self-styled authority on Holy Writ, a tireless discourser on every question under the sun, and, barring the subject of flamingos, a complete fraud. We stopped along the coast to pick up Montour's "flamingo boat," a homemade contraption of the size and appearance of a coffin. We lay off the steep rocks of the shore while the flamingo expert, who had walked the few miles up the beach to join us, launched his strange craft and paddled furiously toward us. As he drew near he began shouting lustily for a rope end. "She fillin' fas'! She fillin' fas'!" he yelled. "Rope! Rope! Heave me a rope! Good Lord, sen' me a rope!" In spite of this bit of dramatics, he was alongside in another half minute, still well afloat, and still talking. We were much amused, especially Forsyth, who has a well-deserved reputation as a boat designer. When we had hauled the craft and its owner aboard, Forsyth said, "Montour, what in Heaven's name are we supposed to do with this leaky coffin?" Montour pretended to be quite offended, sputtering with injured dignity. "You vill see, Commissioner," he protested. "My mind tell me you vill see and approve, sor. Yes, yes, see *and* approve. And the Lord vill be with us, indeed He vill." "My man," said Forsyth in his best magisterial tone, with a forefinger raised admonishingly, "don't change the subject. The Lord is too busy with important matters to be interested in your miserable excuse for a boat. And what I want to know is, what are you intending to do with it?" But Montour was really injured now and, mumbling to himself, he turned the little craft over on the foredeck and lashed it securely.

Just before dark we approached Green Turtle Cay, sailing along easily in a light breeze. On three tiny cays that were covered with opuntia cactus, sooty terns were evidently nesting, and Rodney pointed out that because of the spines in the thickly growing plants, the eggs would be safe from marauding natives. Running on in the early darkness until long past eight o'clock, we anchored off the settlement at Green Turtle Cay for the night. Going ashore for some stores that had not been available in Marsh Harbour, we found the doorways full of people, although not a light was showing. The wooden houses, nearly half of them deserted, are crowded closely together, with scarcely two feet between many of them. And the entire village, in consequence, is jammed all in a heap at one end of what is actually a rather large island. The ancestors of these people were supposed to have been city bred, London dockside in large measure, and even in five generations they had not learned to live like country folk, with the comfort and freedom of wide spaces around them. At Marsh Harbour, while waiting for Rodney, we talked with a number of the inhabitants. Many of the oldest Abaco families have been in the Bahamas since the end of the American Revolution, when officers and men of Cornwallis's army were settled here as colonists. There had been the usual hard times, but along in the nineteenth century prosperity had come to those who excelled at the boatbuilding trade, while others had done well for themselves during the

American Civil War, when blockade running was a risky but profitable business. Green Turtle Cay had been a major headquarters for these operations, and the first mention that I had been able to find in ornithological literature of a flamingo colony at Abaco (though not the first report, which had been Governor Blake's) was the account of a ship captain from Florida who said that while blockade running out of Green Turtle Cay, around 1863, the local people brought in flamingos from a colony some ten miles to the west, and sold them for food. Today many of the younger people have migrated to America or to Nassau, where they can find employment. Except for two or three yards, boatbuilding has dropped off and is rapidly becoming a lost art.

One evening I heard Forsyth, who is well known there on account of his work with the sponge fisheries, lecture a group of older residents on the subject of shipbuilding, but I suspect it was in vain. He remarked that in these days every other householder had set up a little shop, sometimes with nothing more than a few cans of pork and beans, and soda pop on the shelves. He asked for the names of those who were running this shop and that one, and then inquired if the father (or perhaps the grandfather) had not been So-and-so, the boatbuilder. Yes, that was so. But they have given up the trade? Yes, that was so. Ha! says F., you have the mistaken idea that to be a merchant is to move up in the world. You foolishly believe that a storekeeper is better than a builder of boats, but in this you are greatly mistaken. It is just the other way around. No one agreed or disagreed. Nearly all present were small shopkeepers, and nearly all were descended from some of the most skilled builders of sailing sloops and schooners in the islands. Of course, it could be that in this mechanized age there is little demand for the products of that once flourishing trade. All of which seems something of a pity.

There was one gentleman who was not only busily engaged in his boatyard, putting the finishing touches on a large and sturdy sloop, but who was also a man of many parts, as we learned later, and a leader in the community. When I spoke of how much I had been impressed by him, a resident said to me, "It's only to be expected. After all, 'is people wuz officers." I puzzled over this and finally asked another resident to explain. "Officers of what?" I inquired. This other gentleman looked at me in some surprise, "Why," he said, "in the British Army." And then, after a pause, "You know, when you folks 'ad your Revolution." I couldn't believe my ears, for such long-cherished ties with the past seem strange to an American. But, without a doubt, the active boatbuilder and pillar of his community, for whatever reason, was an outstanding citizen.

Long before daylight the next morning we were under way, passing by Spanish Cay and around the north side of Little Abaco Island to the Haulover. This is a narrow spit of rocky land that joins the two extremes of Little Abaco near its middle. Years ago keel boats were laboriously hauled across at high tide, but a Captain Lowe had gone to work with dynamite and blasted a narrow channel through the rock. When we arrived the ebb was rushing through like a millrace, but by waiting for the slack we were able to ease the *Ramona* through without difficulty, with young Rodney's keel boat towing from ahead, on which we attached a small outboard motor. Once on the other side we were "west of Abaco" with clear sailing to the edge of The Marls as far as Mastic Point Cay, where we proposed to begin our explorations. It was on a Sunday when we cleared the Haulover, but squalls, followed by dead calms, plus several stops to look for fresh water, delayed us until Wednesday morning, when we finally anchored at the appointed place. The first stop had been made at the picturesque Negro settlement of Crown Haven, and it was here we discovered that Montour, in addition to his other talents, had a way with the ladies. No sooner had we come ashore, water jugs in hand, than we were greeted by a veritable bevy of dark-skinned beauties, decked in their Sunday best in fluffy white cotton dresses and floppy hats. One young lady even wore long white gloves, though her feet were bare. Ordinarily, on such occasions, the feminine contingent in these settlements remains coyly in the background, but church was just out and, strolling near the sea, loath to go home and remove their finery, these happy belles had recognized Montour in our party and were soon greeting him with familiar shouts, wide displays of large white teeth, and a chorus of girlish simpers. Up the hill we trudged, water jugs and all, and as we came down the last slope toward the village we saw that our Cameron was holding hands with a slim, fetchingly dressed young woman who was fully two heads taller than the old rooster. This was amusing enough, but it had an even better aftermath, for when Montour had gone on by himself to the village well to direct the water drawing, I saw a tall, very angry-looking young Negro step from behind a bush and kick the willowy young woman soundly on her bottom. With a frightened yelp she disappeared into a nearby house.

As we proceeded down the coast we soon found that, as a pilot, Montour was a great hand to strike dramatic poses, lounging in the shade of the mains'l and holding fast to the stays, his straw hat pushed back on his wooly head and a pipe of tobacco in his mouth. He would wave his arms this way and that, talking constantly. So long as we were well offshore he was quite successful at this particular duty, identifying islands and headlands and regaling us with tales, real or imagined, of the former inhabitants, now dead ("God rest their souls, forever, Amen!") or driven elsewhere by hurricanes and other dire calamities. But when we steered in among the islands and cays themselves, seeking an inside channel, it was at once evident that our draft was somewhat greater than he was accustomed to, and the second day on that western coast he had the *Ramona* hard aground. And there we lay, unable to budge her, until high tide floated us off early the following morning. Completely unperturbed in spite of the ragging we gave him, Montour went off in his shallow coffin searching for turtles. These, like the deep channels he had promised, also failed to materialize.

It was the Fourth of July when we dropped our anchor off Mastic Point Cay and set off with the keel boat and Montour's coffin in search of the flamingos. There are an endless maze of channels, many of them too shallow to navigate, and countless little cays, some high enough to support coppices (locally "coppets") of palmettos and a few hardwoods. We saw white-crowned pigeons, willets, tricolored herons, brown pelicans, laughing gulls, and gull-billed terns, but no flamingos. Young Rodney and I, abandoning the keel boat in shoal water, found that we could outdistance Montour in his "flamingo boat" by walking at a good pace along the shorelines and wading the channels from cay to cay. But of course Montour had to stop and bail every few minutes.

Once he caught up with us, late in the afternoon, I asked him where he thought the flamingos might be. "Vell, sor," he replied at once, "ve go in this bight here because my mind tell me the fillamingo nesting somevere up there. My people tell me they always nest in sight of Israel Hill. . . ." And so on, for ten minutes. But when we returned to the *Ramona* at dark, tired and thirsty, we had seen no flamingos.

Next day we moved the big boat to Shallow Water Point, where Montour showed us a well in the hard sand above the beach. It contained water that was slightly brackish to the taste, but as we were running short we filled all vessels and jars. At noon we anchored again, this time off Thatch Point, and I went into The Marls with Montour, who led me directly to the nesting site that he had guarded a decade before. Nineteen of the old nest mounds were still intact, though grown through with red mangrove shoots. It was at this juncture that we saw the first flamingos, flying by overhead on a westerly course. Montour danced for joy. As we returned to the sloop late in the day, five flamingos flew over, heading southwest. Young Rodney had caught a mess of mangrove snappers while off exploring in another direction, and as we ate these, which old Rodney had cooked over a lovely fire of buttonwood coals in the sandbox "stove" on deck, we argued the question of where to continue our search the next morning.

As it turned out, young Rodney and I elected to take the keel boat up the long channel to the north of our anchorage, while Montour insisted on paddling his craft into the easterly channel known vaguely as Cherokee River. Both were good possibilities, but it was Junior and I who found the flamingos. They were nesting on a little islet of mud and sand not far beyond our anchorage. As we moved up the channel we spotted a few adults in the distance, partially hidden by the mangroves of an intervening point of land. Poking along as cautiously as possible, we were able to get within a few hundred feet before they flew. Then we saw the chicks, just a handful of them, swimming away from the islet like young geese, closely attended by the adults, who circled back to them immediately. Standing up in the boat, I counted a couple of dozen nest mounds, not much of a colony, but still a going concern. We moved off almost at once so that the chicks, which were less than a week old, would not swim too far from their base.

Montour had seen nothing at all, and, for once, after he had heard our good news, he was speechless for as long as an hour. But his disappointment was soon forgotten and before we set sail again his usual spirits were completely restored. That night when I fell asleep he was still talking, trying to explain to Forsyth his strange notions about flamingos and the condition of the universe in general. And above Rodney's lusty snores, almost the last words I recall hearing were, "And I tell you, sor, these are not all the fillamingos. No, no, no! My mind tell me, ve can find others if ve look towards Israel Hill. . . ." And so on and on. And then Forsyth's deep voice, sounding far away in the darkness, filled with authority and yet softened by a vast and amused tolerance. "Montour, d'you know, you are an incorrigible rascal!"

*. . . The general decline of the Caribbean fauna is, however, largely a result of human interference and none of the natural destructive factors, at least in the last four centuries, appears to have played a significant rôle.*

J. H. WESTERMANN *

# X : The pearl of the antilles?

Although the Bahamas continue to be, as in the past, the center of abundance for the American flamingo, these birds are likewise found on the coasts of Cuba, Hispaniola, Yucatán (which we had already visited), and across the Caribbean on the islands of Bonaire, La Orchila, and perhaps other insular habitats off the Venezuelan coast. In addition, small numbers of this same race have been discovered nesting on the isolated Galapagos Islands in the Pacific. Of all these locations, Cuba was not only the nearest at hand, but seemed to offer definite possibilities as the site of important nesting colonies of *Phoenicopterus ruber.*

Beginning in 1948, Harold Peters of the U.S. Fish and Wildlife Service made special note of the number and location of all flamingo flocks observed by him while conducting aerial surveys of waterfowl in the Greater Antilles. This information, though limited to the winter season only, provided an excellent starting point. I went to Havana and joined Abelardo Moreno, head of

* *Nature Preservation in the Caribbean.*

the Zoology Department at the University of Havana, on a preliminary trip to Oriente Province and the Río Cauto Delta. We traveled by bus from Havana to Manzanillo, and there I was able to fly in a light plane over the magnificent delta country, where I observed a large flock of flamingos on one of the extensive salinas near the river mouth. There seemed a good chance that they might nest in this vicinity, and a more thorough investigation later on in the season, and by boat, was definitely indicated.

During the return trip by bus I was witness to one small example of the saying that Cubans do things differently from anyone else. There were two drivers on the bus, one a slight man and the other a great big fellow weighing well over 200 pounds. It was dusk when we left Manzanillo, and the road as far as Bayamo had apparently been built for travel by oxcart and never improved. Almost all of the seats were occupied, and for a time, as we pulled out of the town and set off into the night, there was a buzz of general conversation among the passengers. Then, what with the hour and the increasing discomfort of the ride over that roadway, a silence fell on the interior of the vehicle. At this juncture the large bus driver, who had been talking with passengers in front while the smaller man drove, reached onto the baggage rack and produced a guitar. Strumming a few chords and smiling on one and all, he began walking along the aisle and singing. Not a bad voice either. After each song there was a burst of applause, and looking around me I saw that every face was wreathed in smiles. I asked Abelardo what the songs were about and he glanced at me as if to see if I was serious, and then replied, "Why, the songs are about love, of course!"

Next, the driver stopped beside an attractive matron and addressed his song to her, evoking much coyness on her part, and delighted laughter and uproarious applause from the passengers. But his final gesture was even more wonderful. When the bus stopped briefly at a station close to a swamp-bordered stream, I noticed a lot of urchins along the road selling flowers. The large driver stepped off the bus and returned in a few moments with his arms full of wild gardenias. Each female passenger, regardless of age or degree of pulchritude, was gallantly presented with a fragrant gardenia. And along with it a courtly bow, a verse of poetry, or a few snatches of song. I never witnessed anything quite so delightful in a public conveyance anywhere! And yet everyone seemed to take it all more or less for granted.

In the spring of 1951 I began a general survey of the status of flamingos in key spots throughout the West Indies. In late July I was in the Dominican Republic, arriving on the thirtieth on the north coast. My first stop was the little town of Monte Cristi, and there, with great good fortune, I met two young American entomologists who were employed by the local United Fruit Company establishment. One of them, Curt Dowling, had taken a course in ornithology at the University of Miami and was familiar with my spoonbill monograph. When I explained that I was looking for flamingos he said that he was afraid most of the local "flamingos" might turn out to be spoonbills. Nevertheless, I went with them to Puerto Libertador where the manager very kindly put me up at the handsome guesthouse. That afternoon I talked with George Austin, who was in charge of docks and boats for the company, and happened to be interested in birds. He assured me that I would find flamingos, but a trip by boat would be necessary and he would make the arrangements.

Before breakfast the next morning I walked along Estero Balsa, where Austin said flamingos sometimes came to a sandbar to rest and preen. There were none in sight, however, so I strolled back toward the highway along a path that ran through some brush country near the shore. I noticed several thatch-roofed huts on the bank, but some distance off, and saw a few natives squatting about their early morning fires, from which smoke was rising lazily. Then, directly in the path ahead of me, and barring my passage, I saw a fair-sized brown cur dog. It is marvelous how a definite and immediate understanding can be transmitted between a man and a dog. At the first glance I knew from his stance and expression that this dog meant to make me pay tribute for the use of that trail. If he could! And I knew with equal promptness that there was nothing I could do to stop him except retreat, which for some idiotic reason I refused to consider. There seemed to be neither stick nor stone at hand so I approached my adversary unarmed, and with a falsely cheerful mien. "Hello, old boy!" I greeted him in my strange foreign tongue, not slacking my pace. By this time he was twenty feet away and the hackles on his neck and back were standing straight up. "Nice doggy," I murmured. Now I was alongside him and he hadn't budged an inch. Suddenly, with a deep-throated growl he leaped at me and buried his teeth in the calf of my right leg! I have no recollection of what I said to him then, but I know that I was shouting at him and trying to kick at him with my free foot. He let go, quite as suddenly as he had attacked, and still growling in an unfriendly fashion, ran off through the brush. "Foreigners get out" seemed to be the general idea.

I was now in a sweat of anger and apprehension, and the pit of my stomach was doing flip-flops. The bite did not appear to be very deep and it was not bleeding very much, but what if the dog had been mad? I hurried on to the highway, stopped a passing car, and was driven to the company hospital. It was too early for the doctor but I showed my wound to a Spanish-speaking colored gentleman who was wearing a white coat and appeared to be some kind of attendant. He merely stared at the tiny punctures in my calf and said nothing. I got out my indispensable Spanish-English dictionary and leafed through it for the proper words. With appropriate gestures and facial grimaces I showed how Fido had clamped his jaws on my leg. "Perro!" I said, growling deeply and snatching at my injured limb. "Si," said my friend, without much interest. I went back to my dictionary. On page 170 I found "rabies (rébiz) *s. rabia, hidrofobia.*" This I showed to him, repeating my pantomime, baring my teeth, growling, etc. Still he was unimpressed, simply staring at me as if trying to decide whether I might not be dangerous. Finally, in desperation, I pointed to some bottles on a shelf and then to my leg. With a shrug he took down one of them and, finding some cotton, did a reasonably good job of cleansing the wounds. With that I departed, glad to escape.

I did spend an anxious day or two, but the dog hadn't been rabid. He just didn't like strangers.

It was past noon that same day when we got off for the Río

Tapión, myself, the captain, whose name was Alejo, and a grinning assistant whose name wasn't mentioned. In a good-sized skiff propelled by a 10-h.p. outboard, we headed out across the bay toward the river mouth. The name Tapión may come from the verb *tapiar*, "to block up," for we soon came upon narrow places in this tidal stream where sticks formed a sort of crude stop net to keep fish from getting out during low water. In other respects as well, the Tapión is much like the rivers of southwest Florida. The shores are lined with a dense growth of red mangrove that becomes narrower upstream until, with the channel barely wide enough for our boat, the tangle forms a solid roof overhead.

The tide was ebbing rapidly. Off in the northeast we could hear thunder, and shortly after one o'clock, when we were well up toward the head of the river, it began to rain. We had seen one roseate spoonbill, a yellow-billed egret, a green heron, and a few white ibises. With our motor stopped by the soft mud, we poled on until we could go no farther. In a mangrove maze we found a small colony of tricolored herons, little blue herons, and egrets, with young just newly hatched. Suddenly, hearing something above the chatter of the heronry, Alejo raised a hand for silence. Pointing off toward the far bank, he whispered, "*Flamencos!*" Climbing through the mangrove in that direction we came out at length into a long open mud flat. There were legions of fiddler crabs, the males with enormous claws. At the far end of the flat we came into a weird-looking area of black mud and hundreds of dead mangrove stubs. In this rather dismal setting we counted some sixty flamingos, moving about in small groups and feeding. With them were numbers of willets, stilts, herons, egrets, and roseate spoonbills. Food supplies seemed to consist of an abundance of algae, countless aquatic insects, a few mollusks, and at least one variety of killifish. Alejo volunteered the interesting information that the *flamencos* didn't nest here but came over from Florida! It is likely that they actually come from the big colony on Inagua, which lies only some 60 miles due north of Ile de la Tortue on the nearby Haitian coast.

Finding no more flamingos or rumors of flamingos on the north coast, I moved on to Barahona, on Bahía de Neiba to the south, and there found transportation to Jimini, at the western tip of Lago de Enriquillo. The vehicle was a broken-down Plymouth that carried mail and passengers over the dusty 97 kilometers, through Cabral, around the south shore of Laguna del Rincón, through La Salinas and Duverge to the south shore of Enriquillo, and finally to the border town of Jimini. There were two other passengers to begin with, and as we stopped at native villages along the route, more piled in until there were eventually eight of us, in addition to the driver. No one spoke English, so we had a hilarious time trying to talk back and forth with the aid of my pocket dictionary. At one stop, a Negro village of thatch huts, the last passenger crowded aboard. She was a hefty colored woman and she was carrying a small dog and three large melons. With much laughter and a rapid-fire barrage of Spanish from all sides, she sat down in the only space that remained, which was squarely in my lap. And there she rode for the remainder of the voyage. The melons were deposited on my feet, both of which promptly went to sleep, and the dog, which she kept shifting from one arm to the other, would lean over and lick my face each time it came toward me. Since my arms were literally pinned to my sides I could do nothing to defend myself.

The next day I went on a birding expedition to the big lake with the governor of the province, César Alberto Meyreles, and the local justice, Dr. Santiago López. I had met these two gentlemen at dinner in the hotel, and the governor, who had once lived briefly in Harlem, was delighted at this opportunity for practicing his English, which had grown pretty rusty. We rode to the vicinity of Enriquillo in an official jeep and then started walking through the brush and cactus to the shore. At one point, when we seemed to be hemmed in by cactus, the governor, a big man standing well over six feet, reached into his waistband and whipped out an evil-looking bayonetlike weapon that had been concealed in his trouser leg. It had a blade fully eighteen inches long, and from the way he whacked the offending cactus apart it must have been as sharp as a razor. I hoped that we would remain friends!

Lago de Enriquillo lies below sea level and is more than twice as salty as the open sea. There is abundant evidence that it is an ancient sea bed, with corals and the worn shells of large marine mollusks scattered along the shore. On all sides rise the slopes of cedar-covered mountains, quite possibly the breeding site of the rare black-capped petrel (*Pterodroma hasitata*), perhaps in the region of Morne la Selle to the southwest of Enriquillo. When we reached the open shore we counted 49 flamingos and 54 roseate spoonbills feeding not far out. The governor told me that Enriquillo was named for one of their great Indian chieftains, adding that 60 per cent of the people in the Dominican Republic have some degree of Indian blood. He likewise showed me where there is an old Indian rock carving of a human face on the hillside above the lake.

Flamingos once nested on the shores of Enriquillo, but it is evident that they could not do so successfully today, as there are well-traveled roads all the way around the lake, many native villages, and no active law enforcement. Dr. López told me that although flamingos, spoonbills, and "all singing birds" are protected by law, people do shoot them, "and we have no way of knowing." In short, there is no special enforcement agency.

That evening I met a young American surveyor named Byars. The next morning he drove me up into the mountains directly south of Enriquillo, to the beautiful valley in which Lago del Limón is situated. Here we were again very close to the Haitian border, and at the little native village of Limón we were stopped by the troops that are garrisoned there. After a brief delay and much talk we were permitted to go on. Near the lake, which is fresh and surrounded by marshes, we left our car and walked to the shore at several points. There were over 350 flamingos, as well as many stilts, glossy ibises, egrets, and amazing numbers of coots and yellowlegs. It was impossible to get close to the flamingos, which kept well out on the lake, so that this lovely place is a fine natural refuge.

The following day, Byars and I circled the shore of Enriquillo and explored remote parts of its shoreline. We saw several of the amusing little broad-billed todies, which burrow into earth banks like kingfishers. Also palm crows and a lively colony of village weavers, obviously doing very well so far from their native Africa.

And, on the far side of the lake, we also counted nearly 100 flamingos. It seemed apparent that the old nesting sites must have been located in the shallows at both the east and west tips of Enriquillo. The Jimini end is especially suitable, but it is doubtful if they will ever nest there again.

Back in Ciudad Trujillo I met the Director General de Fomento y Turismo and discussed with him the great attraction that these colorful birds might have for tourists. He was politely interested. Then, after a short visit to Haiti—where I was told, in effect, that so long as the people were hungry, and poorly housed and clothed, nothing could be done about flamingo protection—I headed for Cuba. It was evident that flamingos were no longer nesting anywhere in Hispaniola, except possibly on Ile de la Gonave off the coast of Haiti, but I had great hopes for Cuba. I meant to find out for myself if it took me the rest of the summer.

The entire region near the delta salinas of the Río Cauto in Cuba is one of great beauty. Whether you come overland by omnibus, more than 500 miles by the Central Highway from Havana, or fly in by way of Camaguey, you see crowded little towns, broad valleys, with their magnificent clusters of stalwart royal palms, and the miles upon miles of living fence rows, the posts all rooted, and branched, and green with fresh leaves. Then, as you get into Oriente Province, at the eastern tip of the island, you see the mountains—the Sierra Maestra and Pico Turquino, highest peak in Cuba. From the sea, off the coast near Manzanillo, it is a sight worth stopping for, even when you have traveled that far just to see flamingos.

I had arranged, through one of my Cuban friends, for a cruise into the Río Cauto with the local members of the Navy. It sounded like a very good arrangement, as these *marineros*, besides affording the protection of their official craft and personnel in that isolated district, were said to be commanded by an officer, *el capitán del puerto*, in fact, who was reportedly much interested in flamingos. Soon I was in the humid little seaport town of Manzanillo and walking with my friend, Arturo, toward the waterfront building occupied by *el capitán*.

He was a slight, sharp-featured man of about sixty years, alert and smiling, with many wrinkles around his eyes. When we entered his office he quickly shoved something that looked like a glass into a desk drawer. He was dressed in a neatly starched khaki uniform with large stiff epaulets that signified his rank. A sailor in whites, with shore-duty leggings, was thumping at a typewriter. As soon as the captain saw Arturo he pulled the drawer out again, lifted a bottle and some glasses from it and placed them, with an apologetic little flourish, on top of the desk. Introductions were accomplished and then nothing would do but that we must join him in a drink. The local rum, not very good (he shrugged and smiled, turning this way and that so as to look each of us disarmingly in the face), but then it was better than some he had tasted. We joined him. His English was barely sufficient for the simplest conversation, but it was better than my Spanish, so we continued in a mixture of basic English and, for more enlightened discussion, rapid Spanish, Arturo translating for me in frequent asides.

After a little, we got around to the subject of the navy craft that was to take us up the river. A most unfortunate accident had occurred. The *ingeniero,* that is, the sailor who served as engineer, or *mecánico,* had broken his arm. Very painful (*el capitán* grimaced, screwing up his face until he looked like a mummy with its eyes open). But worse still, no one else in the detachment could crank the engine that propelled the boat, much less keep in running (more shrugs). It was unspeakable. In fact, let us not speak of it again. There are other boats, many other boats. In good time we will find another boat, perhaps a fishing boat, and possibly a fisherman who knows the river well. (I began to think that perhaps the captain didn't know it too well himself.) There will be no trouble about it. *El capitán* will gladly accompany us, you can be sure of that. Gladly! But before we talk of these things further, we must join him in another small drink of the local rum. He will not accept a refusal. It is not so bad, this *ron,* quite good, in fact.

Growing a little doubtful of the ability of our navy friend, I had no choice but to sip a second go-'round of the local product and assume a philosophical point of view. I knew there was no hurrying these good people, and it is always necessary to see these little social amenities through to the end. However, there was, it seemed, another problem. The captain turned his mouth down at the corners. His eyes grew round with the enormity of it. Just that morning a message had come by radio from his superiors in Santiago de Cuba. Here! this is the very copy (handing me a half sheet of brown paper on which several lines were typed in Spanish). There! It is signed by the *comandante*, it is *oficial* and very *secreto*. No one must know of this or all will be lost. *El capitán* became so excited at the possibilities that he ran on in unmitigated Spanish, waving his arms and glaring wildly around the room. For the next five minutes or so he and Arturo talked back and forth at a furious tempo. I caught very few words and no sense whatever. Abruptly Arturo raised his hand to me, as a signal, and said, "Le's go!" (Arturo is vain about his American idioms, using them at every opportunity.) "But Arturo," I protested, "what's this all about? What about our plans?" "Never fear, we will talk of plans," he replied darkly, and with scarcely a nod to *el capitán*, who was pulling violently at the handle of his desk drawer again, we went out into the brilliant sunshine of the street.

I think that all Cubans must love dramatic overtones and revel morosely in an atmosphere of conspiracy. If possible, they will squeeze histrionics from even the most commonplace incident. Given the makings of real drama they really overplay it, or so it impresses a mere Anglo-Saxon. Arturo was simply brimming with excitement, but his love of the theatrical was so intense that he couldn't get an intelligible word out. He kept looking to right and left, shaking his head, pursing his lips and putting his finger to them for silence, until I had just about decided it really was a secret. Then, in a torrent of words, half of them Spanish, it came tumbling out. Apparently the authorities had been warned that an attempt would be made to land contraband arms from a boat that would come inshore in the vicinity of Niquero, a village some 50 kilometers to the south. *El capitán* had been instructed to prevent such a landing at all costs, and to apprehend the contraband crew, if possible. Great haste must be made, as I would readily understand, and secrecy was of the utmost importance. These enemies of the government were probably Communists seeking to start a revolution among the cane laborers, or something equally frightful. There were fellow Communists in every *cantina* and on every other park bench in the plaza. We must be very careful. "But Arturo," I protested, "what has this to do with us? We are not going after *el capitán's* gun runners!" Arturo looked at me with a great show of surprise, and perhaps a dash of pity at my naïveté. "But we are!" he announced. "I told him we could not go up the river after flamingos without him, and it is obvious that he cannot go with us until these bandits of contrabanders are caught, so we must go with him, of course. It is only being polite to do so. It would have been very inconsiderate if we did not offer to help him with the contrabanders, when he, *el capitán* himself, has offered to help us with the flamingos!" Although I found the logic of this rather heavy going, I saw nothing to be gained by not falling in with it. After all, with Arturo and *el capitán* both occupied with gun runners, I would only be cooling my heels until they returned anyway. So I said that it was agreeable with me. We would go to Niquero. "But not until tomorrow," Arturo hastened to say. "We must find transportation, and mañana will be time enough."

Back at El Gran Hotel Inglaterra, I struggled with the typewritten menu, fought off the flies and mosquitoes that swarmed in the dining room and, at length, under a copious *mosquitero*, fell asleep, still a trifle uneasy at the unexpected turn of events. Gun runners! I was interested solely in flamingos, but this was Cuba, and I should have known that gun runners would always come first.

That overland journey to Niquero was something that could happen only in Cuba. Arturo, who was a shoe salesman when not looking for flamingos or contrabanders, had found a fellow drummer, a pleasant and quite handsome young man by the name of Aurencio. Aurencio had an old Ford car; he was driving to Niquero in any event, and he would be delighted to have us as fellow travelers. After much talk, comfortably seated in rocking chairs in the open lobby of the Inglaterra, we were joined by Arturo's brother, a big, brawny individual named Carlos, engineer on a small coaster that traded with ports in Hispaniola and Central America. All five of us then piled into the Ford and, with a troop of ragged bootblacks and stray dogs yapping in our wake, we were off.

A party of *viajeros* setting out from a small Cuban town and heading off along a dusty road that can lead nowhere but a dead end down the coast, is evidently quite an event. We reached the open fields on the edge of town, where there were only scattered huts, and the ground was stripped clean by hundreds of goats, and people stopped to stare openmouthed. We tooted our horn, bouncing over the rough trail in reckless abandon, and waved joyously to each and every citizen. Most of them waved back, shouting something cheerful, or shaking their fists in some cases. Arturo told me sagely that some of the shouts were "sort of jokes," others were blessings, and a few were curses. "We have all kinds of people in Cuba," he explained.

On the coastal road to Niquero there are four or five large sugar mills, each with a little town clustered about it. The cane is raised in the hills farther inland, cut by hand, loaded on great oxcarts, and laboriously hauled in to the narrow-gauge railway. Transferred to the little flatcars, it is then carried by rail to the mills. Our experience at the first mill was repeated at each one we reached. In every village our host, Aurencio, had business of his own, and a brief stop had to be made on that account. However, before business came the social courtesies, the salaams, kowtows, loving cups, and Latin embraces. The potentate of each village was, of course, the manager of the sugar mill, and we called on each of them immediately upon arrival. Most of the mills are located on an eminence high above the sea, and swept by cooling breezes. The Ford worked its way to the top, bounced to a stop in front of the main office, and, with the gay informality that appeared to be the tone of our expedition, we marched into the potentate's presence. *El capitán*, as an august official and representative of the government, was pushed forward as exhibit number one. He had assumed a genial dignity, with just a touch of the grim purposefulness that was appropriate to both his rank and the seriousness of his mission. I, as a visiting *Americano*, was exhibit number two. There was always a little joke about Americans not speaking anything but American, but everyone was very jolly and polite. Regardless of the hour, drinks were served, not a local rum on these occasions, but an imported cognac, in thick little glasses from the manager's desk—glasses that were probably never washed, from the looks of them. After which we trooped out again, waited in the shade while Aurencio concluded his business at the company store and in a shop or two in the town, and then we were once more on the open road.

Late in the afternoon, after a series of social calls on a series of sugar-mill potentates, we came bumping and bouncing into the muddy little coastal town of Niquero. The first thing was to stop at the Hotel Sixto, which seemed to be the social, governmental, and business center of the community, arrange for rooms, and shake hands solemnly with the manager of the local sugar mill (who was holding court from a high stool in the bar), the mayor, the justice, the chief of police, the entire navy personnel (one man), and other dignitaries. By the time this was accomplished it was getting dark, and *el capitán*, who had fallen in with a lot of old cronies, was telling everyone about the contrabanders, warning them in a loud and dramatic whisper that it was a great secret and that they mustn't breathe a word of it to anyone.

In the midst of this opéra bouffe, in came Arturo's father-in-law, who is a planter with a couple of thousand acres of sugar cane up in the hills. He immediately invited our entire party to his place for supper and we were soon in the car again, following the señor's truck up a narrow and rapidly climbing trail that would have been difficult for a jackass to navigate. After bogging down in a mudhole and getting splattered from head to foot moving the Ford out of it, we arrived at the *hacienda*, where we were served a splendid supper.

As it was growing late and we were some distance from our rooms at the Sixto, Arturo proposed we go back to Niquero and take our rest. I was more than ready, by this time, but *el capitán*, who was enjoying himself hugely, saw no reason for undue haste. "Tomorrow," he said profoundly, smiling broadly and holding out his empty glass, "is tomorrow."

At length we made the journey downgrade to the town, where Aurencio and his brother left us, and we then prepared for bed. Through the local *marinero* we had arranged with a fishing-boat captain, who was being hired for the occasion, to meet us on the beach at four o'clock, and it was high time we turned in. However, *el capitán* had found his chums again and they were having a great old time of it in the bar. Arturo and I borrowed an alarm clock from Señor Sixto and, setting it for three-thirty, went to our room. In my experience all small Cuban towns take a long time to close down for the night, and Niquero was no exception. We turned out our light and lay there in the stuffy, windowless cubicle, trying to sleep. The shouts and bursts of song from the bar seemed almost in the next room, and, indeed, there were only half walls, the space beneath the ceiling being open all around to permit the hot, sticky air to circulate. Unfortunately, the noises circulated also, the inmates of other rooms moving about, talking, coughing, and raising the devil in general. Smoke from strong Cuban cigarettes and cigars drifted in clouds against the ceiling. Automobiles tore through the streets outside, racing their engines and sounding their horns as if it were high noon instead of midnight. Indeed, at high noon all of these carousers had been sound asleep, which probably accounted for their unrestrained gaiety at this ungodly hour.

When the alarm clock went off before dawn, I found the bare light bulb, turned it on, and sat for a moment, blinded by the glare and listening to the comparative quiet of the slumbering Sixto. The chorus of snores that I heard was impressive in its range and variety, and, after the uproar of the night before, relatively tranquil. Arturo roused himself with difficulty, but as soon as he was out of bed he went down the hall to get the captain on his feet. After an interval, they appeared in the blackness of the hall and beckoned me silently to follow them outside. It seemed that we were conspirators again!

The *marinero* lived with his wife, one parrot, and a small radio in a thatch-roofed house near the beach. We found him standing in the doorway in his navy uniform, a .45 automatic in a holster on his hip, and a flashlight in one hand. Without words we trudged on, beneath rows of coconut palms that cast long, confused shadows, until we found ourselves in the soft sand of the beach. There we were met by our fisherman, who, having had a full night's sleep, was all ready to be on his way. *El capitán,* on the other hand, was not feeling too spry, and both Arturo and I could have done with a little more sleep. So, when *el capitán* asked his subordinate if we might not return to his home for coffee, ere embarking on our perilous adventure, we were not unwilling. Of course the *marinero* agreed cheerfully to haul his wife out of bed again and have her make us some coffee.

We entered the thatched-roof house and settled ourselves in chairs in the living room, which had a wood floor, although the floors in the bedroom and kitchen were of the original earth. *Señora marinero* appeared, very pleasant and attractive, and there was then a great deal of banging about of pots and pans in the kitchen. While we were waiting, greatly subdued, *el capitán* sat with closed eyes, the corners of his mouth drawn down around his sharp little chin, a picture of weariness and dejection. Arturo asked him if he was asleep. "No," said the captain, "not asleep. My eyes are closed for looking inside." Arturo then asked, "And you don't like what you see?" The little man grinned wryly. "I am supposed to be seeing red," he murmured, "but I see nothing but black—black coffee!"

That coffee did wonders, and by the time we had also partaken of the hot milk and cocoa that followed, along with two large rolls of crusty Cuban bread, we were ready for the contrabanders.

It was breaking day when we boarded the fishing boat, a narrow-beamed little launch with an ancient 8-h.p. gasoline engine. Having found ourselves places in the cockpit, we watched the fisherman struggle patiently with the huge flywheel until, after some delay, he had it turning over reluctantly. There were no gears and we leaped ahead at once, narrowly missing a small sloop anchored nearby. With the rhythmic chug-chug of the engine in our ears, and a few last stars twinkling overhead, we crossed the harbor and headed into the Golfo de Guacanayabo. Our adventure had now really begun.

At dawn the breeze was from the east, off the cane hills and the rugged slopes of Sierra Maestra. There was a little sea running and the breeze appeared to be picking up. In the gray light all faces, except that of the ruddy fisherman, looked peaked and unhappy, especially that of *el capitán*. Not a word was spoken. What a contrast, I thought, with last night! But then, that was *bromista,* fun and frolic, while this was the serious business of life. The most serious. Naturally, there is a difference in one's deportment.

With sunup, the breeze increased and we were dipping our narrow bow under. Spray was coming aboard with every pitch and once a few tubfuls of cold green water. Drenched to his hide but still every inch a captain chasing contrabanders, our commander gruffly ordered the craft's speed reduced. We now wallowed along at an erratic 4 knots, the coast dropping out of sight and only a broad expanse of sea and a few distant *cayos* to be seen. The *marinero,* meanwhile, had loosened the flap of his holster (he was the only man aboard who was armed with anything more dangerous than a fountain pen), and was anxiously scanning the horizon. He had an old pair of low-power glasses on a string around his neck and every now and then he would sweep the rim of the sea with them. They were nothing more than opera glasses and he couldn't have seen much through them, the boat pitching and rolling as she was, but he stuck at it, as determined as Drake before Cadiz.

The fisherman, who knew what we were looking for, of course, and who seemed to have become infected with the excitement of the chase, sang out all of a sudden and pointed off across the water. The *marinero* stuck his glasses to his head, Arturo opened his eyes and looked about him, and *el capitán,* rousing himself with an effort, stood in the swaying craft as if coming to attention before the admiral. "*Barca! Barca!*" the fisherman was yelling. Everyone began shouting questions at the *marinero,* who kept on looking. I had a good pair of navy-style binoculars with me, expressly for magnifying the image of any flamingos I came across, but if this was a contraband vessel I might as well magnify its image too. So I got them out and looked carefully at the object that could be dimly seen off the starboard bow. "Why," I said, lowering the glasses and offering them to the captain, "no *barca*, no *barca* at all; it's only a great dead tree come aground on that mudbank there." We were approaching one of the *cayos* that abound in the gulf, and at its southerly end there was a long, narrow bank of sand and mud. The object that was causing so much shouting appeared to me to be a huge dead tree that must have floated down the Río Cauto at flood time, and been cast up on this bank by the tides. It was some distance off the *cayo* and, I must admit, did look just the least bit like a small, two-masted schooner under bare poles. The captain blinked and winked his red-rimmed eyes and then fixed them at the optic end of the binoculars. At the same time, the *marinero*, his *pistola* in one hand, was shouting to the boatman to speed up his engine. Regular fire-eater. *El capitán* kept on looking, shaking all over with excitement or chill or a sudden fit of ague and saying nothing. Finally Arturo, unable to endure any more of this inconclusiveness, took the binoculars away from the captain, who probably couldn't see anything through them but water anyway, and had a long look. "I don' know! I don' know!" he kept saying. The boat was now speeded up to its full 6 knots and as the fisherman had altered the course, so as to head straight for the *barca*, we careened wildly in the trough, shipping water and getting soaking wet all over again. After a few more minutes of this, with the *marinero* standing forward by the stubby mast, where each sea that broke over the bow soon had him nearly drowned, the salt water running down the barrel of his gun in a stream, we were close enough to see that it was nothing but a harmless tree, even without benefit of binoculars.

The *marinero* registered utter disgust. He was so undone that he even forgot to put his weapon away, but just slumped down where he was, next to the mast, the gun in his hand, and stared moodily at the deck. *El capitán*, while still saying nothing, the wise old fellow, was obviously relieved and unable to restrain a deep sigh of thankfulness. The slow-witted fisherman, bringing his craft around just in time to avoid crashing headlong onto the bank, slowed the engine and asked the captain, in a plaintive voice, where he should steer now. *El capitán*, in high good spirits once more, waved his hand vaguely toward the open gulf and said that anywhere out there would do. Anywhere at all.

When we had come around the end of the bank into deeper water the sea was considerably rougher, and even at slow speed we were pitching about most uncomfortably and getting wetter and colder by the minute. *El capitán* began looking off this way and then that way, fidgeting and turning himself clockwise and counterclockwise like some kind of mechanical toy on a spring. I saw what was on his mind and was not the least surprised when he proposed that we turn back. "In weather like this," he said, "no contrabander would dare come near to the coast."

So we were soon once more in Niquero, and, before *el capitán* could find his cronies again, Arturo located another car that was heading back the way we had come. Two pesos each was this chap's fare, and although there was quite a wrangle over this, we paid it and I, for one, felt that it was well worth it. In spite of the dust and the heat we slept all the way back—50 kilometers and not a stop. After a rousing adventure such as we had been through we needed sleep. Especially *el capitán!*

Although the difficulties of ornithological investigation in a gay and freedom-loving country like Cuba were becoming painfully apparent to me, I did not lose heart. There still being no boat available for a trip into the Cauto Delta, I joined my imperturbable friend Arturo on an expedition to Puerto Padre on the north coast. It was generally known, said he, that flamingos nest near that place. We took a train from Manzanillo to Bayamo and then went on by auto to Puerto Padre, arriving in the early afternoon on the nineteenth of August. Then began the business of arranging to go in search of flamingos, a process that involved, among other things, lengthy discussions with nearly everyone in town. Between these energetic conferences we sat in the hallway of Arturo's uncle's house while various friends and members of the family trooped in and out, remaining just long enough to stare openly at me with what appeared to be morbid fascination. They had never seen a flesh-and-blood American before!

It was finally decided to take a large truck belonging to Arturo's uncle and drive to Jeibara, a fishing and salt-raking village on the shore of Bahía Malajeta. From there, I was told, we could reach the flamingos by boat. Everyone of any importance in the town agreed with this, and I need have no fear, we could find them. Everyone was exceedingly optimistic about it. Next day we made an early start. The truck driver was a gay blade whose weakness for the local version of *aguardiente* I was to learn of later. In addition to Arturo and myself, there was the uncle, Señor Antonio, and a local fisherman and self-styled *flamenco* expert, who had been thrust upon us to serve as guide. His name was Nicolas and he was so shifty-eyed and evil-looking that I had grave misgivings about him from the first. He looked exactly like a paid assassin in a Sicilian melodrama. However, I quite naturally kept these thoughts to myself.

Jeibara was enchanting. There is an extensive beach of hard sand and the shallow waters of Bahía Malajeta are an unbelievable shade of green. On the edge of the beach several thatch huts had been built, and a stout and very pleasant gentleman named Felipe, who seemed to be the head man of the place, told us to move in. There was no bedding, or even a bunk of any sort, but Felipe gave us some old gunny sacking and with this we made passable hammocks. As suppertime was drawing near a spry little man, bare of head and of foot, came to our door and asked cheerfully if we wanted a cook. What pay would he expect? "Oh, fiddledeedee!" said he, or an expression to that effect in Spanish. "Money is no good, I will work for two bottles of *aguardiente* a day." One the first thing in the morning, and the second exactly at sunset. I turned to Arturo, and in his usual way he shrugged, pursed his lips, and elevated his expressive eyebrows. Meaning, why not? Or, what can we lose? So the sunset bottle was found (it was amazing how readily those bottles of *aguardiente* appeared), and within an hour we sat down to a fine supper of beans and rice, canned meat, fried bananas, and black Cuban coffee.

The next day it was arranged that we should begin our explorations. In a leaky boat, pushed indifferently along by an ancient 2½-h.p. outboard, we beat our way across the bay, passing ten forlorn-looking flamingos on a sandbar. On the far side we began walking in search of a salina where it was believed the flamingos might have nested. The ground was well elevated and grown to buttonwood (*Conocarpus*), with many wild orchids that appeared to belong to the genus *Epidendrum*. In an open place we came upon three boys, charcoal burners by trade, dipping water from a stinking mudhole among some exposed rocks. They told us that two months before, in mid-June, there had been *muchos flamencos* in the salina nearby. Apparently they were preparing to nest, but some men came with guns and shot several birds. After which the flock left and did not return.

Later in the day, back at Jeibara, we had scarcely stepped out of our boat when another craft arrived. There were three men on board and they had a dead flamingo lying in the bow. It seems that they were salt rakers, and today, having nothing to do, they had gone *caimán* hunting. But their luck was very bad and all they had shot was this one *mucho delgado* creature. It would hardly make a meal for the three of them. Nevertheless, it was quickly skinned, cleaned, and thrown into a pot. As I sat around the fire sharing Felipe's excellent coffee and strong Cuban *cigarros* —I staunchly refused to taste the flamingo—I could hear the ever-present mongrel dogs growling over the severed head and feet of the poor bird. And this was taking place within the boundaries of the National Flamingo Refuge, established some years before by presidential decree!

We later visited the Laguna de Amarillo, so named, no doubt, from the heavy growth of algae, and which Arturo and I finally located after our so-called "guide," Nicolas, had become completely lost. We saw nothing to indicate that flamingos had been there within recent weeks. Next day, leaving the perfectly useless Nicolas behind, we went by boat to the region around Covarrubia, a fishing settlement. There we talked with a number of rough-looking characters and they had the usual report of many flamingos earlier in the season, but all had moved on. As we were talking I noted a severed flamingo head and a partial skin among the debris on the beach.

Back at camp we found that the rest of our party, with all day to themselves, had decided to make the most of their opportunities. Our cook lay stretched out full length on the beach, his bare feet in the surf and an empty *aguardiente* bottle clasped to his bosom. He was out like a light. In the shade of the truck lay our driver, in like condition. And when the horrified Arturo located Nicolas he found him asleep in our quarters, surrounded by empty fruit-juice cans. He had consumed our entire stock! Of the three culprits only Nicolas was sober, so Arturo descended on him with enough wrath for all of them. "I told him," he advised me, "that his father must have been a *caimán* and his mother an *aura*." Apparently the unfortunate Nicolas objected strongly to these insults, for who could be proud of an ancestry that combined the unattractive qualities of a crocodile and a vulture!

The night that followed I shall never forget. Señora Felipe stepped into the breech and treated us to supper (the errant cook, it turned out, was her brother), and after our usual coffee around the open fire we climbed into our improvised hammocks. It was a still night and the mosquitoes and sandflies were worse than ever. In the thatch over our heads crabs moved about, rustling the dry fronds and dropping things on our faces. Finally, worn out from our long day in the sun, I fell asleep. Sometime after midnight I was awakened by blood-chilling shouts. There was no light but I could sense that on the dirt floor next to me two figures were thrashing around as if locked in a death struggle. Then Felipe and the cook, the latter now more or less sobered, came dashing in with a lantern. In the dim light we saw that Nicolas lay on the floor with Arturo holding him by the throat. Near them lay a thin-bladed knife.

It was some minutes before anyone could calm down sufficiently to tell me what was being said. It seemed that Nicolas had brooded over the names that Arturo had applied to his progenitors and had decided to slit Arturo's throat. Fortunately, Arturo was only half asleep and when Nicolas had made his lunge he had caught the fellow's arm and twisted the weapon from his grasp.

For safety's sake we trussed up the glaring Nicolas and laid him away in a corner, while the cook made us some coffee. And there we sat, for all the world, as I thought to myself, like a company of good-natured pirates, fighting off the mosquitoes, gulping our coffee, and harking to the cook as he recited patriotic Cuban poetry. At least that's what Arturo said it was. I only know that it was undeniably dramatic and the cook, who must have had another bottle stashed away somewhere, rose to heights of superb eloquence, bringing tears to the eyes of everyone and loud shouts of *viva* from all throats. The dawn came quickly.

After breakfast Nicolas was turned loose, without ill feelings, and we all boarded the truck and returned to Puerto Padre. Once again I had found no flamingo colony, but I felt that I had learned at first hand some of the reasons why there was none to be found. A refuge cannot exist without the support of government, or without the basic and essential bulwark of favorable public opinion. In Cuba these things seem very far away. Nevertheless, there is still hope. The people of Cuba are resourceful, energetic, and extremely conscious of the beauty of their land. The educational and social improvements now taking place may well turn the scales in the right direction, and in time to save the great natural beauties of this lovely island, truly the Pearl of the Antilles.

*. . . It is possible—yes it is probable—that the United States might run Cuba much better. As I get older, however, I become more and more convinced that good government is not a substitute for self-government.*

DWIGHT MORROW

# XI : Trouble in paradise

The delta of the Río Cauto was still a definite possibility. In March of 1952 I returned to Cuba and again turned myself over to the uncertain hospitality of El Gran Hotel Inglaterra. But not for long. My friend Arturo, remembering the disappointments of my previous visit, wasted no time in taking me to the waterfront shack where dwelt the latest *flamenco* expert, a shrimp fisherman who knew all things about the Cauto Delta and what went on there. Or so he said.

His name was Julio. He claimed he could take us to a place where *los flamencos* nested. Oh yes, no doubt of it at all. *Muchos flamencos!* He leaned over and made patting and slapping motions with his hands to show us how the mud-nest mounds of the flamingo were made. Beside him a tattered Cuban fighting cock strained to the full length of its tether and laid its head on one side, watching his hands. Julio's watery eyes, meanwhile, were watching me and greedily trying to guess how many pesos I should pay for the use of his boat. In the doorway the oldest son—or nephew, I never knew which—Rafael, who looked as if he might have been part Chinese, watched diffidently, picking his strong teeth with a splinter of wood. I never saw Rafael smile. In the sleeping room, to one side, several smaller children of assorted sizes also watched, the older ones perhaps wondering if old Julio would buy them some candy if the *Americano* gave him pesos for the use of his boat. Three of them had certainly had a Negro mother. I asked Arturo if he thought Julio's price was too steep. Arturo raised his brows, pursed his lips, shrugged expressively, and spread his hands. "I do not theenk so," he said at length.

So it was agreed that we would meet the following night exactly at midnight, and set forth then on account of the favorable tide. Julio was paid a small advance, and a few pesos extra for gasoline, and shaking hands all around, we walked back to the town.

The next night, loaded down with groceries, we met on the long stone quay that juts out into deep water on one side of the harbor. The boat was a sorry affair, but had been the only one available. It was an open launch, sixteen feet over-all, and the heavy-duty engine occupied at least a quarter of the space inside. Added to that it smelled strongly of dead fish, mixed with oil, grease, and raw gasoline. A pile of dirty nets cluttered the forward half, and with boxes of grub, two large water tins, odd jugs and bottles, and a half drum of gasoline in the after portion, there was scant room for the crew and passengers. It was a still night, with a bland three-quarter moon. We sat down on the stones of the quay and tied handkerchiefs around our faces to keep from breathing mosquitoes into our noses and mouths, flailing our arms about like men trying to keep warm. At length Julio was ready to go, so we went aboard, Arturo and I first and then Rafael, who was the *ingeniero*, followed by three other fishermen who were going as far as Maboa, the first fishing village up the coast. It made quite a load, and once under way our freeboard was next to nothing. Clear of the harbor, and with the mosquitoes behind us, Arturo and I stretched out and napped by fits and starts. It was a wet journey.

Two hours later, the boat stopped off a dark shore that was barely discernible in the blackness. Then a dog began barking, and next thing a dim light appeared. There were shouts and sleepy replies, and Rafael and another younger man among the fishermen aboard stripped off their clothes and went overboard, shoving and pushing our heavy boat as far toward the beach as it would go. With that they waded on ashore, disappearing in the darkness. Shortly we heard them sliding a light canoe across the mud and shoving it into the shallow water between us and the shore. In this we were transported to the beach.

There was a little cluster of thatch huts, the roofs made of palmetto fronds, the walls of the tough sheets of fiber that are stripped from coconut trees. In one of these, which had an open front and served as a cookhouse, several figures were gathered. When all the gear and supplies had been ferried ashore, Julio built a fire on the sand floor of a raised platform against the wall, and while water was coming to a boil in a large tin can, he set up a soiled, cone-shaped drip bag for making the excellent Cuban coffee. The mosquitoes were as bad as usual and I stood as close to the fire as I could get, for they were less troublesome there. The fishermen crowded around, but chiefly out of curiosity. They had seen very few *Americanos* and stared at me with considerable interest. They were all squat little fellows and strange-appearing, for there is a good deal of Chinese blood in that part of Cuba. Although I am of medium height, I towered over them, and one old man with a cheerful, wrinkled face, scraggly beard, and lank white hair, remarked that all *Americanos* must be *alto*. I explained that where I came from I was—what was the word for short?—*corto*. This brought forth many exclamations, and much discussion followed. There were ten natives present, and eight of them (all except Rafael, who always stood aside, and Julio, who was busy making coffee) lined up, shoulder to shoulder, to see who was the tallest. This one was then shoved forward and stood next to me. The top of his head barely passed my shoulder. More exclamations! By this time the coffee was ready, and when we had finished it, Julio took us to another hut next door where we were all to sleep. We lay down on mats on the ground, just as we were, in our clothes, and Julio fixed patched-up *mosquiteros* over us. As a result of this protection we slept soundly until sunup.

The Río Cauto (*cauto* means "cautious") is the longest river in Cuba. It rises to the north of Santiago de Cuba and follows a winding course northward and then west, for about 150 miles, flowing into the Golfo de Guacanayabo northwest of the seaport of Manzanillo. It is the delta that is especially interesting to an ornithologist. Some 25 kilometers in breadth where it meets the gulf, the delta is bordered by dense mangroves to the south, and wide mud flats and salinas to the north. On our first morning with Julio it was evidently his plan to take the boat up one of the several fingers of the delta, Río Jutia, thence by *piragua* up the smaller Gutta Jutia and from the head of that, on foot, to the large salina where he said the flamingos had nested. I say "evidently" because Julio's plan was always a trifle uncertain and, since he spoke not one word of English, I was never too sure of his intentions, even with the advantage of Arturo's free translation. In fact, Arturo admitted later on, in a moment of confidence, that he too found the old man's mental processes somewhat vague, if not just plain downright irresponsible. Or words to that effect in the Spanish manner of expression.

So we chug-chugged up the coast and into mangrove-lined bays and channels, routing out sizable flocks of white ibises, which the Cubans called *coco blanco,* and troops of cormorants and water turkeys. Their name for the cormorant is *corua,* and for the water turkey, *corua real,* intimating, perhaps, that the cormorant is a fake, an imposter, while the water turkey is the real cormorant. This was especially interesting to me since I had run into a somewhat similar distinction among the Eskimos several years before, when Bob Smith and I were counting waterfowl along the Arctic coast. The Eskimo's name for the Canada goose is *ulualik neglek* —"the goose with the cheeks"—but the black brant of that same region is called *neglekenak,* which means "the *real* neglek"! To pass the time of day, I tried to get Julio's opinion on the distinction between the cormorant and water turkey, but he didn't seem to understand. Arturo became interested, being fascinated with the strange behavior of the *corua reales* anyway, and I explained to him that we have several names for this particular bird, which also occurs in the southeastern United States. Besides water turkey, which stems from the appearance of the tail, there is snakebird, from the long reptilianlike neck and its habit of slithering through the water with only its head and slender neck protruding. Then, of course, there is the scientific name, understood by ornithologists of whatever tongue. This is *Anhinga anhinga*, from which we also obtain yet another common name, anhinga.

Arturo was now laughing uproariously, and it was not so much at the thought of this, to his mind, silly-looking bird having so many names, this bird with his nose stuck out of the water and his suspicious eyes, as it was the unexplainable appropriateness of *Anhinga anhinga*. Between laughs he kept saying the words over and over again, "anhinga-anhinga, anhinga-anhinga"—although, as he pronounced them, it sounded like "anheenga-anheenga." We all had a good laugh, funny or not, even Julio joining in and Rafael coming as close to a smile as he did the entire trip.

In a short while we were aground and had to transfer to the *piragua*, leaving aboard only Celedonio, a Negro boy who had become a member of our expedition in some inexplicable way. Celedonio was a mute and was supposed to be *loco*, in a mild sort of way, but actually he proved more willing than the others, and very helpful at certain tasks. For an hour we paddled up a narrow mangrove creek, the Gutta Jutia, collecting little tree-climbing periwinkles and coffee-bean shells from the branches overhead. Then, even our canoe could go no farther. Julio made it clear that Arturo and I should stay where we were, while he and Rafael went off through the mangroves looking for the salina. We fought mosquitoes for an hour, and finally the two explorers returned, looking very hot, and confessing that they had been unable to find their way. It later turned out that we had paddled up the wrong creek! To cheer, or possibly to deceive me, they had a few cast feathers of the roseate spoonbill, the *sevilla* of that region, that they had picked up, and I believe that Julio's first intent was to pass them off as flamingo feathers. However, without thinking, I had said "*Sevilla!*" upon seeing them in his hand, so he had laid them carefully in the boat without comment.

As we started back down the *gutta* I had my first really serious misgivings regarding Julio.

Back aboard the launch we set off on a hot and frustrating afternoon of aimless wandering. The tide was running out, and the farther upstream we pushed the less water we had under our keel. We wandered into the Río Jucaro, but were soon aground. The two youngsters pulled off their clothes and hopped naked into the mud, waist-deep. To lighten the load, Arturo and I clambered aboard the *piragua* and paddled about, searching for a channel. Old Julio was now overboard too, heaving and sweating. Late in the day we reached a great open place in the river, with high cut-banks to one side. The ground above the banks looked firm and dry, and it was proposed that we camp there for the night. All hands were more than agreeable, so we ran the launch ashore and carried our cooking gear to the top of the bank.

The place was known as "the Canes" (*Las Canas*), and had for some time past been used as a pit by charcoal burners. There was also an old, long-abandoned cane patch, but the site was dominated by a great blackened area where many tons of charcoal had been burned. Julio had a fire going at once, right in the middle of the pit, where there was a plentiful supply of first-rate fuel, and Rafael set to work preparing an excellent supper of fish and rice, boiled together in a big iron pot, with chopped onions and green peppers that I had brought from town thrown in. As we were sitting down on the blackened ground to eat, it started to rain.

There were no tents, tarpaulins, or blankets, and none of us had even so much as a jacket with us. For more than an hour it blew and rained very hard, a regular sea squall, and we could only huddle by the remains of the fire and wait it out. When the sky cleared it was quite dark, and the rising wind was cold. Julio, a sorry sight like the rest of us, built up the fire, and shortly, with the wind to help, had a nice glowing bed of charcoal. I reminded Arturo that Julio had told us to bring no equipment with us, that everything would be provided. Arturo looked sheepish and said, "Our idea of equipment and Julio's mus' be two deefferent theengs." I agreed.

The night was very cold. We lay down on the damp charcoal, as close to the fire as we could crowd, and dozed off and on until just before dawn. With hot coffee we then began another uncertain day. Some charcoal burners that came along now advised us that a large flock of *flamencos* was feeding near Cayo Norte, less than two hours "over that way." We got aboard the boat and started off, not at all sure if Julio knew where Cayo Norte was or not. But he found it, after ambling up several blind alleys, and soon we saw a long line of red against the opposite shore. Julio was so pleased he was nearly in tears. I don't believe he had honestly expected to find any flamingos at all, but here they were! I could see that they were not a nesting group but merely a feeding flock, and the first job was to get a rough count. By stopping the boat alongside the mangroves at one end of Cayo Norte, we were as near as we could get to them without having them fly. I asked Arturo how many flamingos there were in the flock. He was quite excited and said at once, "Oh, there mus' be thousands!" Julio was unwilling to guess, but the usually reticent Rafael also thought there must be thousands. They were scattered in a long line that made an approximate count relatively easy. I counted down the line with my binoculars, twice, and finally hit on a total that seemed reasonably accurate: 610. Large, brilliantly colored birds often appear more numerous than they are actually. However, my companions regarded me doubtfully, suspecting, perhaps, that I couldn't count very well.

After meeting a group of fishermen, from whom we bought a fine mess of freshly caught shrimp, besides getting fresh directions, we wended our way back into the main channel of Río Jacaro again and at length, about 1:30 P.M., discovered ourselves at the mouth of Gutta Nueces. We were back on the track once more! One of the shrimpers had told us that it was too dry to expect our birds to be nesting in the salinas now (it was early March), but that a good rain and high water in the main river would make conditions right. Near the head of the creek we left our launch and paddled up a narrow, ditchlike stream to the very rim of the big Nuecas Salina. Julio reiterated his claim that this was the place where he had seen old nest mounds. It was a broad V-shaped salt flat, now dry and the entire surface cracked open by the sun, so that it was criss-crossed with little wrinkles and miniature ravines, an endless pattern of tiny chasms and gulleys. We had come into it near the head of one of the long arms so that the lower end or tip of this inverted V lay away from us at some distance. Julio pointed off that way and all four of us started walking. Apparently neither Julio or Rafael were used to this kind of cross-country romp, and they soon fell far to the rear. The sun was blazing down and reflecting mercilessly from the surface of the salina, where a dull white crust of salt still clung. We made the turn at the tip of the V and trudged on, the other arm of the flat stretching before us like a desert. Halfway down we waited for our exhausted guides, and then kept pace with them for the next mile or so. This brought us to an irregular shoreline of the salina, with a background of dead trees, killed by repeated doses of salt water, their bare trunks white against the coppery sky. Here, Julio began talking rapidly in Spanish and gesticulating. Arturo turned to me with a weary but triumphant grin and said, "Over there are the old nes' moun's!" I could see nothing, but walked on to where Julio was pointing. The dry bed of the salina was heaped and mottled with hundreds of low circular mounds. I could see at once that they were merely the heaps of mud that remain after flamingos have fed, as they often do, by dancing around and around in one spot, their feet digging a regular trench on the outside of the circle and their bills, on which they pivot, working the mud in the center until it is heaped into a low mound. The French call these *ronds* or *cones alimentaires*. I looked at Julio and shook my head. His watery eyes were watching me and showed at once that he understood, but I could not decide if he had really thought these were old nests or if it had been a case of deliberate deception. In any event, our long trip had been for naught and I was feeling somewhat let down. I could have cheerfully booted old Julio where his ragged pants had the most patches, but it would have done nothing to improve our circumstances.

After another couple of days exploring other parts of the delta, without learning anything conclusive about the nesting place of the flamingos, we went on back to town. As our little craft nosed up to the same stone quay from which we had set out, a man on the shore shouted something at us in an excited manner. Arturo shouted back and the man went on with a long, rapid account that included much arm-waving and other gestures of a dramatic nature. I had been in Cuba often enough to learn to keep my blood pressure down to normal in the face of the most violent goings-on, but this had all the earmarks of something really serious. Then Arturo, who had been listening openmouthed, turned to me with round eyes and said, in his inevitable idiomatic American, "There ees a revolution! Batista has seized the government in Habana an' the president has fled! We mus' get to town at once an' see wha's cooking!"

It was all too true. Shortly after we had set off for the Cauto, there had been a swift, almost bloodless military coup. President Prio was an exile in Mexico and General Batista, who had been one of several presidential candidates in the forthcoming elections, was in charge. We hurried through the town—where crowds were gathered uncertainly in the streets—I to my hotel and Arturo to his home.

After a hot bath and a change of clothes, I met Arturo again and we walked along to the plaza. Here excitement was at fever pitch. In the center of the plaza there is a large band-shell type of structure, fashioned in what I took to be an Arabic style, with a huge dome and long rows of Arabic symbols on the supporting columns. I suppose the significance of this is that the province is called Oriente. Two men were using it as a dais, making impassioned speeches to two different crowds, one on each side. Others moved through the crowds, giving out printed handbills. Arturo read them to me. They were signed by various political parties and called on all Cubans to rise and resist. The speakers on the dais were evidently saying much the same thing. Now and then there were cheers, but on the whole the crowd seemed dazed and uncertain. Police officers stood by, obviously apprehensive. On a side street a group of students was gathering, while a man in a black homburg hat perched precariously on a high iron fence and harangued them.

The tumult in the plaza was mounting rapidly, and an explosion of some sort seemed imminent. All at once, across the park, a different sound was heard, followed by a sudden hush that fell like a low whisper over the entire crowd. Then we could see that people were running headlong, and with strange, frightened expressions on their faces. Men stumbled and fell, tripping over one another or barging blindly into benches and shrubbery, and then leaping up and running again, some of them leaving hats or coats where they dropped them. In back of this suddenly terror-stricken crowd we could see the uniformed figures of troops on horseback, each swinging a bare saber or brandishing a service revolver. The Army had evidently decided to break up the demonstration before it got out of hand. Arturo and I, after one glance, scattered with the rest.

Later in the day I learned that the main airport at Havana, Rancho Boyeros, had been taken over by Batista's men and that all international flights were canceled. I could not leave the country. Neither was I able to get messages out. Banks were closed down, and most business places, excepting, of course, the bars. In one of them, over a cold bottle of *cerveza,* a citizen I had talked with before told me in halting English, "We are crushed by the fact that *this—this*—could happen again to Cuba." I asked what the local army garrison, the authorities in the town and the people themselves would do about it. My friends looked at me sadly. "*Nada!*" they said. "Everyone," Arturo added, "will be waiting and watching."

Later on, at the hotel, the manager, in some agitation, told me that a man had been there looking for me. The manager thought that he was "a kind of policeman." Feeling that his excitement was probably just Cuban love of dramatics, and that it was merely someone from the police wanting me to register as an alien, or something like that, I told him not to worry and went up to bed. But next morning Arturo was much concerned when he heard of it—on top of other rumors with which he was overflowing—and urged that I go with him to his father-in-law's sugar plantation down the coast (the one we had visited briefly before) and stay there until things simmered down. I had to pass the time somehow, so we clambered aboard a dusty and already overcrowded omnibus and made the long, hot journey south. No one stopped or questioned us.

I was now farther away from flamingos than ever, but there was nothing to do but make the best of it. The foothills of the Sierra Maestra in that region are cleared and planted in sugar cane. We passed several days wandering about the countryside, looking at birds and visiting little settlements in the hills, some of them quite primitive. The revolution and the unrest in the town seemed far away, and these hill people seemed almost wholly unconcerned. At one little place we were entertained by a family who operated a bakery. In a separate building there was a huge ancient brick-and-clay oven, and when we entered they were just pulling out great trays of gingerbread. One of the sons, a good-looking boy of ten or twelve, stacked the loaves into baskets that were slung on either side of a gentle little horse, and climbing onto the beast's rump, he then set off along the winding, hillside trails to sell the bread from village to village.

I was anxious to get on home. It had been my original plan to cover the bays and *cayos* along a portion of the north coast, as far as Cayo Romano, but the revolution seemed at that time an uncertain quantity, and I felt it would be wise to postpone any further searches along isolated fringes of the Cuban coast. So some days later, when word reached us that international flights had been resumed, I made my way by various stages to Camagüey and eventually found space on a flight to Miami.

It was more than a year later when I returned once more to Cuba. Conditions there were far from tranquil, but persistent rumors had been reaching me of a flamingo nesting place on one of the bays along the north coast—the region I had meant to visit the previous season—and, like Tartarin, the moment arrived when I had to go. By prior arrangement I was met by Erasmo, a Havana taxi driver who hailed from a village near the coast and who claimed to know exactly where the flamingos nested, a refrain that by now had a familiar and slightly unpleasant ring. Steve Briggs had met and talked with Erasmo entirely by chance, in front of the Hotel Nacional, and Erasmo had insisted that he knew whereof he spoke. As his information dovetailed rather well with other rumors, I found myself borne along with the tide.

My new friend was visiting his family in the vicinity, but on my arrival he gave himself entirely to the business of showing me the flamingo colony. Our first stop was a little place on the coast called Piloto, overlooking Bahía de Gloria. It is a cluster of thatched fishermen's huts around a larger edifice containing rooms and a large bar serving rum and beer. After we had unloaded our gear the first hitch occurred. The boat captain who was to meet us there, one Miguel, was still off in one of his boats and no one seemed to know when he would be back. Another boat, a large sloop, lay at anchor near the wharf, but her crew was also among the missing. Eventually, in midafternoon, two smiling Negro boys came in and were soon talking in animated fashion with Erasmo. It seemed that they were the crew of the sloop and Miguel had instructed them to carry on in his absence.

It was blowing briskly out of the east, the direction in which we must proceed, but without further loss of time we clambered aboard and set sail. Both Erasmo and Pupo, his son, immediately became seasick.

The two boys who made up the crew were known as "Monono" and "Vikini," and they were brothers. Erasmo told me very gravely that, "They are not exactly white but some kind of native. A little mixed up." As a matter of fact, both were quite black and kinky-haired. Erasmo then asked Monono, the elder, if he was a Cuban. To which Monono replied, very serious of mien, "Yes, I am a Cuban, but I don't know what my brother is." Erasmo translated this for my benefit and we laughed uproariously, both boys joining in, even if they didn't know what the joke was all about.

The sloop was named the *February 24th*, after one of Cuba's Independence Days. Twenty-five feet over-all, she was gaff-rigged and open-hulled, except for a tiny, unventilated cuddy in the bow where the boys slept. After beating to windward the rest of the day, we anchored on the far side of the bay, in the lee of Punta Robalo on Cayo Guajaba. There was a typical meal of beans and rice, sweet potatoes, fried bananas, and strong Cuban coffee, and feeling somewhat heavy amidships, we lay down on the greasy floorboards and prepared to sleep. The breeze continued, blowing away most of the mosquitoes, but the little vessel rolled and wallowed in the darkness and the floorboards grew harder with each passing hour. Pupo lost his supper after a little, but otherwise the night passed quietly.

Early the next morning we sighted our first flamingos, small groups of adults flying in swift-moving files toward Cayo Romano. There was a good breeze and we now set off on a new series of tacks, towards the ruins of Puerto Viaro, a little seaport long since deserted and fallen into decay as a result of the building of a railroad through from Morón to Nuevitas. Each time we came about, the boys, with much laughter at the way we all jumped, would shout their version of " 'Ware boom!" This was "*Cuidado con botabara!*" They gave loud emphatic emphasis to the last two syllables. Finally, off Mojarra Island we came up into the wind, dropped our sail, and Vikini threw the anchor overboard. We had arrived. From here, I was told, we could reach the flamingo colony by small boat. But all I saw was water and sunlit sky and mangrove. Not a flamingo in sight!

It was still early in the day, so Erasmo proposed that we eat before journeying into the swamp. Naturally, I agreed, for I wanted a contented boat crew if the going was to be as hot and uncomfortable as I expected it to be. A tarpaulin was stretched over the *botabara* and then, still in no hurry, we all piled into the small boat, equipped with a gill net, and pushed into the edge of the mangroves looking for fish. A number of fair-sized barracudas were seen but our only catch was a small mojarra. Back aboard, with the sun blazing down on us from directly overhead, we sat around beneath the tarpaulin while Erasmo prepared another rice-and-fried-banana meal, embellished with warm Cuban beer and *café solo*. Vikini played tuneless airs on a mouth organ and everyone talked and ate and talked, despite the heat.

At length, further delay being out of the question, we set off in the small boat and began a slow, hot, mosquito-plagued run into the swamp. I am sure that the almost total absence of flamingo flocks along the outer shore or flying back and forth overhead, as one would expect in the vicinity of an active colony, had

Erasmo worried, although he said nothing. But I sensed a reluctance on his part to move on into the swamp and settle the question.

As we wound through the narrow mangrove channels, with Monono picking the way with the unerring skill of long practice, all of us began to feel the rising exitement that always comes with the moment of actual arrival at a long-sought-after goal. I could feel it very strongly in my own case, for I had been searching for a Cuban flamingo colony for so long that its discovery now meant much more than it had at the outset. And in the faces of my companions I could see a similar fever, for this sort of thing is strangely contagious. But when we emerged from beneath the final canopy of mangroves and shoved our way out into the open desolation of the swamp proper, I could see at once that something was wrong. The swamp had once supported a heavy growth of black mangroves, but these had evidently been killed by repeated doses of salt water, possibly a result of a shift in the course of the nearby river which had allowed the tide to overflow its banks and cover the area. Now only the stark skeletons of trees remained, their trunks bleached white by salt and sun so that not a green leaf was visible as far as the eye could see. But more desolate even than this was the obvious fact that there were no flamingos. Not one red feather, nor the sound of a single flamingo voice!

The bottom was a soft black mud, doubtless alluvial in character, and so matted with dead mangrove roots that walking proved extremely difficult. Nevertheless we clambered overboard, and after striking off in a westerly direction for several hundred yards, came upon undeniable evidence that this had been, no more than a year since, a thriving flamingo city. For there were the deserted nest mounds, hundreds of them, standing well above the surface of the water and spread out over a considerable area. Last year, my unhappy guides told me, this very place had been alive with flamingos, a heavenly sight, brilliantly red in the sunlight, a vision of loveliness! I could well believe it for there were no less than 2,000 mounds, far more than I had expected to find in all of Cuba. But this year there were no birds; that was all too clear.

Then I saw the nets. They were old fishing nets stretched between bare tree trunks or poles shoved into the soft mud. In one, scarcely recognizable, was what remained of the body of a young, half-grown flamingo. These nets, the boys readily explained, were used to capture the young birds before they were large enough to fly. Oh yes, they had helped in this capture. Each year the flamingos nested here and each year, when the young were the right size, the nets were spread and several hundred birds driven into them and caught. Some alive, some dead, all to be sold or eaten. Not many—four hundred, five hundred perhaps. A good haul was made last year. Strange that none had nested this season. It was mid-May and ordinarily they should have hatched most of their chicks by now. What could have happened?

I thought I knew what had happened. There had been one raid too many. I had found my Cuban flamingo colony—one year too late!

Would the birds return to this unlucky site? Would the deeply etched influence of their long-established behavior patterns overcome, once more, the panic, the death, the fear, and the frustration these repeated raids must have occasioned? I sat dejectedly on an abandoned nest mound—a beautiful mound of black mud set with purple Venus's-shells that glistened hopefully in the bright sun—and I pondered this imponderable equation. My disappointed friends stood awkwardly in the mud, fingering the torn nets and sharing my distress, even if they did not fully understand it. At any rate, I thought, we now know where the flamingos will build their nests on the Cuban coast, if permitted to do so and if allowed to rear their young in peace. Perhaps, with this knowledge as a new starting point, something can be done to provide these lovely and harassed creatures with the protection and security they need so desperately.

"It's too bad," I told my friends, "that the flamingos can't stage their own revolution."

*. . . Much of the beauty and wonder of nature is based on the fact that organic life is directed towards goals—towards survival, reproduction, and the attainment of higher perfection.*

KONRAD LORENZ *

# XII : The flamingo quadrille

As it turned out, Inagua was the best possibility after all. Not only are there more flamingos on that island today than anywhere else in the range of *Phoenicopterus ruber*, but conditions there proved to be excellent for setting up a practical protection program. If necessary we could make a stand at Inagua and, conceivably, hold off the eventual extinction of this species no matter what happened elsewhere.

It was a March morning when I first stepped ashore on Great Inagua island in the Bahamas. The final lap of the trip was made in a light skiff that had been among the flotsam cast up on the island's shores during World War II. It had been retrieved and mended by one of the local natives, a sturdy islander named Sammy, and it was in this skiff, a few days after I landed on the island, that Sammy and I were poling across the shallow length of Lake Rosa, headed for the flamingos. It was still dark, being only a little past four o'clock in the morning, but Sammy had

* Foreword to *The Herring Gull's World.*

insisted on an early start because of the distance we had to travel and the enervating heat that would be our lot after midday.

As we moved along our jerky and yet surprisingly steady course, I thought how unfortunate it is that we must serve such a long apprenticeship before we are ready to finish what we set out to do in this world. It had been thirty-five years since I had first hoped to visit a flamingo colony, and in that time some fifteen nesting sites of these beautiful birds in the Bahamas and the Caribbean area had been abandoned, chiefly as a result of the rapid growth of the human population in this same region. This is nearly one-half of all the sites deserted since late in the seventeenth century when the English navigator and sometime buccaneer William Dampier visited Bonaire Island and observed the first colony of nesting flamingos to be described in existing literature. However, at the outset of my survey of the flamingo population for the Audubon Society it was fairly clear that the largest surviving group of these birds would probably be found here in the isolated back-waters of Lake Rosa. There was still a lot of searching for me to do after Inagua, but from all reports this island would harbor the largest nursery, and on that dark and star-filled morning I felt that my long search, in this one respect at least, might be near its end.

It was growing light when we came abreast of Horse Cay, which Sam wanted to look at closely, for the birds had nested there the year before and were to nest there again the next year, as it happened. But on this occasion we neither saw nor heard any sign of them. We were now nearly a quarter of the way down the lake, which is about 16 miles in length, west to east as we were traveling, and from 6 miles in width at this point to little more than 2 miles at the far end. The entire island is some 45 miles by 18 in fullest extent, so it is apparent that the lake occupies a considerable portion of the interior.

It is a salt lake, as one would expect, since it is the home of our race of *Phoenicopterus*, the red flamingo, a salty creature if ever there was one. Like the paler race of the Mediterranean our bird seems to be wedded to salt, as if unable to live away from it unless it has had its great wings pinioned to prevent its certain return. Long ago the lake must have been connected with the sea, probably at a point on the western shore of the island, but for an undetermined length of time it has been landlocked, and its shallow depths have been supplied by a series of underground tunnels that reach to the sea and are known locally as "ocean holes." Gilbert Klingel, who wrote a fascinating book about his experiences after being shipwrecked on Inagua in the late 1930s, has had much to say about these tidal openings. They are one of the peculiarities of the island, which is unusual in other respects, as it is composed largely of coralline rock and dolomitic limestone, yet is on the edge of the volcanic region that rises from the sea in the towering bulk of Hispaniola, immediately to the south. The foundations of Great Inagua must be honeycombed with caverns and channels and underground pools, all linked beneath its surface with the surrounding sea. Some of these Stygian tunnels are certainly miles in total length.

On the surface of the island all that one sees is a great shallow lake bed, much of it dry, its waters supplied by periodic tidal gushings and the flow from networks of lesser rivulets that trickle from the crevices that riddle its floor. Most of the ocean holes that are open and active lie toward the eastern end of the lake, and as the prevailing winds are from the east, the accumulated flow is carried westward in a steady movement. Near the head of the big lake I saw one opening that measures three by five feet across, with the sea pouring out of it as from an artesian well. Others, smaller in size, may spout like miniature geysers, but the greater number of holes one comes across are choked with sand and shell. They are barely wet when the tide is running full, and quite dry at low tide. Smaller and somewhat deeper bodies of water, the Upper Lakes, are scattered across the island to the east of the big lake, now called Lake Windsor in honor of the Duke, who was once governor of these islands. In these smaller lakes the ocean holes may be very large, and we saw good-sized fish in some of them, including tarpon and bonefish.

These water sources are vitally important to the flamingo. They are the avenues and the threads of life to everything that lives in the lakes. The bed of Lake Windsor is so capacious, for the amount of water it must normally hold, that it is in effect a huge evaporation pan. As the wind drives the water slowly across its broad shallows, the unhampered tropic sun does the rest. Although the water that comes out of the holes is of a lesser salinity than normal sea water, the various salts are gradually concentrated by evaporation until, by the time the flow reaches the far end of the lake, the salinity reading may be more than four times the density of the sea. And it is no longer clear and green, but brownly opaque and streaked with gypsum. One can scarcely imagine, on first examination, that anything organic could live in such a devil's brew, but creatures do live and find sustenance therein, and one of these is the flamingo. In addition to the microscopic organic foods that are provided by these saline waters, the nest mounds are built around a cluster of ocean holes so that clear brackish water is always available for bathing and drinking. On that first morning, however, all this was still a mystery, and as the blazing sun, copper-red and unhindered by cloud or mist, rose sullenly above the flat horizon, I looked off across that wild expanse of foam-flecked inland sea and felt a great wonder that this was the place I had been searching for.

Yeates, in his delightful account of the Camargue flamingo colony of the Rhone delta, summarizes briefly the rather varied, yet singularly identical, characteristics of flamingo breeding grounds in Europe, Asia, and Africa. Although he was able to leave his base in a comfortable French farmhouse and travel the short distance to the nest mounds in carpet slippers, it may be quite a different story elsewhere. In southern Spain, Johnston contracted fever and Abel Chapman "lost a week through ague brought on by constant splashing about in comparatively cold water with a fierce sun always beating down on one's head." The worst plight, however, was that of McCann's associate, Captain Webster, in the Great Rann of Kutch in northwest India. He returned from a day in the saddle with his face "red, swollen, cracked and peeling in several places, his arms . . . not much better . . . he was a picture of misery." To which McCann adds: "Only those who have experienced the Rann can appreciate the dreadfulness of the conditions at such a time." In all this literature I had found only Yeates's carpet slippers to reassure me, and no mention anywhere of the palm-fringed tropical setting that had waved languorously through my boyhood dreams.

Far ahead, hazy in the heat waves and elongated out of all proportion, lay a gray smudge that Sam announced was Cotton Cay. "When we get there," said he, pointing with his pole, "we maybe hear the fillymingos." "And see them, too?" I asked. Sam scratched his head beneath the band of his well-ventilated Bahamian straw, as if invoking deep thought. "Maybe yes, maybe no," he said doubtfully. "Ah hopes an' prays th' Lord yes," he added with his usual piety, gazing at the enigma of the distant horizon.

Not long after this we sighted a few small and far-off files of flamingos, outriders of the colony, flying one behind another in an easterly direction. As the numbers of these increased Sam could scarcely contain himself. "Them is sure 'nuff goin' straight into the nestes!" he exclaimed, nearly dancing with excitement. "We find 'em sure, we find 'em sure!" The lake had narrowed, and as we approached Cotton Cay, the outline of the horizon to the east was broken by the tops of black mangroves and tropical buttonwoods on Long Cay and the unnamed spits and shorelines of the Upper Lakes region beyond. Then, about eight o'clock, as we were wading laboriously, pushing and shoving our way through jagged coral rocks close to Cotton Cay, Sam heard a new sound and raised his arm for silence. We stood as we were, poised like a pair of sun-blasted statues. In a moment I, too, could hear it, a rumble of distant sound, low and high at once—pulsating—rising until it was clearly audible, then falling until the ear almost lost its vibrations in the murmur of the wind. His broad face turned toward me, radiant with pleasure, Sam anticipated my own words. "That's 'em!" he cried. "The Lord be praised! That's th' fillymingos!" Hauling the now useless skiff up on a dry rock, hastily securing its painter and grabbing the water jug, he started walking rapidly toward the east, his muscular legs swishing and splashing through the warm, salty water. Equally excited, I scrambled along in his wake.

Now and again we stopped to listen. The sound soon became a distant uproar—a din, a clamor, a constant and prolonged uproar. Now it seemed high-pitched and toneless, the sort of sound that can only be made by the dissonant unison of thousands of voices. Still, we could see nothing, except the now more frequent and more lengthy strings of flying birds, their long slender necks stretching out in front and their equally long and slender legs out behind, so that each bird seemed like an animated spear hurtling through the air. When they passed close to us these swiftly moving lines honked much like flocks of geese, but we scarcely heard them against the growing volume of sound in the background.

We reached Long Cay, passed quickly through the shade of its buttonwoods, where the fulsome scent of wild jackasses lay heavily on the air, and emerged into the sun and wind on its eastern face. The breeze was from its accustomed easterly quarter and now that Long Cay lay behind us, that is, to the west, the sound of the flamingo multitudes on ahead was suddenly louder. We hastened on, greatly encouraged and in a rage of excitement, until at length we came close up against another barrier of low trees. As we drew near to them Sam all at once grabbed me by the arm with one hand and with the other pointed off toward a break in the vegetation about a half mile farther on. Openmouthed, we stood and stared in silence. Through the thin screen of brush we could see a solid band of red. It shimmered and undulated in the heat exactly as if it were a long sheet of flame. I thought at once of Frank Chapman's classic account of a similar view of these birds, a half century before on Andros Island. "It was an appalling sight," he wrote. "One of the boatmen said it looked 'like hell,' and the description is apt enough to be set down without impropriety."

Knowing only that this moving mass of red must be a great assemblage of flamingos, we walked rapidly ahead until we had reached the shelter of a narrow growth of low trees. There we flopped on our bellies and stared out across the large pond wherein the flock was congregated. I guessed that there were well over 1,000 flamingos in the group, but they were packed so closely together—literally shoulder to shoulder—that it was difficult to judge. There might easily have been more than twice that number. They moved this way and that, without obvious purpose, like a hysterical and leaderless mob. Tightly packed as they were, and with every individual jostling his neighbor and all of them jumping about like madmen, the outlines of the flock ebbed and flowed, as if it were molten, red-hot lava. Here and there we could see taller, redder heads and necks of the older male birds, riding high above the crowd and bickering with other birds close to them in what appeared to be a frenzy of emotion. These outbreaks rose to a fever pitch and then abruptly subsided. It seemed to be these larger flamingos that set up pressure, first to one side then to the other, so as to keep the entire flock churning about so furiously.

From so close at hand the din was frightful, every kind of flamingo sound—honks, cackles, groans, high froglike notes—issuing forth in one grand, overwhelming chorus from more than a thousand throats at once and without end. We lay there like earth men who had unaccountably fallen upon another planet and had come without warning upon a great number of its outlandish inhabitants engaging in a wild ceremonial dance. Which was not so far from actuality at that! I was not only stirred to my depths by the spectacle itself, but I felt at almost a complete loss. Eyes and ears were not enough to take it in. Now the whole body of birds churned still closer to our hiding place, bearing down on us as if the entire flock were a huge, many-legged creature, a thing of cohesive living tissue, fluid and unpredictable. Then it moved off, nearly across the pond from us, swelling and receding, sinuous necks waving and thrusting along its rim and black wingtips flashing as if to remind us that, after all, this was only a flock of birds.

We watched until the sun was high in the heavens, until, at length, the birds appeared to have exhausted themselves or had gradually lost interest and scattered to other parts of the lakes. Only then did we realize how hot it had grown and feel with real discomfort the bites of the maddening little mosquitoes that lay in wait in every shady spot. Aware from what I had seen and from what Sammy told me that nest building had not yet started, I agreed that we should retrace our steps and return to the settlement for the time being.

On that first morning of my first visit to Inagua, we had happened to stumble on the performance that is perhaps the most intriguing in the flamingo's entire repertoire. It was March, the season when these birds usually begin the involved quadrilles and cotillions that lead to courtship, and eventually, to what W. S. Gilbert, in the guise of "Bab," once referred to as "connubial fondlings and affectionate reciprocities." The wonderful confusion I saw that first morning became even more wondrous when, on subsequent trips, I observed it with less fluster and more understanding. On another March morning, in our camp on Jackass Cay, the ever reliable Sammy advised that the flamingos were again "commulating" in the Upper Lakes. This appears to be Sammy's own term and, since the prenuptial behavior of the flamingo is pretty much a community or communal affair, it is a peculiarly apt, portmanteau sort of word when applied to this species. We set off at once and even before reaching Long Cay, shortly after six o'clock, we saw the large flock that had been night-roosting in the pond there rise in a magnificent massed flight and head out directly into the rising sun toward the Upper Lakes. Farther along, near the Resting Tree, we could see other flocks coming in from the north and east, all moving in from night ponds and congregating in the First Puddle, as the natives call the most westerly of the Lakes.

The Upper Lakes, probably because of their greater isolation, have long been an important nesting area for the flamingos. They are quite distinct from Lake Windsor but, like that larger body, are supplied with fresh sea water by the movement of tides through breaks in the bottom, or floor, of each of them. With no other inlet or outlet, plus the rapid evaporation of that hot, windswept climate, the salinity will average about twice that of normal sea water. As in the big lake, this salinity factor may limit the number of species that can exist in such an environment, but it does not necessarily limit them numerically. Certain microscopic organisms—diatoms, dinoflagellates, rhizopods, bacteria of several kinds, nematode worms, immature mollusks, and other forms—may be astonishingly abundant. One extremely numerous killifish, the omnipresent *Cyprinodon variegatus*, is also able to pass much of its cycle in these excessive salinities, although their life may begin in the cooler and less saline depths of the ocean holes. These conditions result in a specialized group of birds that can exist within such a restricted habitat. Again, these are limited as to species but not as to quantity. There are stilts, egrets, herons, and others that feed on killifishes and aquatic insects, but the prime example is the flamingo, which may crowd into the Upper Lakes at the start of the breeding season in vast multitudes that, even in recent years, has approached 10,000 individuals, the largest assemblage of this species that now survives anywhere. These great flocks quit the nesting lakes when the young are able to fend for themselves, leaving the remaining food supply to their growing offspring. Nor do they generally occupy the same breeding site two years in a row. There are too many of them, and their demands as to daily supplies of food are too great. The whole pattern seems to be beautifully worked out, and although we are sometimes prone to express bewilderment and impatience with what appears to be the capriciousness of the flamingos, it is likely that they are simply reacting to conditions and influences so carefully attuned, so finely balanced, that we have difficulty in recognizing them or in understanding what we see.

Through the winter months the Inagua flamingo flocks have been content to feed and rest in leisurely fashion in the coastal ponds and lagoons, away from the big lake. They are more vulnerable near the shore, for it is easy to reach most of these places by boat from the sea, but the flocks are scattered and wary, and little harm can come to them. They are not tied down to any one spot, as is the case at nesting time. Then March arrives, pregnant with change, bursting with the promise and the challenge of the vernal equinox. Within the birds themselves progressive changes also have been taking place. Restlessly they begin to move about more and to show signs of involuntary reaction to an inward pressure. What has been called "the hereditary clockwork of the population" is now rhythmically ticking off the minutes of a new phase in the cycle. To the histologist each stage in the physiology of this cycle is measurable—the changes can be interpreted by weights, graphs, metric scales, and photomicrographs. To the ethologist, who studies the psychological aspects, each stage is a series of related behavior patterns and innate releaser mechanisms. To the poet and the unabashed lover of nature, each shifting scene is one of increasing beauty and wonder. All of these together are like mirrors reflecting some small part of the normal development of a reasonably complex organism. This organism—the flamingo—is reacting quite naturally to the well-ordered machinery of its own specific identity, within the particular environment that it has won for itself by its long struggle for existence. Perhaps the most remarkable thing about all this is its perfection. Hundreds of infinitely small parts—physiological, psychological, environmental—must fit together smoothly, consecutively, purposefully. And more often than not they do, with survival the aim and the net result.

As we came to the last fringe of trees between us and the gathering flocks, we could see that many of the new arrivals were funneling into the very core of the great red mass of birds already on the pond. From the high-pitched "*eep-eep, eep-eep*" of their voices, from their smaller proportions and slightly paler plumage, I assumed that most of these milling birds were females. To one side, in several closely ordered companies, stood the undoubted males. They strutted even when standing still, long, deeply red necks held straight and tall, heads raised so that the mandibles were thrust upward, arrogantly. Now and then they would turn their heads halfway around, stiffly, almost mechanically, always to the left. First one male would turn his head quickly to the left—pause—then back to the front again. Another male immediately followed suit, then yet another, until all of them were engaged in this behavior. These head-turnings were never in unison, but jerky, nervous, fitful. I felt a desire to shout, "All right now, boys, when I say the word let's all turn our heads together!"

The head-turning was often followed by another and more complicated male display in which the wings, with primaries held close together, were flicked upward to their full extent, held there momentarily, and then smartly lowered. As the wings came down, the bird rapidly twisted his long neck downward, so that his head, thrust backward, brushed sidewise across his back feathers. The entire performance seemed to say, as effectively as if spoken in so many words, "Behold! I am a male!"

Throughout all this, the females alternately milled about in massed formation and, after reaching a violent and deafening peak of both sound and movement, gradually broke off and reverted to a seemingly unconcerned and probably simulated feeding activity. Then, perhaps in response to a renewed stimulus from within and the visual promptings of the performing males, the milling began again, in another sector of the pond, and again the scene was one of sound and flurry.

Flocks of both males and females were still coming in, the males forming remote little troops of alert, stiff-necked observers on the fringes of the pond, the females either joining the hard mass of dancing birds directly or dropping into the shallows some distance off and then walking slowly, in single file, toward the demonstrators. Suddenly, just as one of the female performances had broken up, several males rose and flew in wide circles over the now scattered flock. As they made several turns the circles grew progressively tighter and tighter. Beneath them the hubbub was resumed, with the low, gutteral voices of the males joining in, "*cak-cak! cak-cak! cak-cak!*," until the whole volume of sound reached distressing proportions. As the males settled into the pond, the excited females now moved toward them, as if pulled inward by a powerful magnet (as indeed, in one sense, they were), until the males, their heads thrust high above the entire assemblage, were in the center of a closely packed, weaving mass of birds. When this demonstration reached its peak and broke off, another company of males arose, circled the flock, and came down to set up a second center. This was repeated until the massed flock, in a final moment of hysteria, had become a creature with several nuclei, of wheels within wheels, each an island of upthrust male heads in a moving sea of paler backs and lesser necks, necks that were lowered in modest, almost demure recognition of the momentary importance of the male of the species.

This gregarious ritual must have for its purpose the intermingling of the sexes under circumstances that promote the various manifestations and labels of sex recognition. Along with the progressive gonadal development of both males and females, which takes place more or less simultaneously, the individual bird produces an outward behavior and appearance that is in evidence only at this time of year. At no other season is the tall male so wonderfully feathered, or so deeply and brilliantly colored. The graceful plumes that extend beyond his tail, curving elegantly, are never so long or so scarlet as now. The yellow and orange of the bill is never so bright as at this time. Even the black at the tip of the mandibles is more glossy than it will be later on. And his bearing is something you will see only during this period. He is like a very dignified gentleman who is all dressed up for an exceedingly festive occasion, but has had one glass of punch too many and so is striding about with exaggerated care, as if walking on eggs. Nor can the more modest female be overlooked. She, too, is more beautiful than at other seasons, but she is a trifle smaller and a trifle less brilliant than the male, while her behavior, except for the excusable frenzy of the dance, is quite unassuming, and never ostentatious, or vain, or overbearing. These seem to be male manifestations, at least in the flamingo.

Once the birds are gathered and the quadrille gets under way, it is apparent that the males act in their own masculine way, and the females after their fashion. They are now readily distinguishable as to sex, whereas at other times, without the emphasis of certain adornments and of specific and unusual behavior, the sex of an individual might not be evident and, for that matter, at such a time, would be of no particular consequence. In addition, pairing off can now follow quite naturally and relevantly. All this leaping and milling about stirs responses that serve to push each individual over the line into an ecstatic state of things that will carry them through courtship and connubial bliss. Then, as the peak of this phase is passed, other objects and other patterns take over—the egg-bearing female, the nest mound, the newly hatched chick—and these release still other manifestations, so that, unless broken off by outside disturbance, the cycle gradually unfolds and step by step is ultimately completed.

But the spectacle of the prenuptial dance, the flamingo quadrille, is the most stirring scene of all, from our point of view. When you have seen that you have seen the flamingo at its best. The interludes that follow, dutifully domestic and charming as they are, do not hold a candle to the earlier period for real excitement and beauty and interest. Even the birds themselves show manifold signs of boredom during the long incubation, four weeks of almost complete inaction. And sitting on that large white egg, out in the hot sun all day, must be tiresome, even when you are a flamingo and the egg is your very own.

Fortunately for themselves and their posterity, the flamingos, being birds, are protected from indulgences that may be described as regrets or romantic longings. Their boredom is purely physical. Otherwise, I am sure the long incubation period, and all that must follow, would prove unendurable. Their thoughts would go back, inevitably to the wonderful excitement of that dance in the First Puddle. And who could blame them for sneaking off and starting another shindig? Naturally, this never happens. These lovely, perfectly adapted creatures have no such impulses and no vain dissatisfactions. They haven't even volition, as we know it, but only a complicated behavior mechanism to which they are forever enslaved. Good thing, too, or they might have been extinct ages ago. We do not understand much of all this, only a fragment or an isolated cluster of causes and effects here and there, but the more one looks into this sort of thing the more one is impressed with its amazing and intricate perfection.

Since those early days of our work with the flamingos, much has been learned and much has been done for their protection. So far as Inagua is concerned, the Society for the Protection of the Flamingo in the Bahamas, with Arthur Vernay at the helm and with the good will and assistance of the Erickson family at Matthewtown, has provided complete warden protection. Chief Warden Sam Nixon and his brother James have not only stuck with the flamingos through thick and thin, and in all seasons, but have gained the respect of all, including the native elements of the island. The program at Inagua was initiated while there were yet relatively large numbers of breeding birds in that area and may well be the one outstanding effort that will turn the tide in favor of a new lease on life for these splendid birds. But the support of government and of privately contributed funds must not be relaxed.

Progress has likewise been made elsewhere. In Yucatán, where we have had the personal interest and efficient help of the Roche family of Mérida, a definite and impressive increase in numbers can be noted. There are still difficulties. As this is written the flamingo continues to be listed as a game bird in Mexico. Before our cooperative efforts with Joaquin and Roger Roche began, less than six years ago, there was no protection whatever, and natives could raid the nesting colonies as they pleased. Fishermen from settlements like Río Lagartos and El Cuyo, roaming along the outer coast looking for turtles or other fair game, helped themselves to young flamingos or fresh eggs whenever they felt like it. But this is now, and we trust from now on, a thing of the past. Recently a new threat has appeared, both here and at Bonaire, across the Caribbean. Tourists, chiefly Americans, are reaching these once remote places in greater numbers each year. In the summer of 1955, the Río Lagartos colony, harassed by heavy rains and high tides, nested much later than is usually their custom. In addition, they moved to Isla de Yamalcán, which is to the east of the fishing village of El Cuyo, and a difficult location to guard with the facilities at our command. Still, two wardens were placed on duty, but they were new men and not broken in to the job. It is a more readily accessible place than the nesting sites farther west and there were numbers of visitors, many of them American tourists. One such group persuaded the wardens to permit them to photograph the colony from a tower they built close by, and these activities were a sufficiently disturbing influence to cause the loss of many small young, and unhatched eggs. A bad season was the net result.

At Bonaire, in the Netherlands Antilles, in spite of the best efforts of the local government officials and of Mr. Gerharts, who has done so much to obtain protection, tourists from Curaçao made their way to the colony, and by walking up to the nest mounds to take photographs, caused most of the adults to desert. After a number of years of hope and effort it looked at the beginning of 1955 as if the Bonaire colony was going to make a real comeback. In forty-five minutes all this was undone by a few unthinking people, and we can only trust that the birds will return and try again next year. Obviously, here as in Yucatán and everywhere else that flamingos nest, a greater sense of responsibility on the part of government and of the public must be evidenced very soon or the American flamingo will soon be a very rare bird. There is no protection whatever at the Abaco colony, and should flamingos return and attempt to nest at one of the traditional sites on Andros Island, as Mr. Forsyth writes me they did in 1953, they will be met by nothing better than hungry and unrestrained natives with a taste for their eggs and an utter lack of responsibility.

We have done some things for the flamingo, but it is clear that what we have done is not enough. At La Orchila off the Venezuelan coast, as a result of the intervention of Billy Phelps, Jr., the president of that country has taken a personal interest in the fortunes of the small flamingo colony. Like the remarkable efforts of the Flamingo Society in the Bahamas, this is most encouraging, but nowhere—not in the Bahamas, or in Yucatán, or in the Netherlands Antilles, or in Venezuela, and certainly not in Cuba—has so much as one square foot of land been set aside, *with realistic provisions for proper enforcement*, as a permanent and inviolate refuge for this lovely and much persecuted bird. If species such as the flamingo are to survive, in the full grandeur of their natural status as wild, free-flying birds, then we must persuade our fellow men that it is time we arranged to share a portion of the earth with them. The results of such an arrangement would be colorful and rewarding beyond all imagination.

*. . . I have looked upon those brilliant creatures,*
*And now my heart is sore.*
*All's changed since I, hearing at twilight,*
*The first time on this shore,*
*The bell-beat of their wings above my head . . .*

WILLIAM BUTLER YEATS

# XIII : We find terra incognita!

The alertness of Canadian Wildlife Service and Forestry personnel resulted in an eventual solution to the mystery of the whooping crane's Northern nesting grounds. In late June, 1954, a forest fire was reported in a seldom-visited portion of Wood Buffalo Park, north of 60 degrees in Northwest Territories. A helicopter was being used by the fire prevention crew at Fort Smith, and on June 30 pilot Don Landells, with G. M. Wilson, Superintendent of Forestry, as a passenger, was in the air returning from the vicinity of Fire 24. In a swampy area several miles southeast of the fire they observed two large white birds whose appearance brought them sharply to attention. Flying in at a lower altitude, the two men saw that the birds were undoubtedly adult whooping cranes, and with them—wonder of wonders—was a rusty-colored juvenile which they described as being about the size of a large rooster.

A radio report of their momentous discovery was dispatched at once to Fort Smith and received there by William A. Fuller, biologist at the District headquarters. The time of the observation and the report was just before 5 P.M. Fuller was advised to stand by so as to join another flight that would take off just as soon as the helicopter could return to Fort Smith for refueling. By 6:35 P.M. the machine had landed, refueled, and was again in the air, this time with Fuller aboard. Within the next hour the pair of whoopers was sighted once more, and, in an adjacent area some miles to the north, a single adult whooping crane was also observed.

The region where these birds were seen is interlaced with a countless number of small ponds and lakes, shallow and swampy in character and poorly drained. Many of them are separated by narrow ridges of spruce and other vegetation. The footing is so uncertain that although the pilot attempted to land so as to measure the birds' tracks, he was unable to do so, although a landing was made later in a more open fringe of marsh. There are no deeper lakes nearby and it is therefore an area that is normally avoided by conventional fixed-winged, float-equipped aircraft, because it offers no water suitable for even an emergency landing. In addition, there is no ready means of access on the ground, and, in fact, no reason for either Indians or whites going there at all in the spring and summer season. Or at any other time.

Here, then, was the long-sought *terra incognita* of the whooping crane, its last stronghold and bulwark against the intrusions of the outer world.

In Ottawa, Washington, and New York, plans were immediately discussed for sending a ground-survey party into the area for detailed observations. However, it was decided that the season was already too advanced, and the expedition was put off until the spring of 1955—provided, of course, that whooping cranes returned to the area. Meanwhile, the 1954 breeding season, so hopeful in revealing the nesting locale of at least a portion of the surviving flock, was the poorest on record with regard to results. Of the 24 whooping cranes that had gone North in April, only 21 returned to the Texas coast in October–November. And not one young bird of the year reached the wintering grounds alive, the first time that a complete failure had been noted in this vital department.

During the first two weeks of April, 1955, all 21 birds set out for the Northern breeding grounds, migrating, as usual, by family groups and in small bands of two or three unmated individuals. There was quite a spread to these departures, for the last whoopers were seen in the vicinity of the Aransas Refuge on April 14 and on that same date 5 whoopers were observed at close range in Saskatchewan, and photographed in flight by Fred Bard.

At Fort Smith, Bill Fuller was on the job. On April 26 conditions were such that the runway there was declared unserviceable for aircraft on skis, and the *Beaver*, used by the government services, was flown to Yellowknife, and wheels installed. When it returned on the twenty-eighth, Bill immediately arranged for a preliminary flight over the crane area the following day. But this was prevented by a low ceiling and intermittent snow showers. These conditions prevailed all through the twenty-ninth and most of the thirtieth. Then, during a temporary lull late on the thirtieth, the plane took off and headed for the nesting grounds. Almost at once the snow flurries resumed, but they found the general area and began observations. Just when they were over the critical spot the visibility improved, and Bill was able to locate a pair of whooping cranes in a small pond not far from the initial 1954 site. He took several photographs of these two birds from an altitude of about 800 feet.

The immediate organization of a ground party was considered. It was not until May 5, however, that a decision was definitely reached for sending a survey group into the nesting area, and on that date I had just stepped off a boat at Matthewtown on the distant island of Inagua in the southernmost Bahamas. A radiogram from John Baker said: YOU HAD BETTER LIGHT OUT FOR FORT SMITH. The big moment had finally come! I cut short my flamingo investigations on Inagua, headed home as fast as a slow mailboat could carry me via Nassau, and began packing for the journey North.

During May there were several additional observations, all within the Wood Buffalo Park area. For about a week, early in that month, three whooping cranes were observed near the Hay Camp, close to the Slave River. This is about seventy-two miles in a straight line southeast of the nearest nesting site. On May 15, Fuller and Ray Stewart were flown over the area by Sergeant Heacock in the Royal Canadian Mounted Police plane. They saw a single whooping crane near the upper Sass River. The next day they flew again, this time with a chartered plane, and again saw a lone whooping crane, apparently sitting on a nest!

On May 18, two days before I reached Fort Smith, Ed Wellein and Wes Newcomb of the U.S. Fish and Wildlife Service, flying a Grumman Goose, and with Fuller and Stewart aboard, made the following remarkable observations:

(*a*) Two whoopers at a nest close to Sass River
(*b*) Two whoopers at a nest just north of Klewi River
(*c*) One whooper in flight near nest containing an egg, at the Klewi River but northwest of site "*b*"
(*d*) Two whoopers farther east along Klewi River

This is a total of four possible pairs, all within an area of approximately 500 square miles.

I was finally able to make the necessary reservations and get away from Florida on May 19, arriving in Fort Smith the next day at noon. For a day and a half, with the help of Bill Fuller and his assistant, Ray Stewart, as well as my old friend Ward Stevens, now Superintendent of Game for the Territories, our gear and supplies were assembled, Indian packers obtained, and all preparations made for the projected ground trip into the crane country. I had been joined en route by Bob Stewart, biologist with the U.S. Fish and Wildlife Service, a last-minute but welcome addition to our party. Our departure by boat down the Slave River, the first leg of the journey, was then set for the morning of May 23. Meanwhile, Bill wanted us to see something of our route and of the nesting area from the air, so a flight was arranged for the evening of the twenty-second.

The *Beaver* was now on floats, and with Pat Carey at the controls we took off from below the Rapids of the Drowned at just after 7 P.M. In forty-five minutes we were over the nesting area. There beneath us was the sight I had been hoping to see for almost ten years—a wild whooping crane on its nest! The incubating bird continued to sit as we flew by, circling in a wide arc at 1,000 feet. Its size and outline, even its posture, were unmistakable. I could see that it was turning to watch us as we passed, its head up and its yellow eyes doubtless glaring at us with hostility and a total lack of fear. We flew back over a portion of the region to the north and east, where other pairs had been observed four days previously, but we failed to catch sight of them. In that crazy-quilt pattern of lakes and ponds it was not surprising.

On our way into the area we had taken a long look at the only stream by which we might hope to enter this all but inaccessible wilderness. What we saw was a narrow, twisting creek perhaps twenty to thirty feet wide, fairly deep and swift, and apparently obstructed all along its lower course by log jams. The airline distance from the mouth of the Sass to the vicinity of the nesting area is only about sixteen miles, but there appeared to be some forty or more bends and oxbows in the first mile of actual distance to be covered, and we speculated that in reality the route would total something like sixty or seventy miles.

The next morning we loaded our gear into two Chipewyan-type river boats, each pushed along by a 10-h.p. outboard, and, towing our eighteen-foot canoe astern, we started off down the mighty Slave River toward the Grand Detour, which would be our first portage. In our party, besides myself, were Ray Stewart, Bob Stewart, and ten Indians and breeds who would assist us in packing our canoe, and more than 500 pounds of equipment over the major part of the first portage. It was a bright day though still quite chilly, especially on the open river. Those who had them sat huddled in parkas with the hoods pulled up around their faces. We made the forty-four miles by two-thirty that afternoon, dodging drift logs all the way. When I went ashore, over silt-encrusted slabs of ice that still littered the banks, I found that the packers had a fire going and were already cooking the buffalo steaks that had been provided for them. In typical Indian fashion they were boiling them in a big pot. With lots of potatoes.

At four o'clock we were ready to start packing, two natives carrying the canoe and the rest of us with good loads on our backs. It had been some years since I had done any heavy packing, and with my crippled spine I was just a trifle worried that I might get into trouble. But all went well, although I was very glad to see the end of it. We were now on Seton's trail, the same one that he and Preble followed in the summer of 1907, and which he wrote about in *Arctic Prairies*. Until I read his autobiography not long ago, I hadn't been aware that Seton also suffered from a severe case of arthritis, both legs being affected at an early age. It probably explains his description of crossing this same route, in which he speaks of "the fearful toil of portaging" and the "mortal agony" of the last miles. Since there was no other, we gratefully used a copy of Seton's sketch map of the Grand Detour portage. It proved accurate in every respect, and a real help to us. The trail led through spruce woods still wet from the melted snow. Ruffed grouse were drumming everywhere. We came out into a marshy prairie, skirted some shallow ponds, and once more trailed through a stand of spruce. There were buffalo tracks in abundance now, for this is also their route that we were using, across to the Little Buffalo and the open prairies near its banks.

The water lay as much as a foot deep in some places, and swarmed with mosquito larvae. On a small prairie farther west we saw our first buffalo, but, alarmed at the sight of such a large party, they turned and galloped off toward cover with surprising speed. It was nearly seven o'clock when we reached the short of Long Slough, where our packers left us, with many head-shakings at the futility of our trying to get up the Sass with such a load. We pitched our first camp and, dog tired, fell asleep with the song of the hermit thrush in our ears.

We still had a long haul next day, down the slough by canoe, as a thunderstorm swept by to the south of us, and then a final carry through a wide trail to the Little Buffalo River. Long Slough was lined with cattails, which were just showing signs of new growth, and there were many pairs of horned grebes, lesser yellowlegs, and waterfowl in abundance. Little brown cranes were numerous, calling from here and there about us. On the big subarctic prairies to the west were herds of buffalo, a magnificent sight. One group included several small calves, light brown in color. By five o'clock we had everything across and plunked down at an Indian winter camp site on the Little Buffalo, except for the canoe, outboard motor, and gas cans which we left for morning. We sat around under a tarpaulin through a sudden hailstorm that covered the ground with hailstones the size of marbles, and then set up our tent and began supper. When we made the first portage into camp we saw a large black bear across the river. He disappeared among the trees, but when we came back with the next load, there he was, standing on the bank as if about to plunge in and join us on our side. Not wanting a camp robber on our hands so early in the game, we yelled at him in unfriendly tones and ran him off.

Beaver were plentiful, and that night we roused many times to hear them playfully slapping the surface of the river with their broad tails. It was a cold night with a film of ice forming on water left standing in cups and cooking pots. But it was not cold enough to discourage the chorus of singing and calling birds—hermit and olive-backed thrushes, robins, warblers (especially the abundant Tennessee), and from a greater distance, the voices of geese, swans, and brown cranes.

The next day, May 25, we made the mouth of the Sass River (*Sass* is the Chipewyan word for bear), and, with considerable excitement, began the ascent. Around the first oxbow we ran into a small log jam, cutting our way through in twenty minutes. Two minutes later we were up against a second, and larger, jam. Going ashore we scouted the riverbank upstream. Immediately beyond the second jam there was a third, still larger. Somewhat dismayed we went back downstream to the Little Buffalo and made camp. In the morning, Ray and I, in an empty canoe, and armed with axes and a big saw, returned to jam number two. When, by dint of a little ax work, we had cut it loose, the entire mass of logs and trees moved off in the very considerable current and started a new jam below us! This was a natural but totally unexpected development. The Sass is deep and narrow, with an unbroken series of bends and oxbows from source to mouth. At that early date the water was still high, and consequently quite swift. From what we had seen of it there are almost no straight courses and few bends that are free of logs. There might be several hundred oxbows and almost as many log jams, from obstructions that consist of a mere half-dozen trees to great piles of logs and down timber, criss-crossed and interwoven in a patchwork that it would be impossible to remove except with dynamite. And even then, many of the logs would simply float off downstream on the high water and form other jams below. In a word, to say that the Sass is not navigable is putting it mildly. We would have to portage almost the entire distance, and this would be a backbreaking and uncertain task.

We were now on the first horn of a many-horned dilemma. Our radio transmitter could not be heard in Fort Smith, but we could hear them all right, and that night we listened to Ward Stevens calling us to advise that Pat Carey would be flying over us the next day to check our progress. Unable to explain our situation and not wanting an alarm to be broadcast when they failed to find us up the Sass, we decided to head for the mouth of the Little Buffalo and try to reach the radio station at Fort Resolution. Setting out early the next morning we ran downstream on a high river, and were at the mouth in eleven and a half hours, ordinarily a two-day trip by canoe. There we found the ice still fairly solid on Great Slave Lake, and Chipewyans that were stranded with their families and sled dogs at the Indian village on the east bank told us that it was impossible to get through to Resolution with a loaded canoe because of the ice piled along the lake shore. The next day, which was the twenty-eighth, we persuaded an Indian to carry a message to Resolution for us, and he reached that settlement shortly after 5 P.M., returning that same night, a round trip of thirty-two miles, much of it on foot through ice-cold water. We then sat back to wait.

Our trip down the Little Buffalo was enlivened by the multitudes of birds along the banks and in the water. Bob Stewart counted 53 species and even listed individual numbers, many of them from the songs or call notes. There were spotted sandpipers, green-winged teal, shovelers, golden-eyes, buffleheads, scaup, pintails, Canada geese, kingfishers, phoebes, white-throated and white-crowned sparrows, and many others. Bob listed a total of 63 Tennessee warblers from their songs alone. Everywhere on the upper reaches there were beaver, but as we came closer to the mouth these became scarce and a few muskrats were seen. Seton wrote:

> The Little Buffalo is the most beautiful river in the whole world except, perhaps, its affluent, the Nyarling. This statement sounds like the exaggeration of mere impulsive utterance. Perhaps it is; but I am writing now after thinking the matter over for two and a half years, during which time I have seen a thousand others, including the upper Thames, the Afton, the Seine, the Arno, the Tiber, the Iser, the Spree, and the Rhine.

But he also said that his trip down the Little Buffalo would have been one "of memorable joys but for the awful, awful, awful—see Chapter IX." The title of this chapter is simply "Mosquitoes," and Seton complained that they are a terror to man and beast, making of the North a hell on earth for six months of the year when it might be a human paradise. As the season advanced we found out what he was talking about!

I had caught a bad cold and on the second evening at the river mouth I was explaining my unhappy condition to a family of Indians that stopped by in their canoe. The squaw, a youngish woman wearing long blue jeans and a rather sporty-looking blazer, spoke briefly in Chipewyan now and then, addressing her husband or one of the four children, and all my conversation was with the head of the family. Then, as he asked me if I was taking anything for my cold, the squaw, with something of a flourish, finished lighting a cigarette and, holding it in a most sophisticated manner, said, with no trace of an accent, "Have you tried Vicks?" Ah, wilderness!

Late Sunday afternoon Pat Carey and his float plane, en route from Hay River, landed on the broad stretch of water off our camp. Fort Smith had radioed him of our predicament and he would carry us and our gear, except for the canoe, back to Smith in two loads. Since I had "the Cold" at that time (all of us had it in regular order), I was taken on the first load and the Stewarts came along next day. On the way in, Pat told me that he had seen a helicopter at Hay River that was working for some oil geologists there. Maybe we could arrange to have the use of it for a day. Thus began a week of radio messages between Fort Smith, Hay River, Calgary, and Vancouver, while we cooled our heels impatiently at the Hotel Mackenzie and the whooping-crane hatching date drew nearer and nearer.

Eventually it was arranged for the helicopter to rendezvous with our float plane at a lake to be selected as near as possible to the crane area. With Pat, we flew a supply of helicopter gas, a sixteen-foot canoe, and other essentials out to the Sass River. Taking a bearing on the limestone escarpment close to our birds, we ran due south and located a shallow lake some ten miles from the point on the river where we planned to camp. Pat brought the plane down, his floats dragging in the mud of the bottom, and we unloaded. This was on Saturday, June 4. The next morning we ferried in the rest of our party and the remainder of our gear and supplies.

We had radioed the helicopter pilot the approximate longitude and latitude of our pick-up lake, and when we got there on our second haul he was waiting for us. He turned out to be a Pole newly arrived in that part of Canada. Nevertheless, he seemed to understand our plans well enough, although he had little to say. We showed him our chart, the position of the lake we were on, and the rough location of the escarpment. It lay between ten and twelve miles due north of us, as we indicated, and can be seen for quite a distance. An excellent landmark, which is why we had chosen it. There was so much gear that our friend estimated it would require four round trips to get us in. Since Ray knew the country better than either Bob Stewart or myself, he was elected to go along on the first run and pick a camp site. So we loaded them up and off they went.

There was a brisk wind out of the west, and the pilot flew very low to keep out of it, which made it difficult to get a good look at the country. After what seemed twice the expected distance, Ray saw a stream that looked like the Sass, and a prominent outcropping of limestone. There was no clear space near the escarpment for a landing so they flew downriver, but here everything seemed to be under water. Turning upstream again the pilot saw an open marsh close to the river and separated from it by a narrow ridge of spruce. Down he went and they started unloading.

Four hours and some minutes later I arrived with the last load.

Although I had only seen the region briefly from a Beaver, flying high at 120 miles per hour, it hadn't looked right when we came in to the landing place. However, this was evidently *it*, and when the pilot said he wanted to get moving because of a squall that appeared to be making up in the northwest, we said, "Sure, get going, we're on our own now!" Which we certainly were, more so than we had any idea at the moment. The helicopter disappeared in an instant, and we toted the remainder of our supplies up on the ridge, fighting off clouds of mosquitoes at every step. The river seemed wider and deeper and swifter than we had thought it would be near the source, but since no one before us had seen it from the ground in summer we shrugged it off as another unlooked-for development. We then made camp, and after a quick supper turned in with the hum of mosquitoes and the sad notes of the olive-backs in our ears. It was very cold that night, and sadder than even the olive-backs knew!

A preliminary investigation next morning revealed a major difficulty. The river was as badly choked with log jams as at its mouth. In a short walk downstream, toward the pond area in which we thought the cranes would be, we counted six obstructions, every one of them a beauty. It was clear that our canoe would be useless. To reach the cranes we would have to walk across-country. "Oh well," we comforted ourselves, "it's only two miles or so airline from here to the closest nesting site. We can probably do it in an hour." So after lunch we started walking. A buffalo trail through swamp and windfall and burn led more or less northward, the direction we figured we must go. In the soft mud were many bear tracks, fresh prints of all sizes, including those of cubs. We trudged on, blazing a return trail. The clouds of what Seton had referred to as those little ------ nearly smothered us. After an hour of hard walking we reached no ponds, but seemed to be plunging deeper and deeper into the forest. Finally we turned back.

Another attempt was made next day on a slightly different course, but the results were the same. It wasn't until Wednesday, June 8, that we had done enough exploring to realize that we had been bamboozled. Our helicopter had dropped us in the wrong place. To tell the honest truth, we didn't know *where* we were!

The next move was the unpleasant one of cranking up the radio and asking Fort Smith to search for us by aircraft and tell us our location. That message was hard to send, but there seemed to be no alternative. We finally made contact on the tenth and then we sat down to wait. The following day a message got through to us advising that our old friend Bob Smith of the U.S. Fish and Wildlife Service had arrived with a Grumman Goose, en route to the Arctic Coast. He was taking off to look for us and we were to send up smoke signals. This welcome news reached us around 5 P.M., and within an hour we heard the roar of twin engines and then the plane was zooming low over the treetops above camp. Ward Stevens, who was aboard, dropped us a message giving our position as less than two miles airline upstream from the mouth of the Sass! Apparently, our helicopter pilot had not allowed for the 32-degree compass variation that must be taken into account in that part of the world. Instead of flying due north he had headed closer to northeast and set us down near the wrong escarpment, more than twelve miles airline from our true objective. In that country it might as well have been one hundred and twelve.

We were marooned for eleven days in that mosquito-ridden spot, an experience that none of us would like to repeat. Our most philosophical attitudes were at first strained and then forced. Morning smiles and greetings soon took on the heartiness of a service-club luncheon, and only the O.P. rum in our five-o'clock tea saved each day from complete disintegration by suppertime. To pass the time, Bob Stewart, in spite of the awful plague of mosquitoes, laid out two 15-acre plots, one in the upland and the other in bottomland white spruce, and made a breeding-bird population study of each. Ray and I undertook to do most of the camp chores and stuck close to the radio, working every possible schedule on the Wood Buffalo network in a futile effort to find a helicopter that could get us out of there. The weather continued to get more and more like summer. From a temperature below 40°F. on the fifth of June, it reached a high of 88° on the eleventh. We sweltered and fought mosquitoes, deer flies, and the first of the miserable little black flies.

Finally, having been advised that no helicopter was in that end of the country, we broke camp on the morning of June 17 and began our carry down the Sass. We would have to come out the best way we could. Even with the reduced weight of our supplies the assembled gear filled the little sixteen-foot canoe to overflowing. There was barely room for me and one paddle in the stern, and my two companions were glad to walk the shore. That trip down the lower Sass will long be remembered by all of us. From our camp site to the open and unobstructed waters of the Little Buffalo is only an airline distance of about one and a half miles, but it took us thirteen hours of backbreaking labor to get there! We estimated that the actual distance we traveled along the bends of the river was approximately 4.5 times airline, or close to seven miles, but the real key to the situation was in the forty log jams and beaver dams. Some we cut through and tore out, others we detoured by making portages. Somehow, by nine o'clock that night we had all our gear ashore at a camp site on the Little Buffalo, the same spot where we had bedded down when first attempting to move up the Sass on May 25–26. "We're practically moving backwards," Ray observed.

We still had the Grand Detour portage to cover, but four packers were sent out from Fort Smith to meet us halfway across, at Long Slough, and on the evening of the twentieth we were once more on the banks of the Slave River, where Captain Billy McNeil met us with the government boat *Buffalo*. Thus we were brought back to Fort Smith, a dirty, bearded, and sorry crew, after twenty-nine futile and frustrating days of trying to reach the nesting grounds of the whooping crane.

As we sat down to breakfast under Louie's attentive eye at the Hotel Mackenzie, we had to admit that we were licked. The only thing to be done, it seemed, was give it up until next season.

But fate was only playing games with us! Later that morning we were met at District Headquarters by Ward Stevens. He was waving a piece of paper in his hand, a radiogram that had just come in, and in another moment we were the slightly dazed recipients of the unexpected information that another helicopter had arrived at Hay River and would be available the following Wednesday or Thursday. This was Tuesday, June 21, so we arranged at once for a rendezvous early on Thursday morning back at Grand Detour, and set to work at once replenishing food supplies and going over our now battered and mud-splattered gear. Bob Stewart, having used up the month he had been assigned, left us to return to Patuxent the next day. Ray and I, still worn out from the long, hard journey down the Sass and across to the Slave, gritted our teeth and made ready for another grind.

At midnight on Wednesday we carted our equipment aboard the *Buffalo,* and with Ward, Billy McNeil, and a crewman, set off down the river through the rosy dusk of the subarctic night. A wooden barge was lashed securely to the bow, and this would be the helicopter's landing strip. Next morning the rendezvous time came and went but no sign of a helicopter. Then, at a little past noon he came into view, flying downriver. He had been lost, and had put into Smith for refueling. The pilot was a young man named Holmgren who had flown helicopters off the battleship *Missouri* during the Korean War. He was from New Orleans, and a soft-spoken, easygoing lad. We cooked up some bacon and eggs for him and his engineer, and went over our plans. At one-fifteen we were in the air, with both Ray and myself aboard, and thirty minutes later we had located our area and were on the ground. This time there was no doubt whatever as to it being the right place! Holmgren then took off again for the Slave and was back in little more than an hour with the rest of our gear, his payload being 500 pounds at the altitude we were working. We made tentative arrangements for a pick-up date some ten days to two weeks hence, and with grins and hand wavings all around he lifted away from us with the unreal, magic-carpet action of all whirlybirds, and we were alone.

We were now within a mile of the nearest whooping-crane nesting pond and, looking around us, we had our first closehand impression of *terra incognita.* At this point it was a trifle forbidding. We had landed close to the Sass River on the edge of an open *brûlé* that is roughly one-half by one-quarter mile in extent. On the aerial photograph it shows up as a slightly ovate area that appears darker than the surrounding patchwork of irregularly shaped ponds and small lakes. Actually it is a burned-over region and, as the photographs were ten years old, the fire may have swept through here as much as fifteen or twenty years ago. Only the dead skeletons of black spruce and tamarack remain, many of them prostrate on the ground, others still standing, naked and bereaved-looking. The ground itself is an uneven, uncertain carpet of mosses and lichens, wet and boggy in the depressions. That afternoon it was hot and windswept, and infinitely dreary. To the east the marsh-bordered curves of the upper Sass must have stopped the fire in that direction, and on the other borders the ground falls off rather steeply into a disorganized maze of shallow ponds and damp thickets of dwarf birch, willows, scraggly black spruce, and small twisted tamaracks, much of it too thoroughly soaked to burn with any prolonged enthusiasm. As we needed both shelter and drinking water we set up our tent as close to the river as the wetness of the ground permitted, in the dubious shade of a half-dozen live spruce. When everything was in order we settled back, too weary to feel any particular elation. We wanted nothing more at the moment but sleep.

The next morning, June 24, we made a tentative thrust in the direction of the crane ponds. Plodding and slogging through the wholly unexpected thickets, we found that visibility was often cut to little more than a hundred feet. Sometimes we came up to a small pond that had remained hidden until we were within fifty feet of it. With aerial photos in hand we attempted to match the outlines of ponds with some of those in the prints. At first it seemed an impossible task under conditions as we found them, but we kept trying.

Suddenly, straight ahead of us we saw a flash of something white, and then a strikingly familiar outline. It was a whooping crane, standing with head and neck upthrust, silent and alert. Then a second bird appeared. It was an incredible stroke of luck! Seeking the cover of the nearest thicket, we walked toward them as

amples that we brought back with us indicate that the
the ponds is almost barren, containing virtually no plank-
mud samples were more interesting. Dr. James B. Lackey
niversity of Florida, who analyzed the mud for us, had
ment to make:

protein content of the mud is far higher than I would
pect, and I would judge it to be due to bacteria, blue-
lgae and diatoms. It is certainly significant. I expected
s and phosphorus to be low because of the paucity of
sms, especially green ones, in the water. . . . The high
tent also amazed me. We finally decided that organisms
in this locality must store up quantities of fat to prevent
tion by freezing in winter.

is highly interesting when you realize that this entire
reezes solid in winter, the shallow ponds being completely
. Yet not only the frogs, snails, and other pond fauna
but several species of small fishes, including the brook
k.

ching on the ground for the actual nest site of the Sass
r nearest our camp, we came out on the shores of a larg-
where these two birds were first observed on April 30, the
y Lake of our maps. It is a much more open area than
he lakes and ponds of that region, and appeared especially
se of the fact that the water level had dropped perceptibly.
re flat grassy shores, extensive stands of *Scirpus*, and many
dden coves and bays of a marshy character. We found
sh whooping-crane tracks, some of which were evidently
ler imprints of the young, but we saw no birds. After
meeting they made a point of keeping clear of us, al-
we heard them, and what were probably other pairs,
ow and then. No doubt on the breeding grounds they have
e rigid territorial setup that we had observed on the
arshes in winter. Discovery Lake may typify the best
nesting habitat for whooping cranes in that region, but
mption is based chiefly on its open and marshy ap-



rapidly and quietly as we could, although we probably sounded like a herd of buffalo. The two birds separated, one leading us straight on toward a smaller pond just ahead, the other disappearing off to the north, evidently with young in its wake. When we came up on the first bird again it rose with a brief series of alarm notes and flew off in a short circle toward the north. As it rose among the trees a short-billed gull, doubtless hovering over its precious brood of downy chicks nearby, attacked the flying crane viciously, the only demonstration of this sort I have witnessed in many years of watching whooping cranes.

We reached the second pond and found numbers of crane tracks, the extreme width between the spread of the outer toes measuring the seven inches that indicates the enormous tread of *Grus americana*. Around other ponds in the vicinity there were other sets of tracks, and holes in the mud where the big birds had probed with their heavy bills.

We had at last met the whooping crane face to face on his Northern nesting grounds!

On the following day we set out to orient ourselves accurately on the aerial photos, and in the course of an exhausting day we managed to do so. In slogging around over the crane country we noted the relative scarcity of other life—a few pairs of short-billed gulls, arctic loons, mallards, and green-winged teal. On some ponds the lesser yellowlegs is a noisy tenant, on others, usually with more heavily wooded shores, the equally noisy solitary sandpiper. If we stopped on most marsh-rimmed ponds long enough we found sora rails and Wilson's snipe present. Red-winged blackbirds were flying in and out of several extensive stands of bulrush, their young already airborne, and in the wet birch thickets the cheerful, bubbling notes of the Lincoln's sparrow is a typical song. Once a bald eagle flew over, and we watched as a duck hawk was run off by an angry pair of gulls.

In general, the region in which the whooping crane nests is a sort of arrested subclimax, neither established spruce forest nor a distinct, muskeglike tamarack and spruce bog, although both these types may be found nearby. Strictly speaking, the birds of the white spruce forest—myrtle warblers, olive-backs, solitary vireos, Tennessee warblers, three-toed woodpeckers—are not present, but are close at hand and sometimes may be seen or, at least, heard in the distance. The same applies to tamarack-spruce species, although these nearly overlap the birds of the crane ponds, with interesting variations. Actually the region is one of very small shallow ponds with bottoms that are soft and boggy, but with sedge, bulrush, spike rush, and muskgrass growing along their borders, and cattails here and there. In this they differ from ponds of a typical muskeg region. The higher ground between the ponds is covered by thickets of mixed birch, willows, stunted black spruce, and tamarack. If there is any plant succession that can be noted it is probably toward a black spruce-tamarack association, although white spruce takes over on the higher ground not far distant. However, one has the impression that plant succession in this area has been arrested, delayed, put off in some manner. We are told that this portion of the Athabaska–Slave River drainage basin was covered by the Keewatin Glacier, and the present flora, of course, has developed since then, a slow, plodding development, probably still incomplete because of the short growing season and the slowness of decay in this latitude.

The limestone escarpments running across the Alberta Plateau, of which this region is a part, are of Paleozoic age. Raup described four planes of elevation within Wood Buffalo Park, of which the third seems to apply to the pond region occupied by the cranes: a lower plain at about the 800-foot contour; level, but with occasional rolling areas and morainic hills, poorly drained clayey soils, and small ponds. A map of the park prepared by Dewey Soper in 1939 shows an elevation of 925 feet near the upper Sass River, and 780 feet to 640 feet along the final escarpment west of the Little Buffalo River, near Lobstick Creek. Farther down the course of the little Buffalo this elevation drops to 545 feet, between the Klewi and the Nyarling. It is 681 feet near the mouth of the Sass, and 495 feet at Great Slave Lake. Thus, although the Sass River drainage, by way of the Little Buffalo, drops some 430 feet within a relatively short distance to the level of Great Slave Lake, adjacent pockets such as those within which the crane ponds



are found show a poor or disorgan
are isolated, and individual in char
Dewey Soper has pointed out th
of the largest, most isolated, and
North America. It consists of 17,30
ness, or a total area of about 11,0
graphical point of view it occupies a
in the Canadian zone, with portions
The plant life as a whole is regar
arctic. A total of 461 different plant
been described from the area, as w
than 216 birds. Soper classifies th
Coniferous Forest formation, with n
tion of the subtype most nearly re
area is as follows: "Open muskegs
ponds, and typical 'quaking' bog co
growth, commonly associated with
tered black spruce and tamarack, a
zone of willows, dwarf birch, etc.; 
sora rail, lesser yellow-legs, Bonaparte
bird."

With only slight alterations this
biotic area in which the whooping cr
Omit the term *muskegs*, add *Scirpu*
along with sora rails, yellowlegs, and
Wilson's snipe, solitary sandpiper,
and short-billed gull—and you have

The fauna of the ponds, except for
selves, seems in no way remarkable.
dragonflies, damsel flies, and May flies
fly, several diving beetles, backswimmer
striders. Also a colorful water mite (*E*
of midges, and many bristleworms.
are the most important whooping-cran
and the chorus frog were observed, wh
forms as pond snails, bladder snails,



others. S
water in
ton, but
of the U
this com

The
ever e
green
nitrate
organi
fat co
living
desicca

Which
country
icebound
survive,
stickleba

In sea
River pa
ish lake
Discover
most of
so becau
There w
partly h
fairly fr
the sma
our first
though
calling
the sam
Texas
possible
this ass

pearance. We also saw the tracks of moose, wood buffalo, and red fox.

In that confusing patchwork of lakes and ponds, amid soft bogs and dense thickets, we soon had the feeling of being hopelessly earthbound. Fighting off the clouds of mosquitoes and the newly arrived bulldog flies, and beginning to suffer from a constant ache in our legs from the rough going, we would have given much for the advantages of a helicopter—or for wings of any kind. It was maddening to know that at least one pair of whooping cranes, with young in tow, were within a half mile of us most of the time, yet we were unable to watch them. Our visions were filled with them, a hundred yards away perhaps, calmly picking up snails, the young one quite possibly darting after a white admiral butterfly! Earthbound and weary, we could not tell. But we were on the spot. We had gazed at its features, and felt of it with our bare hands. It is real and it is reasonably understandable. But most important of all, it is no longer unknown.

On July 2 we were advised by radio that pilot Holmgren would be able to pick us up that afternoon for the trip back to the Slave River. Ray and I had then been in the crane country the better part of ten days. In the morning we made a last trip to the ponds and then returned and broke camp. At two o'clock we started smoke signals, but it wasn't until five-fifteen that we finally saw a strange, rapidly moving dot in the sky, off to the northeast. It was the helicopter, too far east of us and moving on a course that would carry him on to the south of our location. I caught the reflection of the sun in my shaving mirror and moved it back and forth like a searchlight beam. Almost at once Holmgren saw it, and in a few more minutes he was with us on the ground.

By 7 P.M. two round trips between our camp and the Grand Detour had been accomplished. The helicopter was then refueled from gas drums that Bill Fuller, now back from the Yukon, had cached on the riverbank the day before, and Holmgren had taken off for his base at Hay River, two hours away. Bill had also left us a Chipewyan boat and outboard, which we found pulled up against the bank. Best of all, there were two bottles of beer under the stern seat! It was a cold trip upstream, and the river was even higher than it had been in May, with just as many drift logs and great trees floating along in the swift current. At 2 A.M. we landed on the muddy shore just below Fort Smith, having taken seven hours to navigate the forty-four miles.

At the Hotel Mackenzie we routed out Louie, and he told us that John O'Reilly of the *New York Herald Tribune* was asleep in an adjoining room, having just arrived. So we immediately woke John and sat down to tell him of our adventures. As he wrote in his paper, "... They came through the Arctic twilight up the river by skiff to reach Fort Smith for the third time. I was there to meet them when they came out. In the words of Robert W. Service, Mr. Allen 'looked like a man who had lived in hell.' He was bearded, dirty, and tired, but this time he was grinning." I was indeed! This time I had something to grin about.

Even more momentous discoveries were in store for us. On July 6, in a light plane with Bill Fuller, O'Reilly, and me as observers, we made a survey flight over the Sass and Klewi Rivers. All told we sighted two pairs of adults, each with twin youngsters, plus a single adult. Altogether, nine whooping cranes. The occurrence of two broods with two young each was an exciting event, and we wondered if this might not be more normal than we had previously supposed. The fact that few pairs reach Texas with twins might be a result of losses on the migration route. After we had left for home, Bill Fuller continued aerial observations, making six more flights, with the final one on October 12. The largest number of whooping cranes seen on a single flight was on September 12, a total of 11 adults and 6 young, 17 in all. It was a great surprise to me that as many as 6 adults and 2 young were still present in the nesting area as late as October 12.

As October drew to a close and November was at hand we wondered how many of the little band would make it safely to Texas. At Aransas Refuge, Julian Howard was prepared to undertake the careful counts that are his important contribution to these joint efforts. By October 27, 13 cranes had arrived. Then, on November 3, a ground count on the refuge revealed two pairs without young, three pairs with 1 young each, and one pair with 2 young. In addition, another pair with twins was observed on Matagorda Island. This count was checked next day from a plane, and the grand total was 20 adults and 8 young, including both sets of twins that we had first sighted near the Sass River in July, 2,500 miles to the north. These 8 young represented the largest number of juveniles to reach the wintering grounds in Texas since our records began in 1938–1939.

Not only had we learned the location of the Northern breeding grounds and much as to their nature and inhabitants, but in this same year we had seen the whooping-crane population increase at a rate that is more heartening than anything that has happened to them in recent years. Perhaps these great birds and their destiny have now caught the attention and commanded the good will of all who live along the critical route of the flyway. If the shooting of these birds during their migrations has been halted for good, then we can begin to believe that they have at last turned the corner and, God willing, will be able to make the long flight back from the dark and soundless void of oblivion.

*. . . There is no survivor, there is no future,*
*there is no life to be created in this form again.*
*We are looking upon the uttermost finality . . .*
*We are in touch with the reality of extinction.*
HENRY BEETLE HOUGH

# XIV : The long flight back

Of all extinct or near-extinct birds, past or present, none is more symbolic of the fight to save threatened species from extinction than the American egret, the "long white" of the plume hunter's vernacular. Early in the present century, as a result of the demand for their plumes by the millinery trade, the egrets were reduced to numbers that were dangerously low. According to Arthur Cleveland Bent, the lowest ebb was apparently reached in 1902, which was the year in which he visited Florida for the first time. Significantly, it was also the year following the founding of an organization known then as the National Association of Audubon Societies. Mr. Bent saw a few egrets on that first visit, but none of them were nesting. The next year he was in Florida again, and in one of the most remote sections of the state, at Cuthbert Lake in Monroe County, he found a colony of some 4,000 water birds of various species, perhaps the only rookery of that size that survived. Among this congregation of birds were exactly 18 American egrets, of which seven pairs had built nests.

The egret had been reduced to this state from numbers that must once have been tremendously impressive. During the long campaign to obtain protection for their colonies, Gilbert Pearson described this former abundance: "At one time the lake shores of Florida teemed with tens of thousands of these elegant, long-legged white creatures. Several years ago I visited rookeries containing great numbers of them, but even then the work of destruction was going on. While visiting a plume hunter's camp in 1886 I was told that the New York feather dealers paid ninety cents for the plumes of every bird. Since that time the price has gone up and up until recently tourists at Miami and Palm Beach have been paying $10 and more for the scalp of each bird brought in by the white hunters and Seminole Indians of the Everglades country. For several years past the National Association of Audubon Societies has been employing guards to protect the few remaining colonies as far as they are known. These nesting places are distributed from the coastal region of North Carolina southward to the Florida Keys, but it is debatable whether the species can be saved, although without the efforts of the Audubon Society the bird would probably have disappeared entirely by this time."

Of course, as has been pointed out elsewhere, what the egret faced was being completely wiped out in the United States, not total extinction as a species. But the extirpation of a large local population can be the forerunner of the destruction of local populations elsewhere, with final extinction as the eventual result. This was especially true in the case of the egret, whose destruction had a commercial basis. As the Florida colonies were ravaged and depleted, plume hunters and dealers began transferring their operations to untouched fields in South America, and who can tell what the ultimate fate of the egrets there might have been if the plumage trade itself had not been outlawed in the United States a few years later? Now, fifty-three years after Bent's report from Cuthbert Lake—and at the cost of the lives of three Audubon wardens plus other, less valuable, considerations—the American egret is an abundant bird once more, nesting throughout Florida, along the Gulf Coast to Texas, and northward to Oregon, Minnesota, Wisconsin, and New Jersey. With spectacular success the American egret has made the long flight back!

By 1901, the year that the Audubon Society was founded, several North American bird species had already become extinct, or were well along the road to oblivion. In June, 1899, in the third number of what was to be the Society's official organ, *Bird-Lore,* a letter was published from the vigorous pen of Theodore Roosevelt, then governor of New York State. Governor Roosevelt wrote: "The destruction of the Wild Pigeon and the Carolina Paroquet has meant a loss as severe as if the Catskills or the Palisades were taken away. When I hear of the destruction of a species I feel just as if all the works of some great writer had perished; as if we had lost all instead of only part of Polybius or Livy."

Up to this time "conservation," in the sense that we employ today, was an unknown word. Robert Cushman Murphy, in a review of the first fifty years of *Bird-Lore* (now *Audubon Magazine*), recalls the state of things at the turn of the century:

> It was an age of expansion, of thresholds and vast portents, and yet in many respects a gentle, leisurely period, as we view it nostalgically across the decades. No motor cars brought far shooting grounds near for hordes of gunners, multiplying like the rabbits of Australia. Drainage programs had scarcely begun to dry up the West. Many or most midland watersheds still bore an adequate forest cover. And even though millions of birds had been heedlessly wiped out by the combined effects of the cage, hat, and game-market trades, there were still spots of primordial Eden in the long-settled East. The ivory-bill, passenger pigeon, and paroquet at least survived, even though their probable doom could be foreseen. Many a southern swamp was yet green with virgin cypress, and there were countless stands of long-leaf pine that neither lumberman nor turpentiner had ravaged.

But many tragic events were in store, and it was to be some time before there was an awakening. The great auk of our North Atlantic seacoasts had been destroyed as early as the 1830s, and became extinct elsewhere in 1844. The Labrador duck was gone by

1878. Now, in rapid succession, the passenger pigeon and the Carolina paroquet were to disappear from the North American scene, and thus from the earth. Evidently the last wild flock of passenger pigeons became extinct about 1900, although a last living example died in captivity, in the Cincinnati Zoological Gardens, in 1914. Schorger estimates that at the time of the first settlements there may have been between 3 and 5 billion of these birds. Witmer Stone wrote:

> The reduction of this once abundant bird to absolute extermination by man's greed should be a lesson to us all, and stifle all opposition to the efforts now being made by national and state governments in behalf of the conservation of other birds threatened with a like fate. What is a little loss of sport to us compared with the extinction of a wild species—something that the hand of man can never replace?

As for the Carolina paroquet, there have been uncertain or unconfirmed reports since, but the last generally accepted observation is that of Frank M. Chapman who saw thirteen of these birds along Taylor Creek, on the northeast side of Lake Okeechobee, Florida. The date was April, 1904.

What was responsible for the extinction of these once abundant birds? In each case the hand of man is not only plainly discernible, but there are well-documented accounts of the exact manner in which the destruction of each was brought about. It should be clear to us at this point that although—as paleontologists would remind us, and as Darwin himself emphasized—extinction has been almost a commonplace phenomenon since the first dawn of life, there is a vast difference between the slow extermination of a species as a result of natural selection, and an abrupt, callous, and unthinking extermination at the hands of man. Students of progressive evolution, and of the vagaries of animal populations in general, can tell us much about the normal processes of extinction, and those of us who are concerned with species that are being persecuted and reduced by man must be completely aware of the work in these fields, but at the same time we cannot afford to overlook the tremendous impact of unnatural factors. If steps are taken in sufficient time, our efforts, while taking into full account the biological and ecological situation, will often accomplish immediate and remarkable results through such fields as legislation, enforcement, education, and public relations. The story of the American egret is a classic example. The egret has been returned to abundance mainly as a result of legal protection, enforcement, and education, although we remain almost completely ignorant of its ecological and behavior patterns and genetic characters. In this instance we were very lucky, but we should not be misled into thinking that we will have such luck every time.

The story behind the extinction of a species already lost can be of value to us. Even the story of the great auk, gone now these 112 years, is a useful one, if only to emphasize the importance of present-day safeguards and restrictions that we may take somewhat for granted.

The great auk (*Plautus impennis*) once inhabited coasts and islands of the North Atlantic from Newfoundland, Iceland, and perhaps southern Greenland, south to Massachusetts and Ireland, and in winter as far as South Carolina, Florida, and the Bay of Biscay. It became extinct under dramatically tragic circumstances that demonstrate how suddenly an extinction of this sort can be finally accomplished. As in the case of the last passenger pigeon, almost the exact hour of its final demise is known. A powerful swimmer and diver, it was a large bird averaging thirty inches in total length, its plumage black above and white underneath. Once ashore, as on a nesting ledge, it was awkward and easily captured, for the garefowl, as it was called, was a flightless bird. As men roved across the Northern seas they found and destroyed colony after colony, taking the birds for food, both for their vessels and for their settlements ashore. Adventurous French fishermen were said to have reached the Newfoundland Banks as early as 1497, and on nearby islands they raided colonies of the garefowl. Cartier, on his first voyage in 1534, salted down five or six barrels of their carcasses for every one of his ships. These raids were continued until, somewhere between 1830 and 1840, the great auk was extinct in North America.

A few survived off the coast of Europe, however. At about the time they were disappearing forever from American shores, the natural-history museums realized that the species was approaching extinction. There were almost none of their eggs or skins in the collections and now they would have to be obtained in a hurry, and at any cost, or it would be too late. One last breeding place was known, an island known as Eldey off the coast of Iceland. In the year 1830, the museums were offering 100 kronen (about thirty dollars) for one garefowl, a goodly sum to the poor fisher folk of Iceland. So Eldey was raided, and it is on record that 20 skins were delivered in that year, 24 in 1831, 13 and one egg in 1833, and 9 skins and 8 eggs in 1834. For a time the demand was satisfied, and the price dropped. Then it again reached 100 kronen, and, in 1840, another raid netted 4 garefowls and 5 eggs. More specimens were demanded, but the fishermen reported that they had taken the last one; there were none left.

Four years went by and there was a clamor for more. Carl Siemsen, who was in touch with the dealers of Europe, went to a fisherman named Vilhjalmur Hakonarsson and urged him to visit Eldey and have one more try, which he agreed to do.

There were some fourteen or fifteen men in the boat as it approached Eldey on the morning of June 3, 1844, but the seas were rougher than usual, and only three of them managed to get ashore. The stage was now set. Within minutes the great auk would be extinct. The three men were Jon Brandsson, Sigurdr Islefsson, and Ketil Kentilsson. Writing some forty years after the event, the ornithologist Siemington Grieve has given us this description of what happened:

> As the men clambered up they saw two garefowls sitting among numberless other rock-birds (*Uria troile* and *Alca torda*), and at once gave chase. The garefowls showed not the slightest disposition to repel the invaders, but immediately ran along under the high cliff, their heads erect, their little wings somewhat extended. They uttered no cry of alarm, and moved, with their short steps, about as quickly as a man could walk. Jon Brandsson, with outstretched arms, drove one into a corner, where he soon had it fast. Sigurdr Islefsson and Ketil pursued

> the second, and the former seized it close to the edge of the rock, here risen to a precipice some fathoms high, the water being directly below it. Ketil then returned to the sloping shelf whence the birds had started, and saw an egg lying on the lava slab, which he knew to be a garefowl's. Whether there was not another egg is uncertain. All this took place in much less time than it takes to tell it.

Another account told how the necks of the two old birds were wrung in the next moment, and how Ketil threw the egg away because it showed a tiny crack. It was the last great auk's egg on earth, and these were the last two birds of their race. The men left the island at once, and the great auk was then extinct. It had not taken much more than five minutes!

After that, all that remained were some 80 skins in museums and private collections (nearly all of them from Eldey and Gierfuglasker), 23 or 24 complete skeletons, 2 specimens preserved in alcohol, and about 75 eggs. Many bones had also been collected, some of them from Funk Island where great numbers of garefowls were slaughtered for their feathers. Dr. Lucas, who visited Funk Island in 1878, estimated from the great heaps of bones that literally millions of the birds must have died there over the years.

For the great auk this was the "uttermost finality." Their kind would nevermore be seen upon the earth.

The next North American bird to disappear was the handsome Labrador duck (*Camptorhynchus labradorius*). It was a large bird, of greater over-all length than the eiders. The male was black with a white head, and white on the breast and wings. The female was grayish-brown above and grayish-white underneath. Of the extinction of the Labrador duck, Edward Howe Forbush had this to say:

> The most remarkable fact about the Labrador duck, which seems to have been common on the Atlantic coast one hundred years ago, is that it is now extinct and no one knows why. If it is a fact that it bred only on rocky islands about the Gulf of St. Lawrence and the coast of Labrador, the feather hunting of the eighteenth century and the egging and shooting of the

nineteenth probably resulted in its extinction; but no one, now living, knows to a certainty that it bred in Labrador. John W. Audubon was shown nests at Blanc Sablon that were said to be those of this species. Newton writes that it was common in summer on the coast of Labrador until about 1842. Major King writes (1886) that it was common on the northern shore of the Gulf of St. Lawrence and bred there, but gives no dates. I have seen no other evidence of its breeding in Labrador. There are no definite records of its nesting, and not one of its eggs is in existence. It may have bred much farther north but so far the records show that no one has ever seen it to the northward. We must be satisfied, then, with the probable explanation that, like the great auk, the species bred more or less locally and was exterminated in much the same way.

But there was an interesting difference in the original distribution of the great auk and the Labrador duck, as pointed out recently by Amadon:

> The Labrador duck is apparently the *only* bird whose range was restricted to the American coast of the North Atlantic. The other coastal species of this area nest also in northwestern Europe, in Iceland, or in other areas. . . . [To which he adds:] Examination of distributional data will often provide a clue to the extinction or near extinction of certain species. The Labrador duck is a case in point. Bent (1925) and others have correctly stated that the presumed small size of the breeding range of this duck made it especially vulnerable to persecution. . . . Persecution by man led to speedy extinction.

Forbush also quoted Elliot who said that between 1860 and 1870 he saw

> . . . a considerable number of the species in the New York markets, but that a full-plumaged male was exceedingly rare, although no one imagined that the species was on the verge of extinction. The last Labrador duck on record died by the hand of man near Long Island, New York, in 1875. According to Dutcher's summary, there are only forty-two recorded speci-

mens in existence in the museums and scientific collections of the world.

Another report states that a specimen, since lost, was taken at Elmira, New York, in 1878. Apparently this remains unconfirmed. In any case, the Labrador duck is no more.

We have already mentioned the possibility that the passenger pigeon, the next species to disappear, once numbered in the billions. In his thorough-going study of *Ectopistes migratorius*, Schorger describes this splendid bird as follows:

> The passenger pigeon, with its small head and neck, long tail, and beautiful plumage, had an air of uncommon elegance. The length of the male was about 16½ inches, and color ranged from slaty blue on the head to grayish blue on the back. The throat, foreneck, and breast were vinaceous; a metallic iridescence of bronze, green, and purple tinged the hindneck."

They ranged chiefly over the eastern half of the United States, west to Montana and Texas, south to north Florida, as well as in southern Canada from Alberta to Ontario. The principal nesting area was the northeastern United States from Minnesota and Kentucky to New England.

Schorger reviews in considerable detail the many ways in which these birds were taken for food. After 1852, when rail transportation was available between the Atlantic seaboard and Chicago, the traffic in pigeons increased. In 1855, the game markets of New York City alone disposed of 300,000 pigeons annually. At Petoskey, Michigan, there were 600 professional netters in 1874, employed exclusively in the pigeon trade, and in 1878 it was estimated that at least 2,000 people were connected with the business, either as catchers or pickers. By 1881 the number of professional trappers reached 1,200. Estimates of the numbers of pigeons killed are astonishing. Three Michigan nestings were said to have furnished the market with 1,000 tons of squabs and 2,400,000 adult birds. Other nestings, as in Wisconsin, contributed even greater numbers. At its height the trade was "big business." One dealer at the Petoskey nesting was reported to be worth

$60,000, "all made in that business." (H. B. Roney in *Chicago Field*. 1879.)

Schorger states that a precipitous decline in numbers took place between 1871 and 1880. Through the 1890s the once great flocks dwindled to nothing, and by 1900 only a few pallid captives survived. There have been many reasons advanced for the rapid demise—biological "defects," inbreeding, disease, the cutting of the mast-bearing forests, fires, etc.—but the record of their slaughter for the market speaks for itself. Schorger writes (1955):

> Judged from the standpoint of numbers, the pigeon was enormously successful in its way of life. Failure to change its habits cannot be laid to stupidity without assuming that most of the surviving species have a higher order of intelligence. The greater number of the passerines chanced to develop a mode of life that rendered survival fairly simple after the advent of Europeans. Very many of our game birds, shore birds, and waterfowl would today be extinct, or near extinction, were it not for coddling through refuges and protective laws. . . . [And further along:] Every species of animal is doomed to extinction when it fails to produce sufficient young to equal the inherent annual losses. This the pigeon was not permitted to do. [Moritz] Fischer estimated that nearly 12,000,000 brooding pigeons met their death during the decade 1866–1876. This represented a high loss of nestlings. It is certain, assuming the correctness of his figures, that the loss would exceed 6,000,000 young. If both parents were taken, the young was doomed to die; and if only one adult of a pair was captured, the lone parent could not keep its young alive during the first few days after hatching. His assumption that the number of squabs taken was negligible missed the most potent cause of extinction.

This attendant loss of young still in the nests was a major reason for the rapid decline of the egrets in Florida, which was well underway during the 1880s and 1890s. The adults were shot and stripped of the "scalp" of plumes (the entire skin of the back was ripped off), and the neglected young perished of slow starvation. Since much of the shooting took place at the rookeries themselves, the entire nesting population generally deserted—egrets, herons, ibises, spoonbills, and all—leaving their young to die. Thus, other species often suffered severe losses, even though only the adults among the egrets were actually killed.

Thus did the magnificent and incredibly numerous passenger pigeon disappear forever, another victim of a blind devotion to the inconceivably stupid doctrine that the natural bounties of America would flow on and on, without limit and without end.

Meanwhile, the end of the gaudy little Carolina paroquet (*Conuropsis carolinensis carolinensis*) was already in sight. About the size of a mourning dove, this lovely bird was green in plumage, with head and neck of bright lemon yellow and orange or red suffusions on the forehead and cheeks. The tail was conical, with long pointed feathers. It once ranged over the Atlantic-coast region of the Southeastern United States, from Florida and Alabama north to Pennsylvania and New York. In 1881, twenty-three years ahead of time, Maynard prophesied their end when he described what were actually the factors that brought about their extermination. Maynard wrote:

> . . . in Florida their enemies are legion; bird catchers trap them by the hundreds for the northern markets, sportsmen shoot them for food, planters kill them because they eat their fruit, and tourists slaughter them simply because they present a favorable mark.

There has been no certain record of a Carolina paroquet since Chapman's observation of 1904, although the species may well have survived beyond that year in some remote area. It is now generally considered that they have long since joined the great auk, the Labrador duck, the passenger pigeon, and the heath hen in the shadowy realms of oblivion.

Today we look back on these tragedies, and at the practices that were responsible for them, and we wonder that many more North American species did not become extinct during these same years. As it is, our record in this respect is pretty bad. David Lack (1954) has said:

It is claimed that more species of birds have become extinct in North America than in Europe, but various European species doubtless became extinct before bird records were kept. In addition, natural habitats have been altered much more gradually in Europe than in North America, which may have allowed more European than American species to become adapted to cultivated land.

But was adaptation possible in situations like those that faced the great auk, Labrador duck, passenger pigeon, Carolina paroquet, and heath hen? There was not enough time. And just as the causes of extinction in these instances are perfectly clear, so are the measures that prevented further rapid and perhaps more extensive losses, as suggested by Schorger. It should be apparent, however, that refuges and protective laws are merely the bare framework on which the conservation edifice has been built. These measures are the fingers thrust into the hole in the dike, for in the long run the job must be completed through education.

There is also the ever present need for more knowledge through research. When we consider the fate of the heath hen, which became extinct in 1933, and the probable and more recent fate of the eskimo curlew—neither of which recovered entirely from the unbridled hunting practices of the early nineteenth century—we can see that these were extinction problems that were handed down to us from the past. There are current examples of bird species that continue to struggle uncertainly for existence because of the nearly fatal blows that were dealt them sometime in the last century—the ivory-billed woodpecker (perhaps already gone), the whooping crane, California condor, American flamingo, and Attwater's prairie chicken. Others, in less critical situations but still far from a return to the normal status of their heyday, include the roseate spoonbill, reddish egret, trumpeter swan, and perhaps a good many more. Some of these birds have already demonstrated an ability to respond to protection under ideal conditions, but it is increasingly apparent that we need to know more as to what these conditions are and how they are to be obtained in each specific case. We should maintain research studies that will keep us constantly alert to fluctuations on the bedside chart of each patient.

From a biological point of view this means, in large part, a sound knowledge of *species characteristics*, of which we remain woefully ignorant in most instances. Can we hope that twenty-eight whooping cranes will have the genetic vigor to increase their numbers and survive indefinitely as a race? Do we know if our present estimates of safe productivity rates for the flamingo are correct? Do we understand the exact ecological demands of our roseate spoonbills, and can we be sure that they will be capable of the adaptations that may be required of them in the next twenty years? Unless we can continue serious work in the direction of such answers we will be giving little beyond lip service to our endangered species. We will be preparing their obituaries instead of saving their lives.

Although most of our presently endangered species can trace the original causes of their problem back many years, the world in which they live so precariously today is providing new threats, streamlined and modern, and armed with potentials that are not pleasant to contemplate. A basic reason for many of these new threats is the skyrocketing human population—in North America, in Africa, in the Caribbean countries, in nearly every part of the world. It has been the most potent cause of the American flamingo's present dilemma. In Latin America and the Caribbean islands the human population is multiplying two and a half times as fast as anywhere else, according to the tabulations of the Population Reference Bureau in Washington. This has been aptly referred to as a "population explosion" (*Time*, October 19, 1953). A few steps are being taken with regard to the preservation of wildlife. In Venezuela, the International Committee for Bird Preservation has prevailed on the government to do something for the flamingo and the seriously endangered red siskin (*Spinus cucullatus*). Elsewhere this same organization has been giving attention to the scarlet ibis (*Guara rubra*) in Surinam, and has set up a special study of the problems faced by the Cuban race of the ivory-billed woodpecker (*Campephilus principalis bairdii*), and the Haitian parrot (*Amazona vittata*). Before he had to give up his work with the Foundation for Scientific Research in Surinam and the Netherlands Antilles, Dr. Jon Westermann published challenging (and distressing) reports on the destruction of the flora and fauna of the Caribbean area. He listed 15 mammals already extinct in that region and some 20 mammal forms now threatened with extinction. In addition, he listed 11 species of birds and 10 subspecies already extinct, and pointed out that in the Caribbean area "within the past 100 years some 14 forms have disappeared, a number surpassing that of entire continental America. Some 15 species are now particularly threatened with extermination, while another 20 or 25 forms are considered to be so reduced in numbers that their survival in the long run is doubtful." Of land reptiles and amphibians, 20 species and 5 subspecies are already gone.

In North America we are now faced with enough problems in this field to keep us occupied for some time to come. What has happened to those critical species which have been the subjects of our Audubon Research Program? The ivory-billed woodpecker has disappeared from both the Singer Tract in Louisiana and the Santee River swamps in South Carolina. The valuable timber of the Singer was cut and removed, in spite of earnest efforts by conservationists and government to find a compromise solution that would leave some of it as a wilderness preserve. The Santee swamp was flooded by the construction of a dam in order to provide electric power for expanding industrial and human needs in that region. A few ivory-bills may survive in parts of northern Florida but their presence there has not been verified, and there now appears to be no possibility of a practicable program for their preservation. In this case the last-ditch fight was evidently made and lost in Louisiana and South Carolina prior to World War II. It was made too late!

The case of the California condor is more encouraging. Carl Koford studied these great birds and their "conditions of life" from March, 1939 to June, 1941, completing the field work in 1946. In his excellent monograph (1953) he lists wanton shooting, collecting, the use of poison, trapping, accidents, fires, construction of roads and trails, oil development, and photographers as the major causes of mortality. As remedies he suggests stronger protective measures, including a Federal law (also still lacking in the case of the roseate spoonbill), strict closure of all nesting and roosting areas, and a practical educational program. Also, the cooperation of stockmen and trappers should be secured in leaving unpoisoned carcasses on the range, and other means of controlling squirrels than by the use of quick-acting poisons should be investigated and encouraged.

Many of these recommendations have now been followed, particularly with regard to closures. Upwards of 60 condors survive.

The roseate spoonbill has shown a remarkable response. In the winter of 1954–1955 the Florida Bay population climbed to an all-time high of 428 nesting adults. In 1935–1936 the comparable number was only 30 nesting adults, so the nineteen-year increase is definitely encouraging. On the Texas coast, improvements since World War II have been steady, if less spectacular. While the new knowledge of the life history and ecology of these birds, secured during the course of our research studies, has been important in directing our efforts for its protection, we have accomplished a large share of these results through good public relations in the critical areas. But we have only to look to the future to see new difficulties arising. The shallow waters of eastern Florida Bay, where these colonies are established on isolated mangrove keys, are nontidal owing to the barrier of many shoals between them and the open Gulf of Mexico. The spoonbills find some food in the very shadows of their nests, in pools where corixids and killifishes begin their life cycles in tremendous abundance. But for the most part, and especially during the critical period when they are feeding their growing young, the adult spoonbills must fly to tidal sloughs close to the Atlantic side, where food supplies are more abundant. With the rapid development and building program now under way on the Florida Keys, some of these natural feeding areas have already been destroyed—turned into boat basins and building lots by dredging and filling. If steps are not taken soon to set aside a few essential tidal sloughs, from Key Largo to the Matecumbes, it is a serious question whether the new residents and droves of tourists who come to this outdoor paradise each winter will continue to enjoy the sight of the pink flocks that enhance the beauty of this region today. A survey is now planned for the purpose of learning the exact needs of the spoonbills in this respect, and for selecting suitable areas that might be preserved for this use. With the support of local civic groups and county and state officials, such a plan may be carried out soon enough so that the presence of the roseate spoonbill in the fabulous Florida Keys may be assured for all time to come.

The future of the whooping crane and the flamingo is beyond prediction. A great deal depends on public opinion, especially in the immediate areas where the problems these two species face are the most serious. There is considerable evidence that the public that is in direct contact with the whooping crane will not only continue its help in every way, but will increase this support. It may well have been a sign of things to come in this respect when the U.S. Air Force recently backed down on its plan to establish a flash-bombing range on Matagorda Island, immediately adjacent to the main wintering flock of whooping cranes on Aransas Refuge, and on the actual winter territories of some of these birds. Had the range been put in operation the results would undoubtedly have been fatal to *Grus americana.*

Our Canadian friends took this threat so seriously that their government made an official protest to the State Department in Washington. When the military finally gave in, a sigh of relief went up that could be heard from coast to coast in both the United States and Canada. A Toronto paper printed a cartoon that reflected the general feeling. It depicted an adult whooping crane standing straight and proud, a medal pinned to his chest. Beside him a young whooper looked up at his parent with shining eyes. He asked his father to tell him again the story of how he licked the U.S. Air Force. With such a spirit abroad in the land it seems to me that there is hope not only for whooping cranes but for mankind as well.

Will these and the other endangered birds be able to make the long flight back? Or are they doomed, in course of time, to join the ghostly legions of those that have already been needlessly destroyed by man? There are many reasons for the hope that we have awakened in time, and the most important of these reasons are concerned with our growing stature as maturing, civilized human beings.

As for the bald fact of extinction, its stark reality and possible meaning to us was described in striking terms in an editorial that appeared in the *Vineyard Gazette* with the announcement of the death of the last heath hen. The date was April 21, 1933, and the writer was the paper's editor, Henry Beetle Hough. Here it is in part:

> Now we know there are degrees even in death. All around us nature is full of casualties, but they do not interrupt the stream of life. When most living things die, they seem only to revert to the central theme of existence from which they were temporarily detached. There is a spirit of vitality everywhere which enfolds the dead with a countenance of consolation, and bestows upon the living races more than has been taken away. But to the heath hen something more than death has happened, or, rather, a different kind of death. There is no survivor, there is no future, there is no life to be created in this form again. We are looking upon the uttermost finality which can be written, glimpsing the darkness which will not know another ray of light. We are in touch with the reality of extinction.
>
> In recent years an impression has gone forth that man has learned to withhold his hand and let things about him grow and multiply. The gospel of conservation, it is said, has won the day. We know this is not true. May the death of the heath hen serve to bring us nearer a time of realization and fulfillment! Until now, saving only the imperious grace of economic importance and sometimes not even that, a creature that man could kill has had to die.
>
> Is nothing to follow the extinction of this bird except one more lesson in conservation for school books, and a sentimental mourning? On the Vineyard, certainly, there is more. What an awe and fascination have been written into the theses of scientific men who came to observe the heath hen on the great plain! What accents of mystery, beauty and the eternal rites of life

the heath hen, in spring, has given to this strange region! At first sight a visitor has thought the seemingly limitless miles of plain both dreary and uninteresting. But not for long. The most prosaic scientist, full of a passion for metric measurements of feathers or Latin labels, has lain among the black scrub oak in the white mists of a chill April morning, and has returned to write poetry. The meticulous observations and Latin terms appear modestly, softened by a cloak of mystery. We read of birds appearing "as if by magic." We are told that the call of the heath hen did not rise or fall, but "ended in the air like a Scotch ballad." And a naturalist who is also a writer has heard in the peeping of the pinkletinks the voice of Ariel, and in the witch dances and goblin cries of the heath hen the grosser spirits of the Island.

And so it is that the extinction of the heath hen has taken away part of the magic of the Vineyard. This is the added loss of the Island. There is a void in the April dawn, there is an expectancy unanswered, there is a tryst not kept....

*About the author:*

Robert Porter Allen is Research Director of the National Audubon Society and the leading authority on species threatened with extinction. He has devoted over twenty-five years of his life to the study and preservation of the whooping crane, the flamingo, and the roseate spoonbill.

Mr. Allen's interest in birds began at an early age. By the time he was nine he was interested in little else and repeatedly cut school to spend a day to watch the shore birds and waterfowl migrate. It was inevitable that his interest in birds should eventually lead him to the National Audubon Society.

The Allens live in Tavernier, Florida.